The Geopolitics of Globalization

This volume explains how the process of globalization is truncated. It underlines the central role played by geopolitics in the contemporary structuring of globalization.

The book operates on a vast theoretical and empirical canvas. It informs the readers on the nature of globalization and the role of markets and geopolitics. It applies its findings to understanding the developmental success in the original 'Asian Tigers', the Southeast Asian nations, and China. It also provides an illuminating contrast between India and Pakistan in the interaction of geopolitics and economic policy.

D1528018

THE GEOPOLITICS OF GLOBALIZATION
The Consequences for Development

Baldev Raj Nayar

OXFORD
UNIVERSITY PRESS

OXFORD
UNIVERSITY PRESS

YMCA Library Building, Jai Singh Road, New Delhi 110 001

Oxford University Press is a department of the University of Oxford. It furthers the
University's objective of excellence in research, scholarship, and education
by publishing worldwide in

Oxford   New York

Auckland Cape Town Dar es Salaam Hong Kong Karachi Kuala Lumpur
Madrid Melbourne Mexico City Nairobi New Delhi Shanghai Taipei Toronto

With offices in
Argentina Austria Brazil Chile Czech Republic France Greece Guatemala
Hungary Italy Japan Poland Portugal Singapore South Korea Switzerland
Thailand Turkey Ukraine Vietnam

Oxford is a registered trademark of Oxford University Press
in the UK and in certain other countries

Published in India
by Oxford University Press, New Delhi

First published 2005
Oxford India Paperbacks 2007

ISBN-13: 978-019-569303-4
ISBN-10: 019-569303-5

Typeset in Bembo 10.5/12 by InoSoft Systems, Noida
Printed in India by Sai Printopack Pvt Ltd, New Delhi 110 020
Published by Oxford University Press
YMCA Library Building, Jai Singh Road, New Delhi 110 001

CONTENTS

PREFACE

For any developing country's policy makers, scholars, and of course the general public, understanding its relationship to the globalization process is certainly of elemental importance today. That precisely constitutes the underlying motivation for the present study. But understanding the relationship of any particular country to globalization requires a prior comprehension of the nature, causes, and consequences of globalization. It is to that quest that this study is directed. The study is informed by a concern, not always explicit, over what lessons the evolution and contemporary structuring of globalization holds for developing countries.

In the process of exploring the various aspects of globalization, especially the role played by geopolitics in its contemporary structuring, the present study deals with the US as the hegemonic power along with its European allies, who are now consolidated as the European Union. These powers constitute the 'regime makers' in the modern-day international system, whereas the others in the system are to varying degrees simply 'regime takers'. Needless to add, the 'regime makers', most particularly the US, determine the nature, scope, and speed of globalization. Accordingly, understanding their international behaviour and its underlying determinants are crucial for the 'regime takers'.

The present work also deals through case studies with several countries in East and Southeast Asia that have undergone economic transformation of varying proportions during the past half-century. These include Japan, Korea, and Taiwan as the first 'Asian tigers', the ASEAN countries that have sought to emulate the model of the Asian tigers, and China as the upcoming challenger in the international system with its 'economic miracle'. For their combination of outward economic orientation and political authoritarianism, whether of the hard or soft kind, these countries are characterized as 'developmental states'. The case studies offer unusual insights into how these countries accommodated themselves to the geopolitics of the region, and of the world in order to avail of the opportunities provided by the international economy for economic advancement. Taken together, they, therefore, hold important lessons for makers of policy and opinion in the developing countries. The case studies on the developmental states are followed by a chapter each on India and Pakistan that examines the interaction of geopolitics and economic policy, specific to these two major countries of Asia.

ACKNOWLEDGEMENTS

The present study, like my earlier ones over more than three decades, has enormously benefited from the advice and counsel, during many conversations, of my friend and colleague, Jagdish Handa, Professor of Economics at McGill University. I am also indebted to him for taking time out from his heavy teaching and research schedule to give a critical reading to the entire manuscript. Thanks are due as well to another friend and colleague, T.V. Paul, James McGill Professor of International Relations. His initial encouragement of this research project for its distinctive viewpoint, and his subsequent recommendations for changes in the introductory and concluding chapters, have been very valuable. I am also grateful to still another friend and colleague, Donald von Eschen, Professor of Sociology at McGill University, who has not only been a long-time source of support and encouragement, but also read an earlier version of the manuscript and provided his characteristically constructive criticisms. Dr James Putzel of the London School of Economics was kind to apply his regional expertise to improve the chapter on Southeast Asia; his suggestions for revision were most useful. Nina Kim's meticulous help with checking the accuracy of quotations and bibliographic citations is heartily appreciated. As before, SSHRC has been generous with financial support. I would like to thank the editors at Oxford University Press for shepherding the manuscript through the review process. Thanks are also due to *Economic and Political Weekly* for publishing an initial version of Chapter 2, and also to *China Report*[1]

[1] Originally published as 'The Geopolitics of China's Economic Miracle', *China Report*, 40, 1 (January–March 2004), 19–47. Copyright © Centre for the Study of Developing Societies 2004. All rights reserved. Reproduced with the permission of the copyright holders and the publishers. Sage Publications India Pvt. Ltd, New Delhi.

for permission to use in Chapter 10 material published earlier in one of its issues.

My deepest debts are due to my wife, who has been the source of unstinted support in my research endeavours for over forty-two years, even in the midst of her own continued battle with breast cancer over the last decade. Her fortitude and quiet acceptance, her devotion to family, and her love for India have given me enormous strength over the years.

LIST OF TABLES

Chapter 1

GLOBALIZATION, GEOPOLITICS, AND DEVELOPMENT

It has literally become a truism that the world has, since the advent of the last quarter of the twentieth century, been increasingly swept away by a rising tide of economic globalization that is radically transforming it. That tide of globalization has, of course, also generated a flood of literature on the phenomenon. The analysis of globalization has come to constitute a substantial growth industry in the social sciences, across the various disciplines. The literature on the subject has now grown to vast proportions, and the approaches to it are many and varied.

The Variant Orientations to Globalization

As an initial step toward gaining a comprehension of the subject, and with a view to outlining the distinctive claims of the present study, the analysts of globalization can be broadly considered to fall into three groups: the agnostics, the enthusiasts, and the critics. To begin with the *agnostics*, they question whether anything new at all has happened by way of a phenomenon such as globalization, believing instead that increased internationalization of the world economy in terms of higher flows of merchandise, capital, and labour has all been seen before, especially in the decades preceding World War I.[1] Indeed,

---

[1] Paul Hirst and Grahame Thompson, *Globalization in Question: The International Economy and the Possibilities of Governance* (Cambridge, UK: Polity Press, 1996), 27; and Robert Gilpin, *The Challenge of Global Capitalism: The World Economy in the 21st Century* (Princeton: Princeton University Press, 2000), 294, 323. Gilpin also points out that Paul Krugman agrees with this position.

they assert that there was greater integration of the world economy before World War I than at the beginning of the fourth quarter of the twentieth century. Their position on the issue constitutes a fundamental objection, and therefore merits serious attention.

Taking a position diametrically opposed to that of the agnostics, the *enthusiasts* of globalization underline that it represents the occurrence of a massive change in the world economy, marking the triumph of markets at the expense of states. As Gilpin interprets the case of the enthusiasts: 'a quantum change in human affairs has taken place as the flow of large quantities of trade, investment, and technologies across national borders has expanded from a trickle to a flood.... As integrative processes widen and deepen globally, some believe that markets have become, or are becoming, the most important mechanism determining both domestic and international affairs. In a highly integrated global economy, the nation-state, according to some, has become anachronistic and is in retreat....'[2]

Thus understood, economic globalization can be said to mark the emergence of a 'supra-national', borderless global economy with its own laws of motion, encompassing and subordinating the various local economies in a single worldwide division of labour, rendering national governments to the equivalent of municipalities. In the view of the enthusiasts, not only is there definitely the occurrence of a massive change in the shape of globalization, but that such change is profoundly benign. Gilpin points out that, 'Market-oriented proponents of globalization consider this development as signalling a grand moment in human history.' He then adds that, for them, 'The supremacy of the market over the state and of economics over politics means the end of a human institution and of the political struggles responsible for war, domination, and other ills.'[3]

When looked at from the perspective of the implications of globalization for economic development in the less developed countries, the stance of the enthusiasts is especially noteworthy. With their theoretical position founded on neo-liberal economics, the enthusiasts welcome the eclipse of the state, for the ascendancy of markets would, by allowing economic forces to have full play, unhindered by the narrow nationalistic considerations of states, assure the unhindered diffusion of prosperity across the world. The enthusiasts

---

[2] Gilpin, *The Challenge of Global Capitalism*, 18–19, 311.
[3] Ibid.

posit an increasing convergence economically among the populations of the world, thus advancing human welfare to an extent unknown hitherto in history.[4] The supporters of globalization on this account are not limited to just liberals, however. Interestingly, there are now some on the Left who see substantial possibilities for redemption in economic globalization.[5]

The *critics* of globalization as the third group tend to agree with the enthusiasts on the trends delineated about increasing economic globalization. However, they disagree strongly with the positive interpretation put upon them; instead, they deem the consequences of globalization to be malign for the mass of national populations.[6] They fear the results to be an increasing concentration of economic, and therefore political, power in the hands of the multinational corporations, the growth of inequalities, the intensification of marginalization of the lower classes, and worsening environmental degradation. Accordingly, they would like to stem the tide of globalization in order to protect the security and welfare of populations. Interestingly, the critics see the state as precisely the strategic institution to accomplish that purpose.

As ought to be expected, the critics are not uniform in their views in regarding globalization as corrosive of mass welfare and the environment; their views are often addressed to particular sectoral and national audiences. One fault-line around which critics seem to cohere is the division between the advanced industrial countries (AICs) and the less developed countries (LDCs). There can be no doubt that a vast gulf really separates these two sets of countries in terms of economic conditions and, therefore, interests. In the AICs, there are vocal activists who protest against globalization outside

[4] On the position of the supporters of globalization, see Thomas L. Friedman, *The Lexus and the Olive Tree* (New York: Anchor Books, 2000); Francis Fukuyama, *The End of History and the Last Man* (New York: Free Press, 1992); and Kenichi Ohmae, *The Borderless World: Power and Strategy in the Interlinked Economy* (New York: Harper Business, 1990).

[5] See, for example, Gavin Kitching, *Seeking Justice Through Globalization: Escaping a Nationalist Perspective* (University Park, PA: Pennsylvania State University Press, 2001); and Michael Hardt and Antonio Negri, *Empire* (Cambridge, MA: Harvard University Press, 2000).

[6] Richard Falk, *Predatory Globalization: A Critique* (Cambridge, UK: Polity Press, 1999); and Dani Rodrik, *Has Globalization Gone Too Far?* (Washington, DC: Institute for International Economics, 1997).

major international conferences, while important interest groups (such as trade unions and environmentalist organizations) also oppose it. At the same time, there are respectable critics in the academic arena as well who have made a strong case against globalization on the ground that it generates increased unemployment among less-skilled labour and engenders greater inequalities within the AICs.[7] More nationalistic critics in the AICs see a global economic shift under way in which foreign direct investment in search of private profits drives industry and jobs from the AICs to the low-wage LDCs, resulting in deindustrialization and unemployment in the AICs.

If that assessment is correct, then one ought to expect greater support for globalization among the LDCs, for they ought to be benefiting from the transfer of industry and jobs from the AICs. Yet, powerful critiques of globalization prevail in the LDCs as well. The case here is a wide-ranging one, covering every aspect of economic, political, and social life. The malign consequences of globalization are said to include: loss of national autonomy in the spheres of economics, foreign policy, and national security; foreign domination of national culture and economy; the exposure of the national economy to major disturbances from external shocks; deepening underdevelopment; widening of inequalities and the immiserization of the population; and political instability, ethnic conflict, and national disintegration.[8]

Causes and Consequences

In any analytical study, three questions are of basic importance. One, what is the nature of the phenomenon under examination? That is, what is the pattern or central tendency in the events that are being investigated? Two, what are the causes of the phenomenon? And, three, what are the consequences of the phenomenon? The first question

[7] Rodrik, *Has Globalization Gone Too Far?*; and Leslie Sklair, *Globalization: Capitalism and Its Alternatives* (Oxford: Oxford University Press, 2002).

[8] Gilpin, *The Challenge of Global Capitalism*, 298, 311, 315, 316; Sklair, *Globalization*, 1–11, 48–53; Rodrik, *Has Globalization Gone Too Far?*; Aijaz Ahmad, 'Globalization and the Nation-State', *Seminar*, No. 437 (January 1996), 43–48; Amit Bhaduri and Deepak Nayyar, *The Intelligent Person's Guide to Liberalization* (New Delhi: Penguin Books, 1996), 76, 101, 111, 121; C.P. Bhambhri, *The Indian State after Independence* (Delhi: Shipra, 2000), ix, xix, 8, 9, 217, 221.

deserves serious attention, given that the agnostics are skeptical of the existence of any such phenomenon as globalization, even as many others recognize it as a monumental process that dominates the contemporary epoch. Contrary to the position of the agnostics, the present study confirms, on the basis of quantitative and other data, the claim that there is a distinctive process under way of a sharper integration of the world economy, which can be characterized as globalization. Additionally, it argues that the process is of a deeper nature than the one that existed before World War I. Contemporary globalization cannot, therefore, be dismissed away as something that has all been seen before. Chapter 2 offers an elaborate treatment, supported by considerable statistical data, of this issue relating to globalization.

On the other hand, despite the apparent stance of the enthusiasts of globalization, the world economy, as it is presently constituted, is nowhere near the stage of integration that they envision. Therefore, taking the nature of globalization as it now exists as the point of departure, the present study further claims that, while powerful social forces favour the advance of economic globalization, there are also strong forces—not least, states and their geopolitics—that serve to constrain it. As a consequence, while there is considerable diffusion of economic globalization across the world, there is (at the same time) a heavy concentration of its central features among a few key economies. The spread of globalization is thus uneven and asymmetrical. Convergence in the sense of uniform prices or of universal development can hardly be said to exist, except perhaps in the case of crude oil prices, which are largely dictated by an oil cartel.

In short, globalization is at present *truncated*, and, in line with this study's argument, it is likely to continue to remain so for the foreseeable future. Accordingly, a softer version of the concept of economic globalization, which treats it less as an end stage and more as a process, is considered to be more appropriate in this study. During that process, the 'international economy' becomes more closely integrated, with domestic economic agents increasingly oriented to the global market rather than to their own particular national markets, but the nation-state continues to remain central to economic management and welfare, both domestically and internationally. Chapter 3 delineates the truncated nature of globalization. This and the chapter that precedes it are grouped together under Part I, titled 'Globalization'.

What, then, are the causes of the phenomenon of globalization and the truncated form in which it presently exists? Implicit in the positions of both the enthusiasts and the critics is that the present global economic order is a consequence simply of relentlessly expanding market forces, spurred in turn by rapid technological change. In the process, the state's position is increasingly eroded while market forces continue on their march to becoming dominant. No doubt, due recognition needs to be accorded to the role of technological factors in the advance of globalization, at times making it seem inescapable and irreversible. Notwithstanding such recognition, another claim of this study is that, behind the truncated nature of contemporary globalization lies the fact of the present-day global economic order having been shaped, as were such orders earlier, by a hegemonic power that has been militarily and economically dominant. Not surprisingly, the hegemonic power and its allies have shaped the global economic order thus to advance their own interests, and they are likely to endeavour to see to it that it continues to do so. In short, economic globalization and its truncated nature have been a function of geopolitics.

The notion of the influential, almost determining impact, of geopolitics runs like a consistent, indeed insistent, thread throughout this study of economic globalization. Geopolitics has been interpreted in various ways, some pejorative and others not. Traditionally, it has been taken to refer to the impact of key geographical features of the globe, no doubt in combination with changing technological conditions, on international politics. Its modern-day founder was the British geographer, Sir Halford Mackinder, who in 1904 posited the immense concentration of power as a result of railroad development in the Heartland or Pivot within the World Island of Eurasia. He projected the Heartland as likely to overwhelm and control the Inner Crescent (the coastal lands) around it, then the Offshore and Outer Islands, and thus the World.[9] The Nazi theoreticians brought the entire field of geopolitics into disrepute with their notion of Lebensraum

---

[9] H.J. Mackinder, 'The Geopolitical Pivot of History', *Geographical Journal*, vol. 23 (1904), 421–44, reprinted in Harm J. de Blij, *Systematic Political Geography* (second ed.; New York: John Wiley & Sons, 1973), 271–95. See also W.H. Parker, *Mackinder: Geography as an Aid to Statecraft* (Oxford, UK: Clarendon Press, 1982); Robert E. Walters, *The Nuclear Trap: An Escape Route* (Harmondsworth, UK: Penguin Books, 1974); and Colin S. Gray, *The Geopolitics of the Nuclear Era: Heartland, Rimlands, and the Technological Revolution* (New York: Crane, Russak, 1977), chapter 2.

('living space') as a justification for the annexation by Germany of territories in Europe.

With the rise of Germany as a challenger in the 1930s, some American scholars became attracted to the subject of geopolitics. In a public lecture in 1942, the American expert on geopolitics, Nicholas John Spykman, reversed Mackinder's ordering schema and made the Rimland (that is, the Inner Crescent), with its concentration of human and economic resources, the key to domination over the World Island. He persuasively argued for thwarting Germany from gaining control of the Rimland. Toward that end, he strongly endorsed a dedicated alliance between the US as the sea power and the Soviet Union as the land power occupying the Heartland.[10] Spykman was profound in his insight about the wartime alliance between the US and the Soviet Union. Of course, after the war, the US and the Soviet Union fell apart. An interesting geopolitical perspective on the subsequent American policy of containment against the Soviet Union would be to view that policy as one gigantic Spykmanian strategic enterprise, to prevent the Rimland from falling under the domination of the Mackinderian Heartland.

In contrast with these geography-specific notions, geopolitics is understood more broadly here as encompassing the politics of grand strategy of states concerning the global distribution of power. As such, it is a matter of the great powers or potential great powers, whose strategic decision-making must take into account the balance of power across the planet. From that perspective, economic globalization cannot be regarded as something that is irreversible; its future is likely to depend on the interests, whether conflictual or cooperative, of the great powers. That, indeed, is the lesson that emerges from the historical interaction of geopolitics and globalization. After all, regardless of whether the earlier globalization was more far-reaching or not than its contemporary incarnation, it nonetheless collapsed suddenly under the weight of the titanic geopolitical conflict that erupted into World War I, and the world economy remained in disarray until the end of World War II. Consequently, no final destination for contemporary globalization, as the enthusiasts are wont to project, can be assumed in advance. By the same token, no permanent triumph of the market over the state can be predicted.

[10] Nicholas John Spykman, *The Geography of the Peace* (New York: Harcourt, Brace and Company, 1944).

At the same time, from the perspective of the minor powers, globalization is inescapable as long as the great powers allow it to proceed or persist.

Chapters 4 to 6 are concerned with the impact of states and their geopolitics in the shaping of global economic relations, and they are placed together under Part II, titled 'Geopolitics'. Chapter 4 deals with the relations between markets and states, the importance of geopolitics, and the evolution of the global economic order before World War II. Chapter 5 focuses on the reshaping of the world economic order under American hegemony. Chapter 6 concerns itself with the diffusion and concentration of power in the post-war period. It also discusses the two parallel phenomena, after the end of the Cold War, of building a comprehensive worldwide multilateral economic order, and the growing fragmentation of the world economy under the impact of the construction of regional economic blocs.

Finally, given the existential fact of globalization, even if truncated in form, what are its consequences? Even though they differ over whether the consequences of globalization are benign or malign, both enthusiasts and critics take them to be, as is already apparent, profound and wide-ranging. A comprehensive treatment of the multifaceted consequences of globalization would be a daunting task. Here, the consideration of the consequences of globalization is limited to the issue of economic growth in the LDCs. The orienting question is whether globalization can be harnessed to overcome its presently truncated nature—thus making for a push toward convergence— through the closer integration of national economies of the LDCs with the world economy, which would likely aid in their development. More pointedly: Does openness to the world economy through an outward-oriented economic strategy aid in economic development, as the enthusiasts assume? Or, does it result in economic marginalization of the LDCs through their exploitation by the multinational corporations, as the critics assume?

The issue of the relationship between openness and development is discussed in Chapter 7, and then investigated through a series of case studies in Chapters 8 to 12 that deal, in large part, with an economically dynamic part of Asia. Of course, economic development is dependent not just on the economic strategy of openness to the world economy. Rather, it depends, too, on several other factors, such as the nature of society (for example, the degree of economic and social equality), and the nature of the state (the degree of its autonomy and strength relative to society). However, it is a particular claim of this study that propitious geopolitical factors have been highly influential, indeed determining, in the successful outcomes in the cases of the adoption of outward-oriented strategies in East and Southeast Asia. That claim should be qualified right away, however, to note that it does not imply that geopolitics constitutes the entire explanation for these successful outcomes in development. Other factors pertaining to state and society, no doubt, also enter into the explanation. Still, favourable geopolitical conditions emerge as having been essential to the success of outward-oriented economic strategies, at least in East and Southeast Asia. That is, geopolitics is seen as a necessary, though not sufficient, cause in these cases.

Chapter 8 deals with Japan, South Korea, and Taiwan, which were among the original Asian Tigers. Chapter 9 focuses on the Southeast Asian states that sought, some more strongly than others, to emulate the example of the original Asian Tigers. Chapter 10 examines the economic miracle of China. Additionally, as a counterfoil to the success of the 'newly industrializing economies' of East and Southeast Asia, Chapters 11 and 12 investigate the performance of India and Pakistan, and assess the role of geopolitical factors in it. Chapters 7 to 12 together constitute Part III, titled 'Development'. Finally, Chapter 13 provides the conclusions of the study, and draws out the implications of its findings.

Realism and the Study of Globalization

As should be readily apparent, the approach of this study falls under the rubric of what is called realism in international politics. Realism comes in two principal variants. One is classical realism, which bases itself on a certain view of human nature, primarily that human beings have the drive for power and domination as their chief characteristic.[11] The other is a version with more scientific pretensions, called structural realism. It is founded upon a particular conception of the deeper structure of the international system, that is, the system's lack of a central authority.[12] Regardless of the variant, realism sees a

[11] Hans J. Morgenthau, *Politics Among Nations* (fourth edition; New York: Alfred A. Knopf, 1967).
[12] Kenneth N. Waltz, *Theory of International Politics* (New York: Random House, 1979); John J. Mearsheimer, *The Tragedy of Great Power Politics* (New

perpetual struggle for power among states. The innovative feature of the present study is that it sets geopolitics as an aspect of realism alongside economic globalization, and conceives the two phenomena with their separate logics to be in interaction rather than seeing the world as dominated, or about to be dominated, by economic globalization alone. It is hoped that this conception provides a truer reflection of the social processes at work in the world.

However, this study takes realism to be an approach to understanding the world, not as given truth. If truth were already known, then universities would not need departments for the social sciences; instead, governments would merely need to institute ministries of propaganda and socialization. So, while the study utilizes the insights of realism, it hopes to avoid being dogmatic about it. Realism's propositions about international politics and the corresponding prescriptions based thereon—such as about the security dilemma, the centrality of power, the balance of power, and the balance between goals and capabilities—are all of great value. Notwithstanding that, the propositions and the prescriptions in the actual world function through, and are applied by, human beings acting on behalf of human groups. However, human beings perceive the world through the prism of their personal preferences and values even as they are also subject to the pressures, often conflicting, of politics, ideology, religion, ethnicity, and economic classes. Accordingly, it is difficult to be dogmatic and to speak with certainty about state behaviour being always, especially over the short term, consistent with realism's propositions and prescriptions. Despite that, there is nonetheless insistent pressure, particularly over the longer term, for state behaviour to be in correspondence with them, because realism's principal and enduring lesson is that the violation of those propositions and prescriptions is likely to be visited by punishment.

On the other hand, while dogma ought to be eschewed, there is no reason to be either defensive or apologetic about realism. Having been the dominant approach in international politics in the post-war period, realism has attracted many attacks from approaches with claims to being alternatives to realism. What is impressive about these

---

York: W.W. Norton, 2001), chapters 1–2, distinguishes between two kinds of structural realism: defensive realism and offensive realism. He classifies Waltz as a follower of defensive realism, while putting himself in the camp of offensive realism

approaches as challengers, however, is their lack of staying power, for one alternative approach has followed another in rather quick succession under a variety of labels: idealism, liberalism, neo-liberalism, institutionalism, liberal institutionalism, interdependence, complex interdependence, international regimes, democratic peace, and now, constructivism.[13] While quite effective as critiques of realism, they have, however, failed to offer an adequate alternative that matches realism in its parsimony and universality.[14] Moreover, ironically, as one century rolls into another, history somehow cunningly keeps continuously operating like a wrecking crew on their assumptions. It does so even as it manifests, sometimes crudely, at other times subtly, the robustness of realism's fundamental propositions on the struggle for power among nations and the centrality of power in determining outcomes in the repeated conflicts among them.

[13] For a lucid and useful survey of the various approaches, see Mark R. Brawley, *Turning Points: Decisions Shaping the Evolution of the International Political Economy* (Peterborough, Ontario: Broadview Press, 1998), Part I.

[14] For a critique of these alternative approaches from a realist perspective, see Mearsheimer, *The Tragedy of Great Power Politics*, chapter 10.

Part I
Globalization

Chapter 2

THE ADVANCE OF GLOBALIZATION
From Shallow to Deep Integration

Economic globalization is nothing but the expansion of the market so as to encompass the entire globe within its sphere; to put it in other words, it represents the integration of different regional markets into a world market. Understood in a commonsense way, the market means the exchange of goods and services at the local community or neighbourhood level. Such a market comes into being because individuals and households find that it is more efficient and beneficial in economic terms to engage in this exchange for the purpose of meeting human needs than it is for them to produce by themselves all the goods and services that they require. Although the household may well be the family's castle, it cannot avoid interdependencies with other households for its economic needs. For, the division of labour and the resulting specialization make for greater efficiency, and therefore better economic gains. Essentially, the same principle extends to the exchange of goods and services between nation-states.

Market Efficiency and Market Expansion

More technically, with the advent of capitalism and the expansion of exchange beyond local communities, the market is understood to be a coordination mechanism for the exchange of goods, services, and factors of production on the basis of relative prices.[1] Ideally, it is a self-regulating mechanism that brings together buyers and sellers on a competitive basis. Driven by the motive force of maximizing

---

[1] Robert Gilpin, *The Political Economy of International Relations* (Princeton: Princeton University Press, 1987), chapter 1.

private profit, the market orders the overall productive system on the basis of demand and supply, and thus determines the allocation of resources among various economic activities. Its principal feature of competition between buyers and sellers acts as the driving force behind the acclaimed efficiency of the system. Such competition determines which economic actors will survive or flourish on the basis of their efficiency. Survival in competition on the basis of efficiency often rests on innovation in technique, in production, and in distribution. Indeed, technology has become an independent factor in production besides land, labour, and capital, and a potent source of economic and political power in the world. Regardless of its other failings, the market system, with its noted superiority in the efficient allocation of resources among different uses in an economy, is regarded by many as without peer through space and time. No economic system, so far devised by any society compares with it in productivity and technological innovation. In the eyes of its supporters, the demise of communism in its rivalry with the market system, and its ultimately succumbing to the latter, serve to confirm the inherent superiority of the system.

The superior efficiency of the market, with its characteristically restless competition among economic actors driven by the motive of profit maximization, leads inevitably to the expansion of the market system, so as to encompass and supersede other types of economic systems outside its realm. The market system is deeply corrosive of other economic systems and tends to dissolve and absorb them. It is corrosive as well of the social values that support such systems, hence the opposition that it invariably arouses in its encounters with them. Be that as it may, the market, therefore, tends to transcend territorial boundaries, whereas states tend to fragment territory and to erect boundaries between themselves. As modern social institutions, both markets and states had their origins around the same time during the course of the long sixteenth century. However, they are based on different logics. The logic of the market is an economic one, that of profit and efficiency, while the logic of the state is a political one, that of power and legitimacy. At the same time, the two logics are not unconnected; indeed, they are interactive, at times collaborating, at other times in conflict, but always affecting each other. Yet, when all is said and done, they are separate; the attempt to altogether replace one with the other often leads to perverse results for society.

Extensive and Intensive Globalization

The tendency of the market toward relentless expansion so as to bring the entire globe under its reign—in other words, economic globalization—has been visible from the time of its birth, though undoubtedly marked by severe interruptions. The *extensive* or widening phase of globalization, in the sense of bringing the entire planet under the sway of the market, had been completed by the end of the nineteenth century. However, World War I soon shattered it, sharply rupturing the world economy. Then the protectionist wave during the Depression years of the 1930s served to continue the economic fragmentation. The thread of the extensive phase was, however, picked up again with the end of World War II, but still only partially, since a considerable part of the globe was under a communist regime that prided itself in being the very antithesis of the market system.

The current *intensive* or deepening phase of globalization, starting around the beginning of the fourth quarter of the twentieth century, followed from the dramatic advances in technology in transportation and communications. Such advances include jet aircraft in aviation, computers, and space satellites that together have made for instant transmission across the world of voice and written messages as well as visual imagery, and containerization for multimodal transportation, including shipping. These technological advances have resulted in a dramatic reduction of transaction costs, that is, costs of international economic transactions.[2] Note, for example, that between 1920 and the end of the century, charges for sea freight came down by about two-thirds and those for air travel by 84 per cent. The same period also saw a decline of 99 per cent in the cost of a three-minute call between London and New York.[3]

[2] Jeffry A. Frieden and Ronald Rogowski, 'The Impact of the International Economy on National Politics: An Analytical Overview', in Robert O. Keohane and Helen V. Milner (eds), *Internationalization and Domestic Politics* (Cambridge: Cambridge University Press, 1996), 24–47. More broadly, they specify transaction costs as covering: transport; infrastructure, such as communications; government policies in relation to trade and investment (for example, tariff barriers, quotas, and capital controls); economies of scale; and total factor productivity.

[3] David Dollar and Aart Kraay, 'Spreading the Wealth', *Foreign Affairs*, 81, 1 (January/February 2002), 120–33.

Reduced Transaction Costs and the Pressures
for Globalization

Such drastic reductions in transaction costs, or conversely large increases in benefits from international economic transactions, have made for the intensification of integration between different parts of the world economy through sharply facilitating the exchange of goods and services.[4] They have made possible the intensive globalization that is characteristic of the contemporary era. In this light, there is in the ultimate analysis a 'technological determinism' at work that has given rise to the phenomenon of intensive globalization.[5] While no doubt carrying an increased risk of exposure to external shocks, the intensive globalization has made for considerable advancement in economic welfare. There is a strong correlation between the degree of integration of a national economy with the world economy and the level of per capita income of its population. Although some may question the direction of the causal relationship, the experience of the East and Southeast Asian countries seems to suggest that their higher rates of economic growth followed the shift to greater openness to the world economy.[6] As a consequence, the possible benefits of openness to the international economy by way of higher income constitute a *positive* or *pull* factor for a state to participate in globalization.

Apart from that, more crucially, the drastic reduction in transaction costs makes globalization compelling for states. Indeed, economic globalization seems virtually unavoidable for states, because of the *negative* or *push* factor of the ill consequences that are likely to follow from not participating in it. This factor exists not only in the sense of missing out on the added economic growth that globalization may make possible, but also in the more profound sense that the national economy is likely to suffer, relatively and absolutely, from not participating in the more intensive international economic exchange. For, insulation from the world economy is likely to make the national economy technologically backward, indeed transform it into a

---

[4] Frieden and Rogowski, 'The Impact of the International Economy on National Politics: An Analytical Overview', 24–47.

[5] Geoffrey Garrett, 'The Causes of Globalization', *Comparative Political Studies*, 33, 6/7 (August/September 2000), 941–91.

[6] The issue of the relationship between international integration and development is dealt with in Part III.

technological ghetto, and turn it into a more inefficient and high-cost economy, whose goods will have little attraction for outsiders.

Failing thus to take advantage of the opportunities provided by the international market, the national economy is likely to depress economic growth even though it may, at the same time, be able to avoid the economic disturbances associated with the world economy. What is more critical, economic insulation cannot even stem the impact of the tide of globalization on the national economy. For, the drastic difference in prices prevailing internally and externally will only give rise to costly economic distortions, such as extreme scarcities of goods and commodities, and strong disparities in the real and nominal values of currencies, which, in turn, are likely to lead to large-scale smuggling, illegal international financial transactions, and both domestic and cross-border corruption.

Perversely, then, excessive emphasis on economic autonomy by the state through refusal to open up the economy to participate in the global exchange of goods and services is likely to end up in undermining the very autonomy that is often the motive for insulation. Again, insulation would need to be accompanied by considerable coercion in order to be effective, which may then have its own economic and political costs. Insulated economies, thus, have perforce to adjust to the pressures of globalization through 'economic liberalization', that is, through relaxation of controls on trade and capital inflows. Economic liberalization is built into the very process of globalization and is a necessary counterpart of it.

In brief, there seems to be no escape from globalization, for exit imposes severe costs. It is in this sense that globalization is often regarded as inescapable. Accommodation or adjustment to globalization is thus an *imperative* for states. It is understandable then that communist regimes—traditionally the very model of the bulwark against international economic integration—and other formerly delinked economies eventually opened themselves up to globalization. Few states are now left outside the scope of globalization; the diffusion of globalization across the entire geographic space of the world is a truly impressive and historic phenomenon.

International Integration in the Nineteenth Century

As noted earlier, this is not the first time that globalization has manifested itself. The late nineteenth century was also marked by a remarkable explosion in the integration of the world economy through vastly expanded trade and foreign investment. This explosion was similarly spurred by a series of technological innovations in transportation and communications, such as the railways, the telegraph, and the steamship.[7] Indeed, there is a school of thought that questions the usage of any special term such as globalization to the contemporary phenomenon of increased international integration, for high levels of trade and capital flows are all considered to have been witnessed before.

On the basis of data for some key national economies, Hirst and Thompson, the premier representatives of this school, took the position in 1996 that trade in 1913 represented a higher percentage of national GDP than in 1973 for several major economic powers.[8] Similarly, they offered data on capital outflows as a percentage of GDP for 1905–14, 1965–75, and 1982–6 for Britain (6.61, 1.17, and 1.10) and Sweden (2.01, 1.02 and 1.48) in support of their contention.[9] While this set of figures is fragmentary, other data on world overseas assets as a percentage of world exports would tend to support the position of Hirst and Thompson: 1885, 2.2; 1900, 2.3; 1913, 1.9; and 1995, 2.1. Moreover, world FDI stock as a percentage of world output was 9.0 in 1913, while it was only 4.5 in 1975 and 5.4 in 1985. Again, net resource transfers through capital markets, indicated by the ratio of current account to GDP as a weighted average for 12 select countries, seems to confirm the high degree of international integration before World War I. In regard to this aspect, Dean Baker *et al.* maintain: 'Considered over a 125-year period from 1870 to 1995, we see that this ratio is substantially higher in the period before the 1930s depression. And while there has been a fairly steady rise in this ratio since the 1960s, by 1990–6 the figure, at 2.7 per cent, is either below or roughly the same as those for any

---

[7] Deepak Nayyar, 'Globalization: The Game, the Players and the Rules', in Satya Dev Gupta (ed.), *The Political Economy of Globalization* (Boston, MA: Kluwer Academic Publishers, 1997), 13–40.

[8] Paul Hirst and Grahame Thompson, *Globalization in Question*, 27. In support of their position, they cited the following percentage figures on merchandise trade as a proportion of GDP in 1913 and 1973: France 35.4 and 29.0; Germany 35.1 and 35.2; Japan 31.4 and 18.3; Netherlands 103.6 and 80.1; UK 44.7 and 39.3; and US 11.2 and 10.5.

[9] Ibid., 27–8.

five-year interval between 1870 and 1929.' Besides, relative to the contemporary period, a tremendous amount of migration prior to World War I was evident, which is said to have remained unmatched ever since.[10]

Little wonder, Hirst and Thompson were convinced of the higher degree of the earlier integration of the world economy. The stance of Paul Krugman and Robert Gilpin on this issue has also been in line with their argument.[11] It has become commonplace to simply assume that there was greater integration before World War I than in the rest of the twentieth century.[12] As Garrett notes: 'This view has been accepted as a statement of fact in numerous influential studies.'[13] Some even refer to the period 1870–1913 as the 'golden era' of international integration.[14] Indeed, impressed by the apparent greater openness of the world economy earlier, Hirst and Thompson rejected the usage of the new-found notion of globalization in favour of the concept of 'inter-national' integration. Leaving quibbles over the

[10] Dean Baker *et al.* (eds), *Globalization and Progressive Economic Policy* (Cambridge: Cambridge University Press, 1998), 9–12.

[11] See Robert Gilpin, *The Challenge of Global Capitalism*, 294, 323.

[12] Note, for example, the assertion by the well-known realist scholar, John J. Mearsheimer, *The Tragedy of Great Power Politics*, 365: 'The fact is that the levels of economic transactions among states today, when compared with domestic economic dealings, are probably no greater than they were in the early twentieth century.' Similar is the comment regarding present-day foreign investment, compared to the earlier era, by the eminent economist, Jagdish Bhagwati, *The Wind of the Hundred Days: How Washington Mismanaged Globalization* (Cambridge, MA: MIT Press, 2000), 329: 'So in the long historical sweep, it is probably untrue to talk of the increased dominance of direct foreign investment.'

[13] Geoffrey Garrett, 'The Causes of Globalization', 942. Among the studies included are: Peter J. Katzenstein, Robert O. Keohane, and Stephen D. Krasner, 'International Organization and the Study of World Politics', *International Organization*, 52 (1998), 647–86; Stephen D. Krasner, *Sovereignty* (Princeton: Princeton University Press, 1999), 220–3; Dani Rodrik, *Has Globalization Gone Too Far?*; and Jeffrey D. Sachs and Andrew Warner, 'Economic Reform and the Process of Global Economic Integration', *Brookings Papers on Economic Activity, 1995*, No. 1 (1995), 1–118.

[14] UNCTAD, *World Investment Report 1994*, 120.

appropriate nomenclature aside, characterizing the present period as one of economic globalization does not necessarily preclude using the same term for the earlier period of international integration. Accordingly, it seems quite appropriate to refer to the 1870–1913 period as Globalization I or the First Age of Globalization, and the contemporary period as Globalization II or the Second Age of Globalization.[15]

Post-war Globalization as Distinctive in Character

Having said that, however, there are nonetheless several aspects, some of them quite weighty, that are quite distinctive of the contemporary period, and these taken together may make it alone as seriously meriting the designation of globalization. As Garrett points out: 'Core features of the contemporary world economy are without historical precedent.'[16] The distinctive aspects of present-day globalization pertain to the level of trade flows, the composition of trade, FDI inflows, the transnationalization of production, and the scale of foreign exchange trading.

Trade Flows

Contrary to the position of Hirst and Thompson, contemporary globalization has surpassed the earlier period in terms of world exports as a proportion of world product. This seems to have been the case even by 1973, which serves as their reference point, when the ratio was 10.5 per cent as against 7.9 per cent in 1913 (see Table 2.1). More remarkably, by the end of the twentieth century, with the share of exports standing at 17.2 per cent in 1998, the world economy was integrated twice as much as it was on the eve of World War I. Significantly, between 1950 and 1999, while the world product increased by about six times, world exports expanded by more than nineteen times.[17]

The rise in exports as a share of GDP is even more pronounced for some of the individual advanced countries that have often been

[15] Nayyar, 'Globalization', 19; and Joseph M. Grieco and G. John Ikenberry, *State Power and World Markets: The International Political Economy* (New York: W.W. Norton & Company, 2003), 5, 208.

[16] Garrett, 'The Causes of Globalization', 942.

[17] Grieco and Ikenberry, *State Power and World Markets*, 5, 208.

Table 2.1: Merchandise Exports as Per Cent of GDP in 1990 Prices, 1870–1998

	1870	1913	1929	1950	1973	1998
France	4.9	7.8	8.6	7.6	15.2	28.7
Germany	9.5	16.1	12.8	6.2	23.8	38.9
Netherlands	17.4	17.3	17.2	12.2	40.7	61.2
UK	12.2	17.5	13.3	11.3	14.0	25.0
Spain	3.8	8.1	5.0	3.0	5.0	23.5
US	2.5	3.7	3.6	3.0	4.9	10.1
Mexico	3.9	9.1	12.5	3.0	1.9	10.7
Brazil	12.2	9.8	6.9	3.9	2.5	5.4
China	0.7	1.7	1.8	2.6	1.5	4.9
India	2.6	4.6	3.7	2.9	2.0	2.4
Japan	0.2	2.4	3.5	2.2	7.7	13.4
World	4.6	7.9	9.0	5.5	10.5	17.2

Source: Angus Maddison, *The World Economy: A Millennial Perspective* (Paris: OECD, 2001), 363.

cited to support the argument about the presumed higher international integration earlier. Compared to the situation in 1913, the share of France in 1998 had increased by almost four times, that of Germany by almost two-and-a-half times, and that of the Netherlands by more than three-and-a-half times. However, the UK, with its share increasing by less than 50 per cent, fell far short of the record of its European competitors. On the other hand, the performance of the two great trading nations outside Europe, the US and Japan, matched that of the mainland European powers. The share of the US had multiplied by about three times, and that of Japan's five-and-a-half times. Not only is it, therefore, no longer tenable to claim that the world economy was more integrated in 1913 than it is now, but with these high ratios there can be no doubt that contemporary integration is of a different order.

That is especially so when this higher level of integration is seen in the context of a world economy that is qualitatively different, both in the density and complexity of economic interaction, precisely because of the quantitative leap in the volume of exports. World exports in 1998 stood at a staggeringly high figure of 5.8 trillion dollars (at 1990 constant prices) (see Table 2.2) (unless otherwise indicated dollars or $ refer to US$). That figure is more than 27 times the figure of 212 billion dollars in 1913, and points to a much transformed world economy. Besides, the rates of growth of world exports during 1950–73 (7.9 per cent) and 1973–98 (5.1

24   *The Geopolitics of Globalization*

Table 2.2: Value of Exports at Constant Prices, 1870–1998 (Million 1990 dollars)

	1870	1913	1950	1973	1990	1998
Western Europe	32,428	127,839	121,535	773,726	1,597,933	2,490,596
Western Offshoots	3,783	27,425	62,892	254,128	570,380	1,071,432
Eastern Europe*	2,100	8,726	14,780	127,285	166,252	237,148
Latin America	2,709	10,910	25,235	66,155	139,611	286,043
Asia	7,000	22,900	41,800	372,170	883,309	1,577,571
Africa	2,325	14,625	29,379	97,184	99,277	154,290
World	50,345	212,425	295,621	1,690,648	3,456,762	5,817,080

* Also includes former USSR.
Source: Angus Maddison, *The World Economy: A Millennial Perspective* (Paris: OECD, 2001), 362.

per cent) are significantly higher than during 1870–1913 (3.4 per cent) (see Table 2.3). This pattern of higher growth rates is replicated in the case of individual countries. Moreover, it is important to remember that exports prior to World War I took place in the context of much of Asia, Africa, and Central America being under the colonial

Table 2.3: Growth Rates in Merchandise Export Volumes, 1870–1998

	1870–1913	1913–50	1950–73	1973–98
France	2.8	1.1	8.2	4.7
Germany	4.1	–2.8	12.4	4.4
Netherlands	2.3	1.5	10.4	4.1
UK	2.8	0.0	3.9	4.4
Spain	3.5	–1.6	9.2	9.0
US	4.9	2.2	6.3	6.0
Mexico	5.4	–0.5	4.3	10.9
Brazil	1.9	1.7	4.7	6.6
China	2.6	1.1	2.7	11.8
India	2.4	–1.5	2.5	5.9
Japan	8.5	2.0	15.4	5.3
World	3.4	0.9	7.9	5.1

Source: Angus Maddison, *The World Economy: A Millennial Perspective* (Paris: OECD, 2001), 362.

occupation of the imperialist powers of the North Atlantic. Some of the exports from the colonies represented forced exports, being more in the nature of tribute rather than simply commercial exchange.

The Composition of Trade

An essential aspect of the contemporary surge in world exports is the dramatic change in their very composition as compared to the period before World War I. In 1913, only the UK (70 per cent) and northwest Europe (52 per cent) had manufactured goods as a substantial share of their exports. While the US and Canada (25.8 per cent) and Asia (21.2 per cent) had somewhat respectable shares, manufactured goods had an insignificant role in the exports of Latin America and Africa (see Table 2.4A).

The situation was entirely different at the end of the twentieth century. In 1999, more than three-fourths of the world's exports consisted of manufactures. As ought to be expected, the share of manufacturing in the exports of industrialized countries at 80.8 per cent was higher than the world average, but it was as high as almost 70 per cent even in the case of the developing countries. On the other hand, West Asia (29.4 per cent) and Africa (18.2 per cent) lagged considerably behind the world average (see Table 2.4B).

FDI and the Transnationalization of Production

There is further the important new development of international integration that is evident in the production of goods and services

Table 2.4A: Manufacturing Exports as Percentage of Total Exports

	1913	1928	1937	1953
US and Canada	25.8	38.5	44.7	60.7
UK	70.0	74.8	72.0	73.7
NW Europe	52.0	65.0	63.1	57.3
Asia*	21.2	30.9	28.1	25.3
Latin America	3.2	2.1	1.7	2.3
Africa	3.7	2.5	3.7	8.5

* Excludes China and North Korea.
Source: Dean Baker *et al.* (eds), *Globalization and Progressive Economic Policy*, 7, which draws on P. Lamartine Yates, *Forty Years of Foreign Trade* (New York: Macmillan, 1959), 55.

Table 2.4B: Manufacturing Exports as Percentage of Total Exports

	1970	1980	1990	1999
World	60.9	54.2	70.5	76.5
Industrial Countries	72.0	70.9	78.0	80.8
Eastern Europe	59.1	50.2	45.4	59.5
Developing Countries	18.5	19.5	53.6	69.0
Latin America	10.6	14.7	31.4	56.8
Africa	7.0	4.0	15.5	18.2
West Asia	4.4	3.0	15.6	29.4
Other Asia	43.5	50.4	76.5	83.1

Source: UNCTAD, *Handbook of Statistics 2001* (New York: UN, 2001), and *Handbook of International Trade and Development Statistics 1992* (New York: UN, 1993).

as distinct from the exchange of goods and services. Even though significant as an indicator of international integration, trade in goods and services, as embodying the *market* dimension of the world economy, represents *shallow integration*. On the other hand, the *transnationalization* of the *production* dimension of the world economy, as reflected in the worldwide activities of transnational corporations (TNCs), alternatively also referred to as multinational corporations (MNCs), is indicative of *deep integration*.[18]

Typically, the TNC is headquartered in one country, where its R&D activities are also most likely to be located, but it has, through foreign direct investment (FDI), established production operations in several other countries around the world. At one time, such offshore production was a mechanism to jump over tariff walls in order to capture overseas markets. However, in the contemporary period of globalization, it is more likely to involve a different modality in an endeavour to cut costs, given the intense global competition. It often means breaking down the production process of a product into several parts and allocating them to different production sites in the world economy, with a view to subsequently integrating them into the final product in one or more places. This technique is adopted not only for local consumption but also for exports internationally, including exports to the home economies of the TNCs. International trade, thus, often assumes the form of 'within-firm' trade by TNCs, and it seems that one-third to two-fifths of contemporary foreign trade is of this nature.

[18] UNCTAD, *World Investment Report 1994*, 117–18.

The transnationalization of production may have at one time been considered to apply only to goods but it is increasingly evident that, with the contemporary advances in information technology (IT), it applies to services as well. The eminent *New York Times* columnist, Thomas Friedman, an enthusiast of globalization, has commented on this particular aspect in the context of the controversy in the US over the outsourcing of white-collar jobs to India. Distinguishing between three eras of globalization, he refers to the first era that broadly stretched across the nineteenth century as Globalization 1.0. In this period, the world was reduced from a size large to a size medium on the basis of falling transportation costs that stemmed from the invention of the steamship and the railroad. Globalization 2.0, covering the last two decades of the twentieth century, was, on the other hand, driven by falling telecom costs and the PC, and it shrunk the world from a size medium to a size small. Friedman goes on to say: 'Now we've entered Globalization 3.0, and it is shrinking the world from size small to a size tiny. That's what this outsourcing of white-collar jobs is telling us—and it is going to require some wrenching adjustments for workers and political systems.' This phenomenon is the result of: (1) the massive laying of undersea fibre-optic cables and the increased bandwidth, which have rendered possible the cheap global transmission and storage of vast amounts of data; (2) the global diffusion of PCs; and (3) 'the convergence of a variety of software applications—from email, to Google, to Microsoft Office, to specially designed outsourcing programmes—that, when combined with all those PCs and bandwidth, made it possible to create global "work-flow platforms".' Explaining the transnationalization of services, he says:

> These work-flow platforms can chop up any service job—accounting, radiology, consulting, software engineering—into different functions and then, thanks to scanning and digitization, outsource each function to teams of skilled knowledge workers around the globe, based on which team can do each function with the highest skill at the lowest price. Then the project is reassembled back at headquarters into a finished product.[19]

Foreign direct investment (FDI) by TNCs has played a crucial role in the contemporary transnationalization of production. Of course, FDI was not unknown in the period prior to World War I, and there

[19] Thomas L. Friedman, 'Sleeping Americans, Working Indians', *Indian Express* Online, 5 March 2004.

even exists the claim that FDI stock as a share of the world product was at a higher level in 1913 than in the subsequent period. Undoubtedly, there was not just 'shallow integration' then, and elements of 'deep integration' also existed before World War I. However, the transnationalization of production in the sense described above, especially on the massive scale in which it is now prevalent, is singularly unique to contemporary globalization. Indeed, as a consequence, the TNC has become the driving force behind contemporary globalization and its acceleration. And, realizing the key role that TNCs can play in the development of an economy by bringing in capital, new technology, and expanded employment opportunities, states have often been engaged in intense competition to attract them, frequently referred to as 'race to the bottom'.

As in the case of exports, so in the case of FDI, it can, therefore, no longer be maintained that there was a higher level of FDI stock existent as a proportion of world output in 1913 than it is presently. In fact, by 1990, the ratio in regard to FDI stock had already surpassed the one that prevailed in 1913. More significantly, within less than a decade, by 1999 it was almost twice as much (17.3 per cent) as it was in 1913 (9.0 per cent) (see Table 2.5), an aspect that is strong testimony to the significant advance in 'deep integration' in contemporary globalization.

Additionally, there is another important feature of contemporary FDI that distinguishes it dramatically from that of the earlier period. It pertains to the nature of economic activity to which FDI is directed. In 1913, 55 per cent of the FDI stock was in the primary sector, while only 10 per cent of it went into manufacturing, and another

Table 2.5: World FDI Stock as Share of World Output

Year	Per Cent	Year	Per cent
1913	9.0	1980	6.0
1960	4.4	1985	7.8
1975	4.5	1990	9.2
1980	4.8	1995	10.3
1985	6.4	1999	17.3

Source: The figures in the first two columns are from UNCTAD, World Investment Report 1994, 130, while those in the last two columns are from World Investment Report 2001, 325, and pertain to 'inward' FDI stock.

30 per cent was directed toward transportation, trade and distribution.[20] However, the position of the primary sector vis-à-vis manufacturing has almost been reversed in the contemporary period. Only 6.3 per cent of FDI stock is in the primary sector while 42.5 per cent of it is in manufacturing, and another 48.5 per cent is in services (including finance),[21] which tend largely to serve the manufacturing sector.

What is especially noteworthy is the phenomenal expansion of FDI, and equally of the number of TNCs, in the last two decades of the twentieth century. In 1982, total FDI inflows amounted to $57 billion, but eight years later in 1990 they had gone up to $202 billion, and another decade later in 2000 to the fantastically high figure of $1.271 trillion (see Table 2.6). In a matter of just eighteen years, FDI inflows had multiplied more than 22 times. In 2001, however, a decline in FDI inflows set in because of the business-cycle slow down in the world economy and the impact of the terrorist attacks of 9/11. Equally astonishing is the number of TNCs that have come into existence. By 2000, there were 64,592 parent TNCs, with 851,167 foreign affiliates.[22]

The Gigantic Scale of Foreign Exchange Trading

Foreign exchange trading on a vast scale, largely unrelated to merchandise trade, is another unique feature of the recent period. Of nominal value at the beginning of the 1970s, foreign exchange trading expanded exponentially thereafter, so that by 1998 its *daily*

Table 2.6: FDI Inflows in Current $ Billion and by Annual Growth Rates

Year	Value $ Billion	Year	Growth Rate %
1982	57	1986–1990	23.0
1990	202	1991–1995	20.8
2000	1,271	1996–1999	40.8
		1998	44.9
		1999	55.2
		2000	18.2

Source: World Investment Report 2001, 10.

[20] *World Investment Report 1994*, 121.
[21] *World Investment Report 1999*, 424–5.
[22] *World Investment Report 2002*, 270–2.

turnover was $1.5 trillion (US).[23] That figure was over 100 times the average of daily world exports in that year at $14.79 billion.[24] Since then, such trading has seen some decline ($1.1 trillion in 2000) under the impact of the changeover to the Euro in the EU, the increased role of electronic broking, and the greater concentration in banking.[25] The high incidence of foreign exchange trading, and more generally the expansion of FDI flows and TNC operations, has been facilitated by the communications revolution that has occurred as a result of the combination of two modern technologies—almost instant satellite-based communications and high-speed computer-aided information processing.[26]

Labour Migration

Finally, if there is one thing in which contemporary globalization can be said to compare unfavourably with that in the earlier period of globalization in the nineteenth century, it is the mobility of labour. As one critic of globalization puts it: 'The fundamental difference between the two phases of globalization is in the sphere of labour flows.'[27] During the earlier period from 1870 to 1914, some 50 million people, forming one-eighth of Europe's population in 1900, moved out of Europe, with two-thirds of them going to the US, and the other one-third to Canada, Australia, and other places.[28] It was a time when there were no passports, no visas, and no restrictions on travel: 'Until World War I, few legislative or political barriers impeded the process of international migration. People were free to travel through Europe and sometimes overseas without a passport; they could settle in a new country with few bureaucratic formalities.... The international exchange of people was more important than the international exchange of goods.'[29]

---

[23] Bank for International Settlements (BIS), *71st Annual Report: 1 April 2000–31 March 2001* (Basel, Switzerland: BIS, 2001), 98.

[24] IMF, *Direction of Trade Statistics Yearbook 2001*, 2. Total world exports in 1998 were valued at $5,396.7 billion.

[25] BIS, *71st Annual Report*, 98–9.

[26] *World Investment Report 1994*, 125.

[27] Nayyar, 'Globalization', 24.

[28] Ibid.

[29] Massimo Livi-Baci, 'South–North Migration: A Comparative Approach to North American and European Experiences', in OECD, *The Changing Course of International Migration* (Paris: OECD, 1993), 37–46.

This idyllic picture of the earlier globalization needs to be qualified, however. As part of that globalization, another 50 million were moved, often forcibly, to work as indentured labour on plantations and in mines in the colonies in the Caribbean, South Africa, East Africa, and Southeast Asia. However, there was no reverse migration from the colonies to the metropolitan countries: 'Immigration from the colonies or other poor countries was not even considered a possibility.'[30] If one were to push the historical account a little further back, one would have to take into consideration also the vast traffic in slaves from Africa to the European colonies in the Western Hemisphere. Eventually, the earlier period of globalization collapsed with World War I, and restrictions came to be imposed on immigration.

Though the scale may not match that of the earlier globalization, labour migration has not been absent in contemporary globalization, however. Table 2.7 compares net migration rates per thousand of population for the 1870–1914 period with several periods after World War II up to the mid-1980s. It is apparent that, for the US and Canada, the post-war rates for immigration are about half than that of the earlier period. Interestingly, post-war Europe, which had traditionally been the source of immigrants for the Western Hemisphere, has itself become a net recipient of immigrants after 1970. In the 1970–80 period, net migration into North America and Europe at the rate of 4.5 per thousand of population was not far removed from the rate of 5.4 of the 1870–1910 period. Thus, labour migration continues to be a significant feature of the contemporary period. Besides, it has its own unique aspects as well. Labour migration has

Table 2.7: Net Migration Rates for the US/Canada and Europe

	1870–1910	1950–60	1960–70	1970–80	1980–85
US and Canada	+5.4	+2.7	+2.3	+4.0	+2.8
Europe	−2.6	−0.8	−	+0.5	+0.1

Source: Dean Baker *et al.* (eds), *Globalization and Progressive Economic Policy*, 12. This source draws its data on the post-war period from Massimo Livi-Baci, 'South–North Migration: A Comparative Approach to North American and European Experiences', in OECD, *The Changing Course of International Migration*, 37–46, which makes reference to 'net migration per thousand population'.

---

[30] Ibid., 37.

now become more globalized in its sources, while in the principal immigrant-receiving countries it has become less racially based.

Another way of looking at the extent of labour migration is to examine the proportion of the foreign born in the population, which is shown in Table 2.8 for the years 1965 and 1990. Among the industrialized countries as a whole, and the regions within them of (1) the US and Canada, (2) Europe, and (3) Oceania, the proportion of the foreign born in the total population has invariably gone up by a wide margin except for Oceania. In Oceania, where the proportion was very high to begin with, the increase has been more modest. While the developing countries as a whole do not compare well with the industrialized countries in this regard, especially striking is the case of the Persian Gulf states where the proportion of the foreign born tripled in 25 years from 12.4 per cent to 36.5 per cent. That exceptional increase has largely been the consequence of the economic boom there, following the OPEC oil price hikes.

Before World War I, the US had been the great magnet for immigration. Later, like other states, it began to impose restrictions, a process that climaxed with the National Origins Act of 1924 based on racial discrimination. That restrictive posture was confirmed again after World War II with the Immigration and Nationality Act of 1952, which imposed quotas for different countries, basically on a racial basis.[31] Consider the fact that as populous a country as India had a

Table 2.8: Foreign Born as Per Cent of Total Population

Countries	1965	1990
Industrialized Countries	3.0	4.5
US and Canada	6.0	8.6
Europe	3.3	5.0
Oceania	14.4	17.8
Developing Countries	1.9	1.6
Persian Gulf states	12.4	36.5
North Africa and W Asia	4.1	6.0
Latin America	2.4	1.6
Sub-Saharan Africa	2.8	2.8
Southern Asia	2.8	1.8
Eastern and SE Asia	1.9	1.2

Source: Same as for Table 2.7.

[31] Ibid., 40.

ridiculous quota of 100 as against the quotas in the hundreds of thousands allowed for European countries. However, in 1965, amendments to the 1952 Act removed the racial restrictions. This removal of restrictions had a tremendous impact: 'By abolishing the national origins quotas that had been in operation since the early 1920s and by giving priority to family reunification as a basis for immigrant admission, the amendments led to levels of immigration that by historical standards are quite high. For example, during the 1980s nearly 600,000 immigrants per year were granted lawful permanent residence in the United States, levels that were surpassed only in the peak immigration years early in the twentieth century.'[32]

A dozen years later, Canada, through its Immigration Act of 1978, also removed the racial bias in its legislation by mandating immigration on a non-discriminatory basis. Thus, in the case of Canada and the US, immigration is now truly global in scope and takes place largely on a universalistic basis. Unlike the past, when immigrants into these two countries were almost entirely white, in 1999 the top five immigrant nationalities for Canada were all Asian while for the US, two were Latin American and three Asian (see Table 2.9). Note, too, that Australia, once with an all-white immigration policy, had China and India among its five top immigrant nationalities in 1999. Indeed, an OECD study states that, 'Asia has for some time been one of the chief sources of immigration towards the OECD area.'[33]

Historically, the US, Canada, and Australia as immigrant nations have been more open to immigration. In 1999, they had a total stock of the foreign born amounting to 28.2 million, 4.97 million and 4.48 million, forming 10.3 per cent, over 17 per cent, and 23.6 per cent of their respective populations.[34] While Europe as a whole, in contrast, has been eager to limit, indeed stem, immigration, there are nonetheless now several European countries that have substantial immigrant populations, and some of them have non-European groups among their top five immigrant nationalities. Thus, France, with a population of 3.26 million foreigners, has four Muslim countries among its top five immigrant nationalities. Similarly, Italy, with a population of 1.25 million foreigners, features Morocco and China

---

[32] F.D. Bean *et al.*, cited in Livi-Baci, 'South–North Migration', 40.

[33] OECD, *Trends in International Migration* (Paris: OECD, 2001), 63.

[34] Ibid., 35 and 37. The figure for Canada is for 1996.

Table 2.9: Top Five Countries in Total Immigration Flows and Stocks of Foreigners in Selected OECD Countries

Top Five Nationalities in 1999	Inflows 1999 %	Stocks 1998 %	Inflows/Stocks
Australia			
New Zealand	23.7	7.5	3.2
United Kingdom	10.0	27.4	0.4
China	7.4	2.8	2.6
South Africa	6.2	1.4	4.3
India	5.0	2.0	2.5
Total ('000)	92.3	3908	–
Canada			
China	15.3	4.6	3.3
India	9.2	4.7	1.9
Pakistan	4.9	–	–
Philippines	4.8	3.7	1.3
Korea	3.8	–	–
Total ('000)	189.8	4971	–
France			
Morocco	16.4	15.4	1.1
Algeria	13.2	14.6	0.9
Turkey	6.6	6.4	1.0
Tunisia	4.7	4.7	1.0
United States	3.1	0.7	4.6
Total ('000)	86.3	3263	–
Germany			
Yugoslavia	13.0	9.8	1.3
Poland	10.7	3.9	2.8
Turkey	7.0	28.8	0.2
Italy	5.2	8.4	0.6
Russia	4.1	1.1	3.7
Total ('000)	673.9	7319	–
Japan			
China	21.0	18.0	1.2
Philippines	20.3	7.0	2.9
Brazil	9.3	14.7	0.6
United States	8.7	2.8	3.1
Korea	8.2	42.2	0.2
Total ('000)	281.9	1512	–

(*Contd.*)

Table 2.9 (*Contd.*)

Top Five Nationalities in 1999	Inflows 1999 %	Stocks 1998 %	Inflows/Stocks
United Kingdom			
United States	16.2	5.4	3.0
Australia	12.0	2.3	5.3
South Africa	8.7	1.8	4.9
India	7.1	6.3	1.1
New Zealand	5.7	1.7	3.3
Total ('000)	276.9	2207	–
Italy			
Albania	13.9	7.3	1.9
Morocco	9.3	11.7	0.8
Former Yugoslavia	9.1	3.3	2.8
Romania	7.8	3.0	2.6
China	4.1	3.0	1.3
Total ('000)	268.1	1250	–
United States			
Mexico	19.9	21.7	0.9
China	5.6	2.7	2.1
India	5.5	2.3	2.4
Philippines	5.2	4.6	1.1
Dominican Republic	3.1	1.8	1.8
Total ('000)	660.5	19767	–

Source: OECD, *Trends in International Migration: Annual Report 2001* (Paris: OECD, 2001), 32–33. Selected countries have over 1 million stock of foreigners in 1998; Switzerland, which had a total stock of 1.4 million foreigners, is not included in this table.

Notes: (1) The figures in column 2 on 'Inflows 1999 %' stand for 'Inflows of foreigners in 1999 as % of total inflows'. (2) The figures in column 3 'Stocks 1998 %' stand for 'Stocks of foreigners in 1998 as % of total stock of foreigners'. The aforementioned OECD document uses the term 'foreigners' in relation to Europe, and the term 'foreign born' with reference to Australia and North America.

among its top five immigrant nationalities. Certainly, Germany is exceptional among the European countries; in 1999, it had a higher inflow of immigrants (673,900) than even the US (660,000); its stock of 7.32 million foreigners as a proportion of its population is higher than that of the US in relation to the latter's population. Turkey ranks third among its top five immigrant nationalities.

As with immigration in general, the foreign or foreign-born labour force forms a considerable part of the total labour force in several OECD countries and its proportion 'has increased significantly' during the last half-decade of the twentieth century.[35] Apart from the exceptional case of Luxembourg, where the foreign labour force formed 57.3 per cent of the total labour force in 1999, the corresponding percentage figures for some other OECD countries were: Australia (24.6), Canada (19.2), Switzerland (18.1), the United States (11.7), Austria (9.5), Belgium (8.7), Germany (8.7), France (6.1), Sweden (4.1), the United Kingdom (3.9), Greece (3.8), Italy (3.6), Netherlands (3.4), and Ireland (3.4).[36]

It is apparent that, while by no stretch of the imagination labour migration comes anywhere near close to capital mobility, in the case of several of the important OECD countries, there nonetheless exists today a substantial volume of immigration. Besides, such immigration is more broadly based now so as to have rendered these countries into multicultural communities. Indeed, some in France and Germany point out, perhaps with exaggeration but certainly also with some regret, that even remote villages now contain at least one mosque.[37] Interestingly, countries that were earlier not exposed to globalization, such as those in eastern and central Europe, have, since the collapse of the Soviet bloc, become home to immigrants from Asia. An important development in Europe has been the acceptance by the EU of the principle of free mobility of labour, even though there has not been much intra-European labour mobility.[38]

The considerable presence of immigrant communities in the advanced industrial countries from the less developed countries has implications for international politics. While there were, no doubt, other more weighty strategic reasons for France's opposition to the American intent to invade Iraq in 2003, a part of the underlying rationale was also to prevent the alienation of its own large Muslim population from North Africa. Along the same line, some observers have advanced the increased presence of the Indian community in the US and active lobbying by it, as one of the reasons for the

---

[35] Ibid., 53.
[36] Ibid., 54. The figure for Canada is for 1994.
[37] Interviews in France and Germany in July 2000.
[38] OECD, *Trends in International Migration*, 34.

American policy to engage India after the latter's nuclear tests in 1998 rather than simply to punish and isolate it.[39]

While labour mobility does not match capital mobility, it has itself certainly become a factor of considerable importance in capital mobility. Note that in 2001, the developing countries received overseas remittances from their migrant workers abroad in the huge amount of $72.3 billion, which was equivalent to 42 per cent of their total FDI inflows. India alone, which ranked number one, received $10 billion; Mexico was second with $9.9 billion, followed by the Philippines with $6.4 billion.[40] The important role of labour in capital mobility in the LDCs can be seen in reference to India: 'Take the year 2000. As a percentage of the country's total exports of goods and services, overseas remittances stood at 18 per cent; as a percentage of official development assistance, they were 779 per cent; and as a percentage of total foreign direct investment, almost the holy grail of policy makers, remittances totalled 494 per cent.'[41] In this fashion, labour migration today is an important contributor to globalization beyond simply through labour transfers. In sum, a not inconsiderable amount of labour migration has taken place under contemporary globalization, though its form, sources, and driving forces are different from those under nineteenth-century globalization.

Summary

One can assert, with some degree of confidence, that economic globalization has made tremendous strides since the advent of the last quarter of the twentieth century, both in terms of shallow and deep integration. There is evidence for this proposition in the definitive trends delineated above in a variety of areas: the huge expansion in world exports, the dominant position of manufactures in trade, the

[39] See the interesting paper by Robert M. Hathway, 'Everybody Wants to Go to Heaven, but No One Wants to Die: The US Congress and the South Asian Nuclear Tests' (1 November 1999 Draft).

[40] Santanu Ghosh, '*Dil Hai Hindustani* for Indians Abroad', *Indian Express* Online, 3 April 2003. India retained its number one position in 2003, when overseas remittances by the Indian diaspora reached the record level of $18.3 billion; see Gayatri Nayak, 'NRIs Send Home Maximum Funds', *Economic Times* Online, 5 April 2004.

[41] 'Workers without Borders', *Indian Express* Online, 4 April 2003.

vast FDI flows, the high role of manufacturing in FDI, the large numbers of TNCs existing now, the transnationalization of production, and the phenomenal growth in foreign exchange trading. Even in respect of labour, there is evidence of considerable migration, and that too, on a more universalistic basis than before. Labour migration, in turn, has been contributing to capital mobility. In the face of these trends, it is difficult to maintain that there is nothing new about the contemporary international economic integration; that it has all been seen before at the beginning of the twentieth century; and that the degree of international integration was higher before World War I than in the present period. Indeed, it would seem that there is nothing in the period prior to World War I that comes close to the kind of deep integration, especially the scale on which it is taking place, that is now under way through the transnationalization of production. To take note of such advance in economic globalization is also to witness the much-proclaimed triumph of the market. Whether this triumph actually means a retreat of the state, however, remains open as an empirical question.

Chapter 3

THE TRUNCATED NATURE OF GLOBALIZATION

Although there can be no doubt about the increasing advance of economic globalization and its wide-ranging geographic scope, it is equally manifest that it is not uniformly spread across the globe. Rather, globalization seems to be heavily concentrated in the developed or industrial countries as against the developing countries. And within the industrial countries, it primarily revolves around the three economies of the European Union (EU), Japan, and the United States, often referred to as the 'Triad'.

In its *World Investment Report* for 1991, UNCTAD had called attention to the shift in foreign direct investment (FDI) from a bipolar pattern in the early 1980s to a tripolar pattern at the beginning of the 1990s. The bipolar pattern had been focused on the US and the European Community (EC) as it was then known, while the tripolar pattern additionally encompassed Japan, thus 'the Triad'.[1] Subsequent annual issues of the Report have continued to emphasize the dominant role of the three economies of the EU, Japan, and the US in FDI. The phenomenon of concentration, however, extends beyond FDI, and applies to other aspects of globalization as well.

Because of the heavy concentration of the world's economic interactions by way of foreign trade and FDI flows in the triad, and more generally in the industrial or developed countries, the rest of the world can appear to have been marginalized economically. Indeed, Hirst and Thompson chose to describe the contemporary process of increased international integration as 'triadization' rather than

[1] UNCTAD, *World Investment Report 1991: The Triad in Foreign Direct Investment,* 32.

globalization.[2] Since the notions of 'triadization' on the one hand, and marginalization on the other are suggestive of economic polarization of the world economy, to avoid such an inference *ab initio* the phenomenon of uneven or asymmetrical spread is here referred to as *truncated globalization*. Such terminology leaves open the possibility that the world economy is not necessarily headed for polarization, though it may well do so.

The argument of this chapter is that the empirical data confirm the highly uneven or asymmetrical spread of globalization. This is true in respect of foreign trade, FDI flows, and the home location of transnational corporations (TNCs).

Trade Flows

In the area of foreign trade, the advanced industrial countries, which had less than 20 per cent of the world's population, had a share of about two-thirds of the world's exports in 1995 and 2000 (see Table 3.1). On the other hand, the developing countries, with over 80 per

Table 3.1: Exports as Share of World Exports

Country/Region	Exports % 1995	Exports % 2000	Population % 1999
Industrial Countries	67.6	63.2	19.5
EU	39.8	35.9	6.2
Japan	8.7	7.5	2.1
US	11.5	12.1	4.5
Developing Countries	32.4	36.8	80.5
Africa	1.6	1.9	
Asia	18.5	19.9	
Europe	4.6	4.9	
Middle East	3.1	4.2	
Western Hemisphere	4.5	5.8	
World	$5,071.0 billion	$6,368.7 billion	6,002.5 million

Source: The figures on exports have been tabulated from data in IMF, *Direction of Trade Statistics Yearbook 2001.* The population figures are from European Commission, *European Social Statistics: Demography* (Luxembourg: Official Publications of the European Communities, 2001), 37.

[2] Paul Hirst and Grahame Thompson, *Globalization in Question*, chapter 3.

cent of the world's population, had only about a third of the world's exports. Among the industrial economies, the shares of the countries in the EU, Japan, and the US in 2000 were 35.9 per cent, 7.5 per cent, and 12.1 per cent, respectively, which together formed 55.5 per cent of the world's total exports. Their collective share was somewhat higher in 1995 (60 per cent). The unusually high figure for the EU, about three times or more than that of the US, is somewhat misleading. It is like the total for the industrial and the developing countries, simply an aggregate of the figures for all its members, even when they are exporting to each other. It is as if one were to take into account interstate commerce within the US for arriving at the figure for the US. This comment, of course, applies to the data on FDI flows as well.

The implication of the figures on exports can be stated simply: In the first place, the developed countries, with a share of about two-thirds of world exports, dominate world trade. Secondly, among the industrial countries, the triad of the EU, Japan, and the US has the lion's share (about 55 to 60 per cent of world exports or nearly 90 per cent of the share of industrial countries). Thirdly, the developing countries have a disproportionately low share of world exports, given that the bulk of humanity (80 per cent) lives there. Taken together, these facts clearly demonstrate that world trade takes place essentially among the 'triad' and that globalization is, indeed, 'triadization'.

Foreign Direct Investment

As in the case of exports so in the case of FDI, the developed countries dominate both inflows and outflows. In 2000, the share of the developed countries in FDI inflows was 82.3 per cent (see Table 3.2). The figure for that particular year, as also for 1999, seems to be on the high side, because of the exceptionally large numbers of M&As (merger and acquisitions). The average over the decade 1990–9 was about two-thirds of world FDI inflows. Even that lower average figure shows that one-fifth of the world's population gets a highly disproportionate share of FDI, and is therefore able to avail of the benefits that flow from such investment.

On the other hand, the developing countries, with four-fifths of the world's population, receive less than one-third of the FDI inflows. Note, however, that the 2000 figure for the developed countries is about the same as the average for an earlier five-year period,

Table 3.2: FDI Inflows and Outflows (Percentages)

Country/ Region	Inflows 1990–4	Inflows 1995–9	Inflows 2000	Outflows 1990–4	Outflows 1995–9	Outflows 2000
Developed Countries	65.3	67.5	82.3	87.8	89.1	92.2
EU	38.2	37.0	54.2	46.8	57.4	70.2
Japan	0.7	0.7	0.6	11.0	4.0	2.3
US	18.2	23.6	20.2	22.1	19.6	12.0
Developing Countries	32.6	29.3	15.9	12.1	10.6	7.6

Source: UNCTAD, *World Investment Report 2002*, 265.

1986–90 (82.4 per cent).[3] Among the developed economies, the EU corners the bulk of the FDI inflows, with its share in world FDI inflows being 54.2 per cent in 2000, and an average of around 38 per cent during the previous decade. The US share was 20.2 per cent in 2000, which was largely in line with its average share during the decade of the 1990s. On the other hand, FDI inflows have only a minor role in Japan's economy, amounting to less than 1 per cent. The triad, taken together, has a share of 75 per cent of world FDI inflows.

In respect of FDI outflows, the share of developed countries in 2000 was over 92.2 per cent, with the shares of the EU, Japan, and the US being 70.2 per cent, 2.3 per cent, and 12.0 per cent, respectively. The share of the EU is again on the high side, compared to the average for the previous decade. As is to be expected, the developing countries have only a nominal role in FDI outflows; in 2000 their share was 7.6 per cent even though in the preceding decade it had been a little over 10 per cent.

Transnational Corporations

The story of the heavy concentration of globalization in the developed economies is repeated in the case of TNCs. Of the 64,592 TNCs in the world in 2000, a total of 50,250 (77.8 per cent) were located in the developed world, while the developing countries had 13,492 TNCs (20.9 per cent).[4] In the developed world, the EU with 35,096 TNCs had the largest number while Japan had 3,786, and the US, 3,263. The

---

[3] UNCTAD, *World Investment Report 2002*, 7.
[4] Ibid., 270–2.

disparity between the developed and developing worlds emerges even more starkly in looking at the top 100 non-financial TNCs (see Table 3.3); only five of these are from the developing countries (Hong Kong, Mexico, Korea, Venezuela, and Malaysia). The EU had 49 entries with a share of 53 per cent in the total foreign assets of the top 100 TNCs, while Japan had 16 entries with 10.7 per cent of the assets, and the US 23 entries with 27.2 per cent of the assets.

There is even greater concentration of economic power as one gets closer to the top of the pyramid. Among the top 20 TNCs, apart from one each from Hong Kong, Australia and Switzerland, the rest are all from the triad. The US has 5, Japan 1, and the EU 11 (UK 3; France 3; Spain 2; Italy 1; and Germany 2).[5] If TNCs are the engine

Table 3.3: Home Economies of the World's Top 100 TNCs in 2000

Economy	Share in Total Foreign Assets of Top 100	Number of Entries
European Union	53.0	49
United Kingdom	21.0	14
France	12.0	13
Germany	9.3	10
Spain	3.4	2
Italy	2.9	2
Netherlands	2.0	3
North America	28.1	25
United States	27.2	23
Canada	1.0	2
Japan	10.7	16
Other Economies	7.6	10
Switzerland	3.4	3
Hong Kong	1.6	1
Australia	0.8	1
Mexico	0.4	1
Norway	0.4	1
Venezuela	0.3	1
Korea	0.3	1
Malaysia	0.3	1

Source: UNCTAD, *World Investment Report 2002*, 93.

[5] Ibid., 86. Two TNCs are listed as UK/Netherlands (Royal Dutch/Shell) and Germany/US (DaimlerChrysler); the first has been included under the UK, and the second under Germany.

of globalization, then the driver's seat is basically a monopoly of the developed countries, primarily the 'triad' among them, and more particularly, the US and the EU.

Summary

Considering the concentration of economic globalization from the perspective of exports, FDI flows, and TNCs, the conclusion is compelling: globalization is largely, though not entirely, an affair of the developed world, especially the triad of the EU, Japan, and the US. With some exceptions, the involvement of the developing countries in globalization is very low. The spread of globalization is, thus, uneven. It would be preposterous to speak of globalization as having already arrived as an end-stage, or of convergence having become a feature of contemporary globalization, as the enthusiasts of globalization assume. Globalization is asymmetrically distributed; it is truncated. How this development has come to pass requires further investigation.

Part II
Geopolitics

Chapter 4

MARKETS AND STATES
The Centrality of Geopolitics

In examining the phenomenon of globalization, some analysts differentiate between: (1) globalization as an economic process, and (2) globalization as a political project.[1] Apparently, the former is taken

[1] Note the following: (1) 'Globalization can best be thought of as *a political project*.... In this sense, it has to be viewed as *an ideological project* as much as an objective description of global reality.' Peter Newell, 'Global Challenges to the Future State', *Seminar*, No. 503 (July 2001), 71–85. (2) 'Globalization has been characterized by him [John Gray] as *the great American project*, holding the key to future global prosperity. As the world's dominant political and military power and home of the world's largest MNCs, the US engineers the forces of globalization, and displays missionary zeal to spread it across the globe.' D.N. Ghosh, 'Globalization and National Politics', *Economic and Political Weekly* 37, 39 (25 September 1999), 2770–1. (3) 'It [globalization] is a move or a series of moves towards what may be described as a global economy. The world is moving towards it but is not there yet. The moves are not merely to be understood as conscious efforts by individuals, businesses or governments. These are often responses to *impersonal forces of markets and technology.*' Manu Shroff, 'Globalization: A Stock-Taking', *Economic and Political Weekly* 34, 40 (2 October 1999), 2845–9. (4) '...we can distinguish between two different generic classes of meanings attributed to it [globalization]. One is *the spread of human civilization*, artefacts, institutions, patterns of living, information and knowledge to span the planet earth (and the stratosphere surrounding it), the other is *a policy deliberately aimed* at spreading certain institutions, modes of doing business, producing and trading commodities, services and information across all the states of the world. An analyst can trace the process of globalization in the various senses of the first generic class without accepting the agenda implict in the second class.' Amiya Kumar Bagchi, 'Globalization, Liberalization and Vulnerability', *Economic and Political Weekly* 34, 35 (6 November 1999), 3219–30 [emphasis added].

to be a function of the self-propelled impersonal forces of the market and, perhaps therefore, to be accepted, availed of, or adjusted to by states and their societies. On the other hand, the position on globalization as a political project seems to be based on the assumption of its being a function of the policies of one or more developed states, particularly the US, driven by the political aim of domination of the world. Indeed, one author asserts outright that 'the word "globalization" is really a contemporary euphemism for American economic dominance.'[2] In this view, the US may bring its enormous power to bear directly on other states to open their economies to penetration by its corporations. Or, it may act through the international financial institutions, such as the International Monetary Fund and the World Bank, where the dominant model, significantly named 'the Washington Consensus', requires less developed countries (LDCs)—seeking help to climb out of economic crises—to open up their economies. Thus understood, it is not technological determinism that explains contemporary globalization, but rather political direction emanating from the advanced industrial countries, particularly the US. As such, though market-oriented, globalization is politically constructed by power-driven states.[3]

As against this interpretation, the first view about globalization as a market-based self-driven economic process is in line with the perspective of the 'enthusiasts' of globalization who see the market as having already rendered, or just about to render, the state as obsolete. This perspective is conveyed sufficiently by book titles such as *Sovereignty at Bay*, *The Twilight of Sovereignty*, *The End of the Nation State*, *The Retreat of the State*, *The End of Geography*, *The End of Sovereignty*, *Losing Control?*, and *One World, Ready or Not*. More broadly, in terms of the dominant paradigms in political economy, which have both analytical and prescriptive dimensions, the perspective corresponds to *economic liberalism*.

Liberalism, Mercantilism, and National Power

Analytically, with the individual as its unit of analysis, economic liberalism proceeds on the assumption that the market is the

[2] Ethan B. Kapstein, 'Does Unipolarity Have a Future?', in Ethan B. Kapstein and Michael Mastanduno (eds), *Unipolar Politics: Realism and State Strategies After the Cold War* (New York: Columbia University Press, 1999), 468.

[3] See Geoffrey Garrett, 'The Causes of Globalization', 941–91.

independent variable, while the state is the dependent variable, and prescriptively it regards that situation as it ought to be. For, unhindered by the state, the market makes for greater human welfare by virtue of the economic gains it makes possible, even though such gains may not be equally distributed. For liberalism, the preference for the market is based on the *absolute*, not relative, gains that it makes possible. The tradition goes back to the founder of liberalism in the eighteenth century, Adam Smith. Such a position, however, is taken to be untenable by the other great paradigm of *mercantilism*,[4] which is the economic counterpart of the theory of realism in international politics.[5]

Mercantilism, or economic nationalism, takes humanity to be divided into different social groups, which are, in the modern era organized politically into a substantial number of territorially, demarcated states of considerable size with a monopoly of legitimate violence within their territories. For it, the state or nation-state is the unit of analysis. On the state falls the responsibility to perform certain fundamental functions for the sake of its own survival and that of the society of which it is a part. For convenience in understanding, these functions can be reduced to basically two, one pertaining to the domestic scene and the other to the external arena.

In order to assure its own stability in the internal context of the society in which it is located, the state is under compulsion to acquire

---

[4] On mercantilism, see Jonathan Kirshner, 'The Political Economy of Realism', in Kapstein and Mastanduno (eds), *Unipolar Politics*, 69–102, and the numerous works discussed and cited therein.

[5] For a survey of the theory of realism and its rivals, see Mark R. Brawley, *Turning Points: Decisions Shaping the Evolution of the International Political Economy* (Peterborough, Ontario: Broadview Press, 1998, chapters 1–2. The standard work on 'classical realism' is Hans J. Morgenthau, *Politics Among Nations*, while that on 'structural realism' is Kenneth N. Waltz, *Theory of International Politics*. Realism lays claim to an extraordinarily rich heritage, not only going back thousands of years in history, but also across civilizations with eminent figures like Thucydides in Greece, Kautilya in India, and Sun Tzu in China. See also John J. Mearsheimer, *The Tragedy of Great Power Politics*, which provides a forceful defence of realism, and a strong critique of rival approaches. Although a structural realist, Mearsheimer describes his approach as that of offensive realism even as he places Waltz in the school of defensive realism.

legitimacy, which means having the support of key groups in society. While key social groups may extend support to the state on the basis of the particular form of that state being a desirable end in itself, often their support depends on the state assuring material satisfaction to them. In order to secure the support of these groups, the state must demonstrate *effectiveness* in providing them economic benefits apart from assuring them of other benefits such as adequate social status and a share in political power.[6] The provision of such economic benefits depends on the economic capacity of the state, which, in turn, is based on the efficient working of markets. The state, therefore, cannot leave markets alone. To begin with, markets cannot function on their own, for their very functioning is premised on the existence of certain rules of the game, such as established rights to property and the sanctity of contracts, which must be guaranteed by an authority outside the market. That authority, in modern times, has been and continues to be the state. However, the need for the state to demonstrate its effectiveness through intervention in the market in order to assure legitimacy emerges as especially acute when there are market failures, regardless of whether the sources of such failures are domestic or international.[7]

In part, legitimacy also depends on the effectiveness of the state in fulfilling its other critical function in the context of its relations externally with other states—the provision of *national security*. Conflict is pervasive in the interstate system and war is an ever-present possibility, because of the absence of a legitimate central political authority in that system—the core premise of realism. In this situation, it is an essential function of the state to assure its own security and that of the society for which it is the overall decision-making unit. A fundamental prerequisite for the performance of that function is power. The interstate system is an arena where power matters crucially and where, as Thucydides pointed out long ago: 'The strong do what they can, and the weak suffer what they must.'[8] In

---

[6] On the concepts of legitimacy and effectiveness, see the classic work by Seymour Martin Lipset, *Political Man: The Social Bases of Politics* (Garden City, NY: Doubleday, 1960). The equivalent Marxist concepts are *legitimation* and *accumulation*; see James O'Connor, *The Fiscal Crisis of the State* (New York: St Martin's Press, 1973), p. 6.

[7] See Karl Polanyi, *The Great Transformation* (New York: Rinehart, 1957).

[8] Thucydides, *Pelopennesian War*, translated by Richard Crawley (London: J.M. Dent, 1903), 394. Another version puts it as: 'In fact, the strong do what

sum, competition, conflict and the struggle for survival among states constitute the *encompassing principle* in the working of the interstate system; cooperation, when it does occur among states, is subordinate to that encompassing principle. That is the central message of realism.

In order to be able to provide security, any given state must mobilize its own capabilities and those of its allies. Military capabilities are certainly key in this regard, but fundamental to military capabilities are economic capabilities, and therefore, again, no state can, as a result, leave markets alone. So, apart from reasons of legitimacy, the state has to concern itself with the market for the sake of security. In this regard, of special concern to the state is the extent to which the domestic economy is vulnerable to developments in the international economy, or to the economic actions of other states. Under the compulsions of the interstate system, what is important to states is *relative gain*, that is, gain relative to other states, not just *absolute gain*.[9] To fall behind other states in capabilities or to be dependent on them creates vulnerabilities for a state in relation to other states. A serious dilemma therefore confronts states. On the one hand, states seek to participate in the international economy in order to avail of the benefits that such participation may bring. To that end, states may engage in international cooperation for mutual gain and adopt policies with elements of economic liberalism and openness to the world economy. On the other hand, states seek to avoid vulnerabilities that spring both from dependence on other states and from exposure to possible disturbances in the international economy. Consequently, states have a strong inclination to follow mercantilist policies.

Although liberalism and mercantilism are on the surface antipodal policies, the pursuit of liberalism is not necessarily inconsistent with mercantilism. For, liberalism can often be simply a mask for mercantilism. Indeed, liberalism can, in fact, be mercantilism precisely in the sense that its adoption or enforcement is often designed to serve the national interests of particular states that are economically strong.

---

they have the power to do, and the weak accept what they have to accept.' See Thucydides, *History of the Pelopennesian War*, translated by Rex Warner (London: Penguin, 1972), 402.

[9] On the issue, see Robert Powell, 'Absolute and Relative Gains in International Relations Theory', *American Political Science Review*, 85, 4 (December 1991), 1303–20.

Liberalism is at heart, a policy of the strong, that is, of states with economies that are more advanced and competitive. As Bhagwati puts it: 'Free trade comes as one's ideological preference only when one is strong: the Darwinian process appeals to those who expect to emerge the winners. It is therefore, the preferred doctrine of those who possess actual or perceived competitiveness.'[10] Strong states, thus, aim for relative gain through liberalism. Mercantilism, on the other hand, is often a policy of the weak, who do not want to be overwhelmed economically by the strong or they want to catch up with the strong. Neither policy is or needs to be followed by states in whole or for all time. Both can be applied selectively in particular economic sectors and during certain developmental stages, or be oriented toward specific states. Such a stance is made vivid by the behaviour of Great Britain.

The Changing Stance of Britain on Liberalism

It is interesting to note that, before it turned to liberalism, Great Britain had for long followed protectionist policies, both in relation to the European powers and to the manufactures of its colonies in Asia. But it continued with its mercantilist policies even after it was far advanced as the pioneer industrial power. Following the 'Torrens thesis', named after Robert Torrens, the opponents of free trade in the early nineteenth century had dreaded the industrialization of other countries, believing it would spell the decline of British industrial advantage. This view was accepted by British officialdom, and consequently the export of machinery and skilled labour was banned. Later, in the 1820s, the Torrens thesis was rejected, but the rejection stemmed from 'the confidence that British technological and industrial supremacy was so great that she need fear no rivals.'[11] Insofar as liberalism in this instance was designed to serve the national interests of Britain, it was mercantilist in intent. And it worked as intended; Britain was able to 'crush rival industries in every part of

---

[10] Jagdish Bhagwati, *Political Economy and International Economics* (Cambridge, MA: MIT Press, 1991), 101.

[11] Robert Gilpin, *US Power and the Multinational Corporation: The Political Economy of Foreign Direct Investment* (New York: Basic Books, 1975), 75.

the world by supplying the market with goods produced on the better and cheaper methods, which were only practiced in England.'[12]

Viewing the situation from the perspective of the German people, who were latecomers to industrialization, Friedrich List saw through the British design and opposed liberalism; instead, he favoured mercantilism. List held England's contemporaneous advocacy of free trade as opportunistic, following as it did an earlier policy of long duration of stringent restrictions on foreign imports, which had enabled England to become an industrial power. More, he took it to be typical English cant and self-interested ideological camouflage 'to conceal the true policy of England under the cosmopolitical expressions and arguments which Adam Smith had discovered, in order to induce foreign nations not to imitate that policy'.[13] Interestingly, List had come to these conclusions on the basis of his understanding of American economic nationalism since the time of Treasury Secretary Alexander Hamilton. The latter had advocated a deliberate national policy for industrialization through protection, proclaiming: 'Not only the wealth but the independence and security of a country appear to be materially connected with the prosperity of manufactures.'[14]

Subsequently, as the German economy emerged as more competitive and productive, and Germany rose, therefore, as a challenger to Britain in the late-nineteenth and early-twentieth century, Britain once again began entertaining thoughts about protectionism.[15] Britain's relative

[12] William Cunningham, *The Rise and Decline of the Free Trade Movement*, cited in Kirshner, 'The Political Economy of Realism', 76.

[13] Friedrich List, *The National System of Political Economy* (New York: August M. Kelley, 1966), 347–51.

[14] Walt W. Rostow, *Politics and the Stages of Growth* (Cambridge: Cambridge University Press, 1971), 189. One biographer notes concerning Hamilton's important 'Report on Manufactures' to the US Congress: 'Hamilton proposed a system of tariffs to protect America's fledgling industries from foreign, chiefly British, competition. He established the doctrine of protectionism. Where Americans could provide their own finished goods, import duties should be prohibitively high.' Willard Sterne Randall, *Alexander Hamilton: A Life* (New York: HarperCollins, 2003), 404.

[15] Paul Kennedy, *The Rise and Fall of Great Powers: Economic Change and Military Conflict from 1500 to 2000* (London: Unwin Hyman, 1988), 228–9; Peter Mathias, *The First Industrial Nation: An Economic History of Britain, 1700–1914* (London: Methuen, 1969), 397; Francois Crouzet, *The Victorian Economy* (New York: Columbia University Press, 1982), 128; Kirshner, 'The Political Economy of Realism', 76 and 94 (n39).

decline resulted in 'a protectionist backlash', and protectionist organizations, such as the National Fair Trade League, the National Society for the Defence of British Industry, and the Reciprocity Free Trade Association grew to press for change in policy.[16] Britain imposed protective tariffs on products of key industries during World War I, but interestingly it continued with them after the war in order to stave off competition from Germany.[17] Still later, when confronted by a drain on sterling balances in the midst of a worldwide financial crisis, Britain ditched the gold standard in 1931. Then, in 1932, it converted the Commonwealth into a preferential trading bloc to advance its imperial interests, abandoning, in the process, a century of free trade policy. During and soon after World War II, Britain fought a hopeless and ultimately futile rearguard battle against American economic coercion to remove imperial preferences, restrictions on American imports, and exchange controls.

What is constant in all these changes in economic policy is consistent with the encompassing principle of international politics, the pursuit of national interest. One of the greatest challenges for the developing countries is, then, precisely how in the era of globalization can liberal policies, or a combination of liberal and mercantilist policies, be employed to serve their national interest in terms of the goals of development, poverty alleviation, and national autonomy.

Authority and the International Economy

Just as the national market requires a political authority in the form of the state to set the rules of the game, so does the international market or economy. Since there is no recognized legitimate central authority in the interstate system, the rules of the game are set by the powerful states. It is, in fact, power that is instrumental in instituting the rules, and it is the powerful that are the shapers of international economic regimes.[18] Although the modern interstate system has since Westphalia in 1648 been based on the doctrine of the sovereign equality of states, in actual fact, there exists an oligarchy of a few great powers that makes, in conflict or cooperation, the vital

---

[16] Bhagwati, *Political Economy and International Economics*, 48–9.

[17] Mathias, *The First Industrial Nation*, 442.

[18] On the subject, see Stephen D. Krasner (ed.), *International Regimes* (Ithaca, NY: Cornell University Press, 1983).

decisions that determine the destiny of the system. Such great powers are the *subjects* in decision-making in the international system; the rest are merely the *objects* of their decisions.

The position of the great powers in the interstate system derives from a combination of military and economic capabilities. Both kinds of capabilities are necessary; neither suffices by itself. As one author has averred succinctly, 'national power depends in large measure upon economic productivity' and 'military power depends upon economic strength'.[19] Paul Kennedy affirms the view forcefully: 'It sounds crudely mercantilistic to express it this way, but wealth is usually needed to underpin military power, and military power is usually needed to acquire and protect wealth…. The history of the rise and later fall of the leading countries in the Great Power system since the advance of western Europe in the sixteenth century … shows a very significant correlation *over the longer term* between productive and revenue-raising capacities on the one hand, and military strength on the other.'[20] Given that correlation, the nature of the distribution of economic power, as also, therefore, the nature of the international economic order which fosters that distribution, is just as critical to the great powers as is the balance of (military) power. Consequently, any notion that economic globalization could represent simply the working of some self-propelled impersonal forces of the market, or that it could be something that is divorced from the interests of one or more great powers, runs contrary to the very nature of the interstate system.

It is true that Marx, in his Manifesto of the Communist Party, had lauded the bourgeoisie for the expansion of capitalism in strictly economic terms. He had proclaimed: 'The cheap prices of its commodities are the heavy artillery with which it batters down all Chinese walls, with which it forces the barbarians' intensely obstinate hatred of foreigners to capitulate.'[21] In actual fact, however, it was the heavy artillery of British warships during the Opium Wars of the mid-nineteenth century that opened China to world trade in a

[19] J.B. Condliffe, *The Commerce of Nations*, cited in Kirshner, 'The Political Economy of Realism', 71.

[20] Kennedy, *The Rise and Fall of Great Powers*, xvi.

[21] Karl Marx and Frederick Engels, *The Communist Manifesto*, reproduced in *Karl Marx: Selected Writings*, (ed.) David McLellan (Oxford: Oxford University Press, 1977), 221–47.

subordinate role through the imposition of unequal treaties. In like manner, it was through military violence that European powers colonized Asia, Africa, and the Western Hemisphere, and launched the extensive phase of globalization. As the adage held, trade followed the flag. British naval power created and sustained the liberal international economic order of the nineteenth century. War inflicted by Europe on the rest of the world was the midwife of the extensive phase of globalization. As an international economic order, globalization, in its extensive phase, developed not simply as a spontaneous economic process, but under the active sponsorship of the militarily and economically powerful states of the day. Can the intensive phase of globalization in the contemporary period be any different?

War and the World Economic Order

It is significant that new international economic orders tend to be founded by the victors at the end of a major war and reflect the new distribution of power. Essentially, the new hegemon[22] that arises at the end of a major war, determines the shape of the international economic order. While the hegemon may establish a new international economic order, however, the situation does not remain frozen. For one thing, the other great powers in the interstate system are determined to change the balance of power in their favour and, to that end, endeavour to advance their military and economic capabilities relative to the hegemon. For another, the market has a logic of its own, and not everything in the world economy can be

---

[22] Although the term 'hegemon' is in wide usage in international political economy, Mearsheimer questions its utility in the study of international politics at the level of the international system. He avers: 'In essence, a hegemon is the only great power in the system…. it is virtually impossible for any state to achieve global hegemony…. there has never been a global hegemon, and there is not likely to be one anytime soon'. This would seem to be a highly restrictive meaning of the term, especially for the present study, which straddles across international political economy and international politics. A hegemon stands apart from the other great powers in terms of its 'ordering' role in the world's economic and political arenas. One can employ the term even within Mearsheimer's own definition as long as it allows some flexibility in interpreting the notion of domination: 'A hegemon is a state that is so powerful that it dominates all the other states.' Mearsheimer, *The Tragedy of Great Power Politics*, 40–1.

controlled by states. Over time, the working of the market may advantage some states as against others. Again, the natural endowments of particular states may lead to differential growth rates and undermine the earlier distribution of power. As the distribution of power changes, conflicts are likely to arise between rising powers and declining powers over the nature of the international economic order.

In a theory that later came to be referred to as 'hegemonic stability theory', Robert Gilpin posited that, over time, the power of the hegemon as the supplier of international public goods suffers deterioration relative to other states.[23] In that circumstance, the hegemon is likely to turn to protectionist measures, and other states may react to such behaviour with similar measures. As a consequence, there is a tendency for the international economy to fragment into economic blocs, and the growing conflict may well result in economic warfare and eventually in war, giving rise to a new hegemon.

Geopolitics and Change in the World Economy

For much of the nineteenth century after the Napoleonic wars, Great Britain was the hegemonic power. It used that position to establish, through unilateral actions and bilateral agreements, what is regarded as a liberal international economic order. However, Britain has received more credit for its liberalism than was deserved, since, in practice, its trade policies toward other states were invariably affected by geopolitical or strategic considerations.[24]

Note, too, the paradox that, while preaching the virtues of liberalism, both economic and political, Britain as well as several other European powers held down vast portions of the world under forcible political subjugation in their empires, and thoroughly exploited them economically. Britain alone held a quarter of the world's territory and population in its far-flung empire where the sun reputedly never set. The economic consequences of colonialism were devastating for the colonized. For example, at the time of the conquest of India by Britain, the two political entities had roughly about the same standard of living. However, during the course of two centuries of British rule,

---

[23] Robert Gilpin, *War and Change in World Politics* (Cambridge: Cambridge University Press, 1981).

[24] Joanne Gowa, *Cooperation Among Nations: Europe, America and Non-Tariff Barriers* (Princeton: Princeton University Press, 1994), chapter 5.

when the economies of the two countries were integrated in a superordinate–subordinate relationship, Great Britain became a modern industrialized country while India was 'deindustrialized' and rendered into a poverty-stricken and stagnant agricultural society. On the other hand, the only one country in Asia that escaped colonization by the European states, Japan, quickly rose to become an industrial workshop and a great power. For countries, that were no longer colonies but were still weak because of economic underdevelopment, the experience of gunboat diplomacy at the hands of Great Britain and the US was commonplace.[25]

Within Europe, the rise of Germany as an economic power in the second half of the nineteenth century, after its unification under Prussian auspices, threatened Britain's hegemonic position. Germany's attempt to carve out its own place in the sun, in emulation of the existing great powers with their vast empires, brought it into conflict with Great Britain as the existing hegemon. The resulting clash of arms in the form of World War I led to the collapse of the old economic and political order. Germany was eventually defeated, but it required the entry of the US into the war on the side of Britain and its allies to achieve victory.

The US had emerged, in actual fact, as the new hegemon. By 1929, it was producing about 45 per cent of the world's manufactures and had a share of one-fifth in the world's exports.[26] The US proved unwilling, however, to take on the responsibility that went with having become the hegemon, even as Britain, weakened by the war and indebted to the US, was no longer capable of assuming that role. As a consequence, the world lapsed into the 'twenty years crisis' between the two world wars.[27] The crisis was manifest in the political arena in the failure of the League of Nations to prevent or to punish

[25] Apart from the notions of 'the white man's burden' and 'the civilizing mission', there is a long tradition going back to Marx that tends to excuse the tragedy visited upon the colonized by emphasizing its historical necessity, and therefore views the role of imperialism positively. See Bill Warren, *Imperialism: Pioneer of Capitalism* (London: Verso, 1980), and Niall Ferguson, *Empire: The Rise and Demise of the British World Order and the Lessons for Global Power* (New York: Basic Books, 2003).

[26] Diana Tussie, *The Less Developed Countries and the World Trading System: A Challenge to the GATT* (New York: St Martin's Press, 1987), 9.

[27] Edward Hallett Carr, *The Twenty Years' Crisis, 1919–1939* (New York: Harper & Row, 1964).

aggression. In the economic arena, competitive devaluations and tariff escalations led to the long Depression of the 1930s. In this anarchical situation, Germany and Japan endeavoured, following the example set by the other contemporaneous great powers, to establish their own regional economic blocs and empires, one in the heart of Europe and the other in East Asia. Their revisionist endeavours put them at odds with the existing major powers and triggered World War II. In that titanic struggle, the military muscle of both the Soviet Union and the US was required to finally defeat Germany and Japan. The end of the war certified the emergence of the US as the new hegemonic power over much of the world, barring that part of it which was physically controlled by the Soviet Union. Out of the ashes of the war was then born a new international order of American design. This time, the US was eager to take on the role of hegemon; it had both the will and the capacity to impose a new world order in accord with its values and interests.

Summary

Economic globalization does not represent simply the working out of the logic of the market. Instead, it is a result of the interaction between markets and states. Especially important in this regard is the larger interstate system that encompasses the relations between states, the key characteristic of which, in the absence of a central authority, is the struggle for power among states. In the course of this struggle for power, wars occur between the major powers, which can confirm the existing hegemonic power in its position or give rise to a new hegemonic power. As in the case of the domestic market, where the state establishes the rules of the game for the market, in the international market or economy the rules of the game are set by a hegemonic power as a sort of proto-central authority among the different states. As Joseph Nye puts it, 'Politics and economics are connected. International economic systems rest upon international political order.'[28] However, given the nature of the international system, the hegemonic power continues to lack legitimacy in the system as a whole; whatever legitimacy it has is simply a function of its power. Over time, the hegemon is likely to suffer economic

[28] Joseph S. Nye, Jr, 'East Asian Security: The Case for Deep Engagement', *Foreign Affairs*, 74, 4 (July/August 1995), 90–102.

decline and challengers may emerge. A new hegemonic power may then arise to set up another world economic order.

In the modern era, Great Britain as the hegemonic power established a liberal international economic order in the nineteenth century, which came under challenge with the rise of Germany. The US joined with Britain to defeat Germany in World War I but proved unwilling to take on the burden of hegemony, with the result that the international economy sank into disorder and another war followed twenty years later. After the defeat of the Axis powers in 1945, the US, strengthened by the war, was now ready and eager to assume its responsibility as hegemon. Both the intensive globalization of the post-war period and its truncated nature are rooted in the new order that the US came to establish.

Chapter 5

THE GEOPOLITICAL RESHAPING OF THE POST-WAR WORLD ECONOMY

Two dominant features of the global economy are manifest. One is the thrust toward globalization that has been evident in the post-war period, especially the advance from shallow to deep integration of the international economy. The other is the pattern of concentration that makes the extant globalization to be *truncated* in nature, with the bulk of international economic transactions focused around the 'triad' of the major economies of the US, the EU and Japan. What is the explanation for both the advance in economic globalization and its truncated nature? This study has already taken the position that there is a strong linkage between changes in hegemony and international economic orders. Consistent with that position, the argument of this chapter is that both the advance in globalization and its truncated nature in the form of 'triadization' have been a function of the geopolitics associated with the accession of the US to the role of the new hegemon after World War II.

Prior to World War II, the great power system consisted of the US, Great Britain, Germany, France, Japan, and the Soviet Union. These states were also the major centres of economic and industrial power. The war, however, destroyed the economies of Germany and Japan, brought enormous ruin to those of Europe, including France's, and devastated the Soviet economy. Though on the victorious side, Great Britain was crippled economically because of the accumulation of vast debts that it now owed to the US, the dominions and the colonies, and also because of its antiquated and obsolescing industrial plant. Of the great powers, the US alone escaped relatively unscathed, with its mainland untouched by war.

The Rise of the United States as Hegemonic Superpower

Not only did the US not suffer economically from the war, but paradoxically it emerged dramatically stronger, indeed as a superpower militarily in an essentially unipolar system, and as a colossus economically that generated about half of the world product. Without a doubt, the US was the new hegemonic power across the globe except for the Soviet-held territory. It was now the undisputed master of the Rimlands and the Offshore and Outer Islands of the World Island—to employ the concepts of Mackinder and Spykman that dominated geopolitical thought of the time—which were dependent on it for both security and succour.

The enormity of the power of the US was matched by its self-perception of having ushered the American Century or Pax Americana, generating among most Americans a messianic complex, somewhat similar to that of Pax Romana for the Romans many centuries earlier. Drew Middleton pointed out how after World War II, the US envisioned 'an unprecedented expansion of power and influence on a global scale', one 'greater in extent than any known to history', and he underlined 'the supreme national confidence it promoted in the American people'. He continued: 'Americans were emboldened to believe that there were no policies they could not implement, no danger they could not overcome.'[1] In giving expression to the feeling of omnipotence that prevailed among most Americans, Dean Rusk once exclaimed: 'When the United States applies pressure on something, anything, it gives.'[2] One State Department policy planning chief commented retrospectively: 'In the period following World War II, our pre-eminent power encouraged us to believe we could shape the globe according to American designs.'[3] Little wonder, the US was determined to impose on the new post-war world an international order fashioned in line with its own preferences.

---

[1] Drew Middleton, *Retreat from Victory: A Critical Appraisal of American Foreign and Military Policy from 1920 to the 1970s* (New York: Hawthorn Books, 1973), 45–6, 213.

[2] Marvin Kalb and Bernard Kalb, *Kissinger* (Boston: Little, Brown, 1974), 65.

[3] Winston Lord, 'America's Purposes in an Ambiguous Age', *Department of State Bulletin*, No. 1845 (4 November 1974), 617–22.

Advance American Planning for the Post-War World Order

The US did not wait until after the end of the war for the construction of the new world order. Apparently convinced that its power would ultimately prevail, it began to build it, brick by brick, early on during the war. Once American troops had landed in Italy in 1943, the conviction grew that the Axis powers were headed for defeat before too long, and, therefore, planning for the post-war world order began in earnest. What is impressive in this planning is the determination of the US to preclude, insofar as it was within its power, the existence of any economic, and therefore military, rival from the new post-war order. It would be a mistaken view to believe that it is only the experience of the long confrontation with the Soviet Union during the Cold War in the post-war period that led to such a determination after the disintegration of the Soviet bloc and the Soviet Union.[4] Rather, that determination has a longer ancestry, though it faced serious problems as long as the Soviet Union lasted. In any case, toward the end of seeing to it that there were no rivals, the US insistently drove hard bargains with its allies, and displayed a remarkable degree of ruthlessness in its efforts in this regard.

Great Britain as Target

With Germany and Japan seemingly destined to go down in defeat and the Soviet Union still beyond the reach of American power, Great Britain with its empire was the only relevant great power as a potential rival to the US in the post-war world. Unsurprisingly, it was the first target of the American effort at reshaping the new world order, notwithstanding repeated public proclamations on both sides about Anglo-American solidarity.

The US sought to accomplish its goal of a new world order by conditioning its Lend–Lease supplies and loans so as to force Great Britain to subscribe to the American vision of the trading and financial architecture for the post-war world. Robert Skidelsky, the biographer of John Maynard Keynes, sharply underlines, 'the intensity and often bitterness of the struggle between Britain and America for post-war position which went on under the façade of the Grand

---

[4] See the draft Defence Planning Guidance Paper of 1992, *New York Times*, 8 March 1992, A14.

Alliance.' During the course of that struggle, 'the Americans tried to use Lend–Lease as a lever to destroy Britain's pre-war financial and trading system, based on the sterling area and imperial preferences.' Skidelsky points out that 'sympathy for "plucky" Britain in its stand against the Nazi bully never extended to generalized support for Britain's world position. This is the clue to Anglo-American relations, economic as well as political, both in the pre-war period and once the Grand Alliance had been forged.'[5] In apparent agreement with this assessment, American historian Randall Woods commented concerning Lend–Lease: 'Shrewder heads on both sides of the Atlantic viewed it as a device that could be used to alter the structure of international trade and finance, and determine the global balance of power in the post-war world.'[6]

Multilateralism as Principle and Interest

The building blocks of the new order were put in place by bending Britain—which was, with its Commonwealth sterling bloc, the chief barrier to the expansion of American economic power abroad—to American will. The centrepiece of the new grand American architecture for the world order was the concept of 'multilateralism', which required the dismantling of barriers to trade, and the removal of currency exchange controls. Against the backdrop of the experience of the Depression years, when protectionist barriers and competitive 'beggar-thy-neighbour' devaluations were pervasive, this policy stance was proclaimed on grounds of principle with the aim of assuring worldwide prosperity, which, in turn, was considered a prerequisite for peace. No doubt, it represented ideological belief on the part of some American decision-makers, but it also embodied American nationalism and national interests. It incorporated as well the interests of what were believed to be profit-hungry business lobbies to open the world economy for American exports, and also those of American politicians who wanted full employment in order to ensure political stability.

---

[5] Robert Skidelsky, *John Maynard Keynes: Volume Three: Fighting for Freedom 1937–1946* (New York: Viking Press, 2002), xxii, 93.

[6] Randall Bennett Woods, *A Changing of the Guard: Anglo-American Relations, 1941–1946* (Chapel Hill: University of North Carolina Press, 1990), 10.

Multilateralism in trade was not new to the British, for, after all, they were the creators of that type of system in the nineteenth century and had nurtured it for about a hundred years. On the other hand, the US had over this period built itself into a mighty industrial power behind high tariff walls, which reached their zenith in the Hawley-Smoot tariff legislation in 1930. Now at the receiving end of the American pressure for economic liberalism, the British were uniquely placed to be insightful about American intentions, given their own history of pursuing interest behind the garb of principle. In the opinion of the wartime British Secretary of State for India, Leo Amery, as expressed by Woods:

> The United States was now advocating multilateralism because its economy closely resembled that of Great Britain during the last half of the nineteenth century. Washington's goal was 'self-sufficient expansionism'. The United States was an interdependent economic entity with a huge and prosperous home market and surplus capital to invest. Its manufacturers were certain that they could dominate any market in the world given an equal chance.

Apropos American insistence on multilateralism, Amery asserted: 'The new blend of Puritan quasi-religious Free Trade fervour with an aggressive Imperialism presents us with a problem of no little difficulty.' Churchill, too, worried whether multilateralism was simply a mask for American nationalism.[7] However, given their weakened state, the British could do little except bow to the inevitable. After a careful review of the historical record, Woods concluded that 'nationalists, bureaucratic imperialists, and special interests modified multilateralism into a machine to enrich America' and that 'multilateralism became the servant of capitalism and American special interests'.[8]

The US was quite tough-minded about getting Britain to bend. Understandably, to the British the American approach 'smacked of unilateralism—that is, requirements unilaterally imposed on Great Britain'.[9] During the war, the US 'laboured to hold British gold–dollar reserves to a minimum, and to commit the United Kingdom to a multilateral trading system in which it could not compete. Great Britain received enough aid to enable it to survive, and to play a role in the war against the Axis, but not enough to preserve its overseas

[7] Ibid., 39, 47.
[8] Ibid., 398–9.
[9] Ibid., 55.

investments and markets, to maintain its military outposts, or to participate in a system of multilateral commerce'.[10]

The New International Trading Order

After the war, the American vision on trade was incorporated in the General Agreement on Trade and Tariffs (GATT) in 1947. A more ambitious undertaking to establish the International Trade Organization—an international agency for trade equivalent to the IMF and the World Bank in monetary and development affairs, respectively—failed to materialize because it was not found acceptable to the US, since it was suspected of potentially infringing its national sovereignty. GATT, as an understanding between the contracting states, remained the framework for almost a half-century within which various states through several periodic multinational 'rounds' decided mutually on reciprocal reductions in tariffs. The founding principles of GATT were non-discrimination and reciprocity. The chief mechanism toward those ends was the 'most favoured nation' (MFN) clause, whereby tariff concessions conceded to one state became available to all the other contracting states. However, notwithstanding the earlier bold pronouncements on multilateralism, GATT did not promise unfettered free trade. Rather, it quite radically modified the doctrine in order to protect the interests of the US and its allies, in consideration of their domestic requirements for full employment and political stability.

Multilateralism was born *truncated*. GATT was essentially a rich man's club, organized to the detriment of the weak. To begin with, it endorsed capital mobility, which was of beneficial interest to the capital-surplus US and the advanced industrial countries, but it excluded labour mobility, which would have been of advantage to the labour-surplus poor countries. Again, it protected the overly subsidized agriculture and the less competitive labour-intensive manufacturing industries of the US and its allies against competition from the LDCs.[11] In retrospect, Ruggie dignified the system by characterizing it as *embedded liberalism*, while Woods was more

---

[10] Ibid., 7, 39, 47, 398.

[11] Diana Tussie, *The Less Developed Countries and the World Trading System*, chapter 1.

forthright in calling it 'a corrupted multilateralism'.[12] This modified form of liberalism—with 'lots of cheating taking place on the domestic side' (Ruggie's words but used here to different effect), designed precisely to serve the interests of the powerful—was intended to externalize the costs of adjustment to the weak abroad. The numerous derogations and reservations to the principle of free trade were intended to ensure that the costs of adjustment to change in the world economy would not be borne by the major economic powers. Rather, they would be transferred to the LDCs, which, consistent with their lack of economic clout, had little role in international economic decision-making.

The key illustration of the fundamental modification of the doctrine of free multilateral trade is provided by the treatment by the US and its advanced industrial allies toward the LDCs in respect of textiles and clothing, first of cotton and wool, but later extended to all man-made fibres as well. Building on earlier departures from principle, in 1974 the more comprehensive Multi-Fibre Agreement (MFA) imposed, in clear derogation of GATT rules, a quota system in order to control textile imports from LDCs; this quota system was in addition to the usual agreed upon tariffs. Within the overall framework of the MFA and its precursors, the quotas were then agreed to on a bilateral basis, which Tussie describes as 'also violating the GATT principle of non-discrimination'.[13] In truth, agreement on a bilateral basis is a transparent euphemism for a unilateral imposition by the strong in response to 'the unchecked power of vested interests organized as protectionist lobbies', that is, in order 'to placate the textile companies and unions'. As the staff of GATT itself put it, the MFA was 'the first important instance in which the generally and solemnly agreed rules of post-war policy conduct—including the keystone of the system, the non-discrimination rule—were formally set aside for reasons recognized as pragmatic.'[14]

Instead of assuring non-discrimination, GATT became, in the case of the LDCs, the instrument of protecting its very antithesis, providing

---

[12] John Gerard Ruggie, 'International Regimes, Transactions, and Change: Embedded Liberalism in the Post-War Economic Order', in Stephen D. Krasner (ed.), *International Regimes*, 195–231; Woods, *A Changing of the Guard*, 402.

[13] Tussie, *The Less Developed Countries*, 64.

[14] Ibid., 79, 81.

'a stamp of legitimacy for the selective protection of textile and clothing industries of the developed countries'. It turned out to be the source of discrimination against LDCs in two ways:

> On the one hand, importing countries are free from their MFN obligations: they can determine which suppliers are the ones disrupting their markets and request them and only them to control the flow of their exports. A central feature of both the LTA [Long-Term Agreement] and the MFA is that they have circumscribed the controls to imports from LDCs (initially, Japan was also included). The United States and the West European countries exempted their own products from the quota restrictions on the grounds that these did not create 'market disruption'. On the other hand, exporting countries have waived their right to retaliate by withdrawing a concession as well as their right to demand an equivalent concession in compensation for the restrictions on textiles and clothing.[15]

Such was the liberal nature of the multilateral order established by the US!

The contemporary relative marginalization of the LDCs in world exports is, thus, not unrelated to the trading system established after the war. With time, the US and its allies, no doubt, lowered tariffs in successive rounds of negotiations in areas of mutual interest to them. At the same time, they refined the system of non-tariff barriers into an art form in order to constrain labour-intensive imports from LDCs with the exception of those that were strategic allies.[16] The boom in post-war world trade was, therefore, largely a phenomenon of the developed world. The share of the industrial countries in world exports jumped from 65 per cent in 1950 to 80 per cent in 1970, while that of the LDCs slid from 35 per cent to 20 per cent.[17] As an otherwise admirer of embedded liberalism, Ruggie was nonetheless compelled to acknowledge:

> Those who are 'regime makers' shift a disproportionate share of adjustment costs onto those who are 'regime takers'.... The compromise of embedded liberalism has never been fully extended to the developing countries. They have been disproportionately subject to the orthodox stabilization measures of the IMF, often with no beneficial results in export earnings but substantial

---

[15] Ibid., 72–3.

[16] For a forceful critique of GATT from the perspective of the LDCs, see Chakravarthi Raghavan, *Recolonization: GATT, the Uruguay Round & the Third World* (London: Zed Books, 1990).

[17] Tussie, *The Less Developed Countries*, 2.

increases in import bills and consequent increases in domestic prices. Moreover, the liberalization produced by the GATT has benefited relatively few among them.[18]

In its broad outline, the international trade regime, structured to benefit the developed countries to the relative disadvantage of the LDCs, has continued into the twenty-first century despite institutional changes over time. Beyond imposed quotas and non-tariff barriers, the US and its allies distorted the world trading system through massively subsidizing their agricultural sectors to the detriment of the developing world. Subsequently, in the shift from GATT to the World Trade Organization (WTO), the developed countries were able to broaden the meaning of 'trade' to bring in foreign investment, intellectual property (patents), and social matters under WTO's purview, again to their own benefit.

The New International Financial Order

American nationalism was no less manifest in respect of international finance than it was in trade. The Bretton Woods agreements arrived at, in 1944, on currency stabilization and post-war reconstruction— which led to the establishment of the International Monetary Fund (IMF) and the International Bank for Reconstruction and Development (IBRD, later called the World Bank)—were the outcome of negotiations basically between the US and Britain. They were essentially of American design, and meant to guarantee that 'a United States monopoly of the world's gold–dollar supply would continue'.[19]

The key decision-maker on the issue in the US government was Treasury Secretary, Henry Morgenthau, a staunch economic nationalist. His aim, according to Skidelsky, was 'to shift financial power from New York and London to Washington': 'The United States, not Britain, would be the leader of the post-war free world, the dollar would replace the pound as the world's leading currency. He would do all he could to help Britain, but as a satellite, not as an ally.' The negotiations between the two allies over the post-war arrangements followed a set pattern: 'The British proposed, the Americans disposed. This was the inevitable consequence of the asymmetry of power.'[20]

---

[18] Ruggie, 'International Regimes', 229–30.
[19] Woods, *A Changing of the Guard*, 3.
[20] Skidelsky, *Keynes*, 99, 310.

The American historian Woods would seemingly concur with the thrust of the argument: 'Treasury looked forward to a post-war financial order in which an American-controlled international agency implemented and supervised a currency stabilization agreement that linked the major trading currencies of the world firmly to each other and to gold.... United States's preponderance on the governing board would ensure that dollars and gold would be sold only to finance current transactions and not to build up the gold–dollar reserves of other nations.' The fundamental intent was 'to ensure United States's domination of international finance'.[21]

After Great Britain and the US had bilaterally agreed on a 'joint statement by experts' on the setting up of the IMF, the US invited forty-four nations to Bretton Woods, New Hampshire, essentially to ratify it. For, as one source put it: 'The delegates did not reach an "agreement". They merely signed a paper which looked like an agreement.' As for the agreement, it was clearly designed to advance American interests. Skidelsky underlines: 'The Agreement reflected the views of the American, not the British, Treasury.... The Agreement was shaped not by Keynes's *General Theory*, but by the US desire for an updated gold standard as a means of liberalizing trade. If there was an underlying ideology, it was Morgenthau's determination to concentrate financial power in Washington.'[22] This assessment is in fundamental agreement with the position of one of the Canadian delegates, A.F.W. Plumptre, who held that: 'It is true, and it was true at the time, that the new international institutions, largely fashioned in Washington, were designed to serve the international interests of the US. The charge that they could in many respects be considered as the creatures of American "capitalist imperialism" can, in a sense, be accepted.'[23]

The British were devastated by the shift in financial power, however; Henry Clay of the Bank of England described Bretton Woods as 'the greatest blow to Britain next to the war'. That sentiment stemmed from the belief that 'London has lost its position as the financial centre of the world.' The dollar was made the sole currency, the par value of which was designated in terms of gold, whereas the

[21] Woods, *A Changing of the Guard*, 3, 62, 75.

[22] Skidelsky, *Keynes*, 357.

[23] A.F.W. Plumptre, *Three Decades of Decision: Canada and the World Monetary System* (Toronto: McClelland & Stewart, 1977), 31.

par values of all other currencies were fixed in terms of the dollar. Moreover, the British could not persuade the US to have the IMF headquartered in London instead of Washington. The US brushed the British off with the comment: 'We are putting in twice as much money as anybody else, three times as much … it is preposterous that the head office should be any place else. We can vote it any place we want … that is why they [the British] don't want it to come to a vote.'[24]

With most nations economically prostrate and dependent on the US, the acceptance of the agreements on the IMF and IBRD at Bretton Woods was a function of American power. The quotas for the subscriptions of individual countries to the IMF were established in secret negotiations, with a French delegate remarking that all this was done 'more or less arbitrarily by the United States in a series of deals'. The largest quotas went to the US, Britain, the USSR, China and France, who a year later were also made permanent members of the UN Security Council, 'affirming the world's political as well as financial pecking order'.[25]

Here in international finance, as in international trade, the LDCs were regime-takers rather than regime-makers and, accordingly, they were to bear for decades to come the inordinate costs of adjustment, through the conditionalities imposed by the IMF and IBRD, in their situation of recurrent balance of payments deficits. In the negotiations leading to the establishment of IMF and IBRD, Keynes had proposed—with an eye to Britain's own anticipated post-war situation—that countries with persistent surpluses in their balance of payments should also be obligated to adjust their foreign economic policies. The US simply dismissed that proposition out of hand. This outcome in regime formation was the direct result of the asymmetry in power between the US and the rest of the world.

The same power asymmetry was to become manifest in subsequent regime change as well, even though the economic position of the US had somewhat weakened meanwhile. In the 1960s, the US began to encounter mounting current account deficits as a consequence of 'imperial overstretch', as evident in the Vietnam war, and of domestic economic expansion as manifest in the pursuit of the Great Society. The resulting lack of confidence in the future value of the dollar, and

---

[24] Skidelsky, *Keynes*, 352, 357.
[25] Ibid., 442–3.

uncertainty over its convertibility into gold at the set value of $35 per ounce, led to increasing speculation on the dollar. The US insisted, however, that other major economic powers revalue their currencies upwards because it did not want to devalue its own currency, for that would have detracted from American national greatness.

When the other major economic powers failed to cooperate on revaluation, the US, in August 1971, suddenly and without any forewarning, took unilateral action known as the 'Nixon shocks'. Through this dramatic action, the US simply jettisoned the Bretton Woods agreement on the convertibility of dollars into gold and on fixed exchange rates, forcing the world currencies eventually to shift to a system of floating exchange rates.[26] In essence: 'Acting unilaterally and coercively, Washington demanded unrequited monetary and trade concessions from its major economic and military partners, imposing a tariff surcharge on their exports to the US until they yielded.'[27] The episode vividly demonstrated that legal parchment has little worth when it conflicts with the national interests of the powerful. The US refused to adjust its state behaviour to the international rules that it had itself established. Following the rules—as France's Finance Minister, Valery Giscard d'Estaing, had indeed bluntly recommended in July 1971— would have meant for the US to go to the IMF, just like other countries, and get loans under the usual conditionalities to cover its deficits.[28] Instead, the US forced the overthrow of the rules in favour of a systemic outcome that corresponded to its own preferences.

Tough American Conditionalities for Post-War Britain

It is clear that economic nationalism had been much in evidence in American planning for the post-war world order during the course of World War II. Such nationalism continued to be manifest as well in the period immediately after the war. The US employed its

---

[26] For a brief case study of the episode, see Brawley, *Turning Points*, Chapter 17. For a systematic and thorough examination, see John Odell, *US International Monetary Policy: Markets, Power and Ideas as Sources of Change* (Princeton: Princeton University Press, 1982).

[27] Ibid., 6.

[28] Ibid., 229–30. Note that five days after the announcement of the 'Nixon Shocks', the IMF Board declared that the US had acted in violation of its obligations under the IMF with regard to assuring the stability of the dollar. Ibid., 272.

unmatched economic power quite sternly in post-war negotiations with Britain when, in its situation of economic exigency following the war, the latter approached the US for a loan in 1946. During the negotiations, Britain was forced to capitulate completely before American terms on exchange controls, and on current account convertibility, notwithstanding the transitional dispensation that had been given to Britain on these issues at Bretton Woods.[29] The harsh conditions that Washington attached to the $3.75 billion loan, however, 'brought England to the verge of bankruptcy by late summer 1947'.[30]

The American approach to the financial management of the world up to this point, thus, turned out to be marked less by the magnanimity that is said to be usually associated with the leadership role of a hegemonic power than by nationalism. In the opinion of the historian Randall Woods: 'Those in the vanguard of the interventionist movement in 1946 ... were pro-business, fiscal conservatives; they were nationalists determined to gain tangible financial and strategic profit from every dollar spent.' However, what is remarkable is that the American posture soon underwent dramatic change when 'the liberal pragmatists seize[d] control of the interventionist movement'.[31] The crucial question that arises is as to what made for the passing of control to these liberal pragmatists.

Geopolitical Challenge and American Internationalism

What turned the US away from its strictly nationalist approach with regard to international commerce and finance was a hinge shift in geopolitics. The consequences were wide-ranging, marking a radical swing from the earlier pattern of American state behaviour. This applied no less to the former Axis powers than it did to the allies and the liberated areas.

Initial American Policy toward the Former Axis Powers

In the period immediately after the end of the war, the American posture toward the defeated Axis powers under its occupation,

---

[29] Skidelsky, *Keynes*, 442–3.
[30] Woods, *A Changing of the Guard*, 406.
[31] Ibid., 406–7.

Germany and Japan, had understandably been punitive. Indeed, during the war, Treasury Secretary Henry Morgenthau had envisioned reducing Germany to a pastoral country, rid of its industrial power, so that it could never rise as a threat again. The plan for the deindustrialization of Germany, however, went beyond being just Morgenthau's personal preference. Churchill and Roosevelt signed on to a joint plan committing their states to shutting down German heavy industry and converting Germany to 'a country primarily agricultural and pastoral in character'. The expected reward for Britain, in return, which apparently weighed in its agreeing to the plan, was the passing on to it of Germany's export business.[32] If that plan had really been implemented, there would have been, with the absence of Germany as the driving force of the present-day European economy, little likelihood of a contemporary Europe united as a common market, emerging as the second leg of the triad in the global economy today.

Similar to the fate reserved for Germany, the US intended to finish off Japan as an industrial power. The sentiment for revenge and punishment was very strong in the US. One adviser to the State-War-Navy Coordinating Committee, a sort of predecessor of the National Security Council, asked for the 'almost total elimination of the Japanese as a race', with Japan to be bombed so ruthlessly as to see that there is 'little left of its civilization'. President Franklin Roosevelt's son, Elliott, wanted the US to 'keep on bombing until we have destroyed about half the Japanese civilian population', while the President himself wanted the Japanese to be cross-bred with the more peaceful islanders of the Pacific. President Harry Truman thought of the Japanese as 'vicious and cruel savages', with the fate that they met at the hands of American atomic bombs dropped on Hiroshima and Nagasaki, being regarded as well deserved.[33] Japan did not really need to wait for any plan of the victors for deindustrialization after defeat in war, however; massive American bombing raids had substantially accomplished such an aim by making rubble of half of urban Japan. General Douglas MacArthur, presiding over the Supreme Command of the Allied Powers (SCAP) in Japan, himself had proclaimed, with some hyperbole but a lot of truth: 'Never in history

[32] Skidelsky, *Keynes*, 363.

[33] Michael Schaller, *The American Occupation of Japan: The Origins of the Cold War in Asia* (New York: Oxford University Press, 1985), 3–4, 26.

had a nation and its people been more completely crushed than were the Japanese at the end of the war.'[34]

After the war, the US had no intention to rehabilitate the economy of that part of Germany which was under its occupation. It had left the matter aside for subsequent negotiation with its allies. More important, as perhaps the most brilliant strategic thinker in the US government at the time, George Kennan, put it: 'We were not even clear in our own minds whether we wanted German economy rehabilitated. Sometimes we thought we did. Sometimes we thought we didn't. Sometimes we just agreed to disagree among ourselves.' The consequence was that the US 'let the economic situation slide for two years', and failed to develop any rehabilitation plan even for its own occupation zone. Its priority at the time was the denazification and democratization of public life in Germany.[35]

Similarly, in the case of Japan, where the US was the sole occupying power, Washington mandated the Occupation authorities with the task of radically restructuring Japan, focusing on demilitarization, democratization, and economic reform. The Basic Post-surrender Policy for Japan, instituted in August 1945, sought to 'insure that Japan will not again become a menace to the peace and security of the world', and therefore laid down that 'the existing economic basis of Japan's military strength must be destroyed and not permitted to revive.'[36] Accordingly, the Occupation authorities demobilized and dispersed the Japanese armed forces, and demolished all military installations and destroyed all military equipment. Other Washington directives required the payment by Japan of heavy reparations, the elimination of industrial capacity in certain key branches and restricting it in others, and the dismantlement of business conglomerates (*zaibatsu*).

[34] Douglas MacArthur, *Reminiscences* (New York: McGraw-Hill, 1964), 281.

[35] George F. Kennan, *Memoirs, 1925–1950* (Boston, MA: Little, Brown and Company, 1967), 333.

[36] Richard J. Samuels, *Rich Nation, Strong Army: National Security and the Technological Transformation of Japan* (Ithaca, NY: Cornell University Press, 1994), 130–1. See also Schaller, *The American Occupation of Japan*, 7–8, 25, 31; Kazuo Kawai, *Japan's American Interlude* (Chicago: University of Chicago Press, 1960), 21, 133; and William S. Borden, *The Pacific Alliance: United States Foreign Economic Policy and Japanese Trade Recovery, 1947–1953* (Madison, WI: University of Wisconsin Press, 1984), 66.

Any consequent hardship for the Japanese from these measures was regarded as just deserts for their egregious misdeeds in the past. Japan was expected to bear the burden of repairing its own war damage, and to reconcile itself to having the same standards of living as the rest of Asia. Patrick and Rosovsky had perceptively noted: 'Right after the war nearly everyone believed that the Japanese were condemned to a long period of national poverty, and—aside from reparations—the world community had little interest in them.'[37] If the US as the occupying power in Japan had persisted in the course that it was set on in the immediate post-war period, there would likely have been absent the third leg also of the triad in the global economy in the shape of Japan as an economic powerhouse.

A couple of years after the end of the war, the policies of the Occupation authorities in Japan were the subject of a devastating critique by Kennan. He was especially biting with regard to trust-busting in the Japanese economy. Kennan thought: 'The ideological concepts on which these measures rested bore so close a resemblance to Soviet views about the evils of "capitalist monopolies" that the measures themselves could only have been eminently agreeable to anyone interested in the future communization of Japan.' As for the 'purging' of individuals from government, business, and the educational system, he believed that 'SCAP had proceeded on a scale, and with a dogmatic, impersonal vindictiveness, for which there were few examples outside the totalitarian countries themselves.... the indiscriminate purging of whole categories of individuals [was] sickeningly similar to totalitarian practices.' Kennan further believed that the complete disbanding of the armed and police forces had rendered Japan vulnerable in relation to its internal security. In sum, he was convinced that 'the nature of the occupational policies pursued up to that time by General MacArthur's headquarters seemed on cursory examination to be such that if they had been devised for the specific purpose of rendering Japanese society vulnerable to Communist political pressures and paving the way for a Communist takeover, they could scarcely have been other than what they were.'[38]

---

[37] Hugh Patrick and Henry Rosovsky, *Asia's New Giant: How the Japanese Economy Works* (Washington, DC: The Brookings Institution, 1976), 911.

[38] Kennan, *Memoirs*, 376, 388–90.

The Soviet Threat and the American Reversal of Course

The punitive phase based on notions of revenge and punishment about the future fate of Germany and Japan was soon abandoned, however, and there was a sudden reversal of course from punishment to economic recovery and advance. The fundamental reason for the course reversal was this: the world that had emerged out of the ruins of World War II was a politically fractured one, divided between the American-led Western bloc and the Soviet-led Eastern bloc, along a demarcating line largely reflecting the physical presence of their respective armies. The line ran through the very heart of Europe, splitting it between Western and Eastern Europe, with Eastern Europe now said to lie behind what came to be called the Iron Curtain installed by the Soviet Union.

With some twenty-four million dead[39] and much of its economy destroyed by war, the Soviet Union was really, despite the apparent awesomeness of its military strength and its opportunistic assertiveness, a frightened power, especially given the American display of atomic prowess at Hiroshima and Nagasaki.[40] At the same time, since it regarded itself as the victorious power that was primarily responsible for defeating Germany, the Soviet Union was intent on keeping under its control areas of Europe that it had militarily conquered, without being excessively bothered about democratic niceties and national sentiments of other states. It was also ready to grab those states that, because of their internal turmoil, would fall into its lap. However, given its economic weakness, the Soviet Union was cautious and eager to avoid direct military involvement in the cause of expansion of its area of influence.

The situation of bipolarity between the US and the Soviet Union—as the two newly triumphant superpowers in war that were in their different ways also messianic powers—with their armies facing across the line of division in Europe, was nonetheless ripe for conflict. The trigger for the conflict occurred with the emergent incapacity of Great Britain as the long-standing imperial power to support

[39] The estimate is from John J. Mearsheimer, *The Tragedy of Great Power Politics*, 443 (n72).

[40] For the revisionist view that the American atomic attacks on Japan were intended to signal the new American power to the Soviets, see Gar Alperovitz, *Atomic Diplomacy: Hiroshima and Potsdam: The Use of the Atomic Bomb and the Confrontation with Soviet Power* (New York: Simon and Schuster, 1965).

Greece and Turkey economically any longer. The prospect, then, was of imminent collapse of these two countries in the face of pressures from within and without, with the two likely falling into the Soviet camp. At Britain's request, the US eagerly took on the erstwhile empire's responsibilities, but it cast them, in view of the need to mobilize political support in the Congress and the American public, in terms of a titanic worldwide struggle between good and evil. It fired the opening shot in 1947 with the Truman Doctrine that saw the world, within a Manichaean framework, divided between the forces of democracy and dictatorship. It further expressed the American determination to support the forces of freedom and democracy by pledging assistance to all states that were threatened by international communism.

Kennan was dismayed by the overblown rhetoric of the Truman Doctrine, which seemed to him to have needlessly elevated a local threat into a global conflict, but the die had been cast. It was a turning point in post-war international politics. The new American strategy toward the Soviet Union came to be termed *containment*, and it marked the beginning of an almost half-century of Cold War between the US and the Soviet Union, that had its scary moments of threatening to take the world into a nuclear Armageddon. The strategy became the sheet anchor of American foreign policy, and it was pursued single-mindedly by the US over the subsequent more than four decades, regardless of the many changes from one administration to another. To the world outside, the intellectual rationale for the policy of containment was provided, even if unintendedly, by George Kennan in an anonymous article attributed to 'X' in the journal *Foreign Affairs*. Its core idea was that the Soviet Union would invariably endeavour, driven by its ideology and history, to spread its power in Europe and Asia to a point where it would tip the balance of power in Eurasia, and thus threaten the national interests of the US. However, Kennan saw it as within the power of the US to contain such a threat and believed that it was incumbent on the US to do so:

> Soviet pressure against the free institutions of the Western world is something that can be contained by the adroit and vigilant application of counter-force at a series of constantly shifting geographical and political points, corresponding to the shifts and manoeuvres of Soviet policy but which cannot be charmed or talked out of existence.[41]

[41] 'X' [George F. Kennan], 'The Sources of Soviet Conduct', *Foreign Affairs*, 25, 4 (July 1947), 576.

Perceiving itself, thus, to be trapped in a life-or-death struggle, the US decided on a worldwide policy of containment against the Soviet Union, and proceeded to mobilize the world militarily and economically toward that end. This was a drastic reversal from the path of wartime alliance with the Soviet Union against the Axis powers. It also signalled a departure from the strictly nationalist approach that the US had hitherto pursued toward its other allies in the closing years of the war and in the period immediately after the war. It marked the shift to a policy more appropriate to the leadership role of a hegemon in being proactively supportive of them. As Woods explains: 'Only after Britain experienced virtual bankruptcy and a dangerous void materialized in European politics, did the liberal pragmatists seize control of the anticommunist phase of the interventionist movement and come to the continent's rescue.'[42] Thus, the perception of a new geopolitical reality inspired fundamental change in strategy.

The resultant containment policy can be considered to have had two components: military and economic. Kennan himself was averse to the military component, tending to see the Soviet threat more in political and economic terms, where the power vacuums in Europe and East Asia issuing out of the war were likely to tempt the Soviet Union to expand its sphere of control and domination.[43] For him, the war-ravaged economies of Europe and East Asia, particularly of Germany and Japan, with their armies of the impoverished and unemployed, offered opportunities to the Soviet Union that it was likely to exploit. Moreover, the existing substantial penetration of the polities of these areas by communist parties and revolutionary groups that were either sympathetic to, or proxies of, the Soviet Union could lead to the eventual defection of these areas to the Soviet bloc, if help was not extended to them.[44] As major centres of industrial power before the war, Germany and Japan plus Great Britain and France were high prizes in the contest between the US and the Soviet

[42] Woods, *A Changing of the Guard*, 407.

[43] Wilson D. Miscamble, *George F. Kennan and the Making of American Foreign Policy, 1947–1950* (Princeton: Princeton University Press, 1992), 74.

[44] On Europe's desperate economic situation in the immediate post-war period and the threat posed by local communist parties, see Miscamble, *George F. Kennan*, 43–5, and David Mayers, *George Kennan and the Dilemmas of US Foreign Policy* (New York: Oxford University Press, 1988), 134–5, 139, 141.

Union.[45] The US could not allow them to slide out of its control except at the peril of drastically shifting the global balance of power in favour of the Soviet bloc, thus endangering its own security in the process. With the economies of these areas either having already collapsed or being on the verge of collapse, the task of denial of these areas to the Soviet Union was considered to be both imperative and urgent.

Although he had been in the forefront of recognizing the Soviet threat, Kennan was convinced that it ought to be tackled through political and economic means. The US was, no doubt, readily persuaded to use the instrument of economic aid to assist the recovery of the war-ravaged economies. However, the dominant perspective in Washington, which eventually came to be accepted as policy, saw the military component 'as an essential supplement' to the economic instrument,[46] lifting the spirits of the war-ravaged countries and allowing them to focus on economic recovery. In the ultimate analysis, then, containment turned out to be double-barrelled, combining both the military and economic instruments.

Military Containment: Implications for Globalization

Militarily, as part of its containment policy, the US reorganized the world outside the Soviet bloc, particularly in Western Europe. It did so through alliances, most prominently NATO (founded in 1949) and also CENTO and SEATO (which followed in the mid-1950s), and through bilateral security treaties, such as between the US and Japan (1951), as a firewall against the feared Soviet expansion. While CENTO and SEATO subsequently withered away because of political and military disruptions among their LDC constituents, NATO as an alliance of the developed transatlantic countries and the US–Japan security treaty remained the bulwark of the anti-Soviet effort.

The success of NATO reflected an underlying fundamental unity of purpose in resisting any possible threat of further Soviet expansion in Europe. Indeed, it could be said that the initiative for NATO initially came from some of the European powers, and therefore the resulting American military domination of Western Europe represented an 'empire by invitation'.[47] NATO fulfilled several functions, which

---

[45] Schaller, *The American Occupation of Japan*, 87–8.

[46] Miscamble, *George F. Kennan*, 134.

[47] Ibid., 138.

were described pithily and colourfully by Lord Ismay, NATO's first secretary-general: 'NATO exists for three reasons—to keep the Russians out, the Americans in and the Germans down.'[48] The success of the US–Japan security treaty—rather more accurately the American military protectorate over Japan—flowed from several factors. Among these were: the crushing defeat inflicted by the US on Japan in World War II, the consequent American occupation of Japan, the American disarmament of Japan, the American-imposed constitution which barred Japan from raising armed forces even for the defence of its own territory, and the innate fear of the Japanese officials and public that building sufficient military power for self-defence may lead to a recurrence of militarism in Japan.

From the start, however, the aims of containment were more ambitious than simply being defensive in terms of safeguarding the security of the Western bloc. Containment's intellectual father, George Kennan, had indeed suggested: 'The United States has in its power to increase enormously the strains under which Soviet policy must operate ... and in this way to promote tendencies which must eventually find their outlet in either the break-up or the gradual mellowing of Soviet power.'[49] That is precisely what ultimately came to pass; indeed, both mellowing and break-up took place, in that order. What is remarkable is the dedicated and relentless pursuit of this objective by the US, unhampered by the transfers of power from one administration to another.

Under the immense pressure of the American challenge to compete militarily, especially during the Reagan era, both the Soviet bloc and the Soviet Union eventually broke up about a decade before the end of the twentieth century. That made the US the sole superpower in a basically unipolar system, and American military power has, as a result, assumed rather unchallengeable proportions in the world. On the one hand, NATO has expanded substantially in membership, encompassing some of the former members of the Soviet-sponsored Warsaw Pact, taking American power to the doorsteps of the Russian rump left over from the disintegration of the Soviet Union. Besides, new military bases in Central Asia leave Russia encircled by American power. On the other hand, the US has become increasingly

[48] Cited in Peter Hennessy, *Never Again: Britain, 1945–1951* (London: Jonathan Cape, 1992), 253.

[49] Kennan, 'The Sources of Soviet Conduct', 581.

interventionist around the world and also unilateralist, alienating even its formal allies in the process.

Regardless, American military bases have, since the end of World War II girdled the globe in greater numbers and in new locations, large garrisons of American troops have remained stationed in Europe, Japan, and South Korea, and vast American fleets have continued to traverse unhindered the world's vast oceans. In a pioneering and insightful work, Gilpin had noted: 'For the United States and the *Pax Americana*, military alliances with the "rimlands" of Western Europe and Asia (Japan) have provided the functional equivalent of the system of naval bases upon which the *Pax Britannica* rested. The American presence in Europe, Japan, and elsewhere around the Soviet Union provided a strategic and political framework within which American hegemony was exercised.'[50]

The American military presence around the world, existent on a vast scale even before the collapse of the Soviet Union, gives the US the semblance of owning a vast empire of unsurpassed size, beyond anything witnessed by the Roman and British empires, rather than simply being a hegemonic power. This dominating American military presence around much of the globe in the post-war world has a critical linkage with the advance of economic globalization. The phenomenon of economic globalization is not something that has occurred as simply the outcome of some autonomous economic processes, but is fundamentally rooted in the geopolitical fact of the global reach of American military power. It is precisely the globe-girdling American military presence that has provided the political framework—because of the accompanying security and stability that it assures—within which the Western regime of 'embedded liberalism' has functioned and the massive flows of post-war foreign direct investment (FDI) have taken place. As Gilpin had remarked: 'The *Pax Americana* provided a political and security structure which facilitated rapid expansion abroad by American corporations.... The creation of a favourable political environment provided the *necessary* conditions for foreign direct investment by multinational corporations.'[51] Consequently, the American military power and far-flung system of

[50] Robert Gilpin, *US Power and the Multinational Corporation*, 105.
[51] Ibid., 113.

military bases around the world, on the one hand, and the liberal world economic order, on the other, have to be seen joined together as twins, not as some entities apart. Thomas Friedman, an ardent supporter of globalization, is certainly correct in averring:

> Sustainable globalization requires a stable power structure, and no country is more essential for this than the United States.... all the trade and financial integration it [Silicon Valley] is promoting through its innovations, and all the wealth this is generating, are happening in a world stabilized by a benign superpower, with its capital in Washington, DC. The fact that no two major countries have gone to war since they both got McDonald's is partly due to economic integration, but it is also due to the presence of American power and America's willingness to use that power against those who would threaten the system of globalization—from Iraq to North Korea. The *hidden hand* of the market will never work without a *hidden fist.*
>
> Markets function and flourish only when property rights are secure and can be enforced, which, in turn, requires a political framework protected and backed by military power.... Indeed, McDonald's cannot flourish without McDonnell Douglas, the designer of the US Air Force F-15. And the hidden fist that keeps the world safe for Silicon Valley's technologies to flourish is called the US Army, Air Force, Navy, and Marine Corps.[52]

All this underlines once again the fundamental fact that globalization, as an economic process, cannot be divorced from globalization as a political, or more accurately, a geopolitical, project.

Containment through Economic Reconstruction

More important, the aim of containment of the Soviet Union led to a massive American programme of financial aid for the economic recovery and reconstruction of Europe and Japan, in an effort to consolidate them politically so as to defeat the threat of communism to these areas from within. The plan for the economic reconstruction preceded the more military cast that was subsequently given to containment, and it is something for which George Kennan as the then Director of State Department's Policy Planning Staff can justifiably claim credit.[53]

Kennan's policy prescriptions for economic reconstruction stemmed from the war-ravaged conditions of the economies of the allies and the former Axis powers that rendered them vulnerable to pressures

---

[52] Thomas L. Friedman, *The Lexus and the Olive Tree*, 464; [emphasis added].

[53] Miscamble, *George F. Kennan*, 73–4.

from the Soviet Union, and possible seizure by communist parties from within. Kennan was particularly persuaded by the need to help Germany: 'In this case that which is at stake is an economic programme of crucial urgency: a programme on which tens of millions of people are waiting as a matter almost of life and death, a programme which may prove decisive for the balance of power in Europe.... it is imperatively urgent today that the improvement of economic conditions, and the revival of productive capacity in the west of Germany be made the primary object of our policy in that area and be given top priority in all our occupation policies.'[54]

The same logic also extended to other needy powers, such as France, Italy, Great Britain, and Japan. Indeed, Kennan's economic prescriptions were premised on a strategic architecture that viewed the power structure of the world as organized around five major industrial centres. As he repeatedly emphasized: 'There were only five regions of the world—the United States, the United Kingdom, the Rhine valley with adjacent industrial areas [i.e., Germany], the Soviet Union, and Japan—where the sinews of modern military strength could be produced in quantity.' He then pointed out that 'only one of these was under Communist control' and he defined 'the main task of containment, accordingly, as one of seeing to it that none of the remaining ones fell under such control'.[55] It followed from this power-centred structure of the world that the US could not allow any of the non-Communist industrial centres to slip into the Soviet orbit, for that would alter the global balance of power in a way that would imperil the security of the United States. In this scheme of things, Germany and Japan were of the utmost importance. As Kennan and his Policy Planning Staff surveyed the world scene in its totality, they came to the conclusion:

> The theatres of our greatest dangers, our greatest responsibilities, and our greatest possibilities at that moment were the two occupied areas of Western Germany and Japan. These places were the centres, respectively, of the two greatest industrial complexes of East and West. Their recovery was essential to the restoration of stability in Europe and East Asia. It was essential, if any sort of a tolerable balance of power was to be established in the post-war world, that they be kept out of Communist hands and that their great resources be utilized to the full for constructive purposes.[56]

[54] Kennan, *Memoirs*, 334.
[55] Ibid., 359. See also Mayers, *George Kennan*, 122.
[56] Kennan, *Memoirs*, 368.

It was within such a strategic framework that the Marshall Plan, named after the then Secretary of State, General George Marshall, was launched in 1947 for the economic recovery of Europe. The resources of the IMF and the IBRD were not adequate for the purpose, and would have been quickly exhausted.[57] Consequently, with its great economic prowess, the US had to undertake the task of organizing and financing European recovery. The massive scale of the Marshall Plan can be adjudged from the fact that an amount of $13.3 billion was spent on economic aid to Europe within a matter of four years.[58] The Plan was a gratifying moment for Kennan, for it 'finally broke through the confusion of wartime pro-Sovietism, wishful thinking, anglophobia and self-righteous punitivism in which our occupational policies in Germany had, thus, far been enveloped.'[59]

The Marshall Plan was accompanied by an American-imposed condition which was of momentous importance for the shape that economic globalization was later to assume. The US made the economic aid to war-torn Europe conditional on economic cooperation among the various countries. It insisted that the European countries work together to develop a coordinated programme of economic recovery 'on a European scale'. Apparently, the condition was inspired by the need to avoid competition among the European nations in making demands that, in the aggregate, would escalate beyond what the US could reasonably meet. The Americans also hoped, in the process, 'to force the Europeans to begin to think like Europeans, and not like nationalists, in their approach to the economic problems of the continent'.[60] The American condition on European cooperation may have also issued out of an American concern that, if they were not pushed into it, the European nations would simply revert to their traditional animosities and conflicts that would require American military intervention once again to settle. In any case, a pragmatic and statesmanlike political compact between Germany and France—

---

[57] Borden, *The Pacific Alliance*, 31.

[58] Mayers, *George Kennan*, 138. One authority places the current value of the Marshall Plan at some $90 billion; see Michael D. Intriligator, 'Globalization of the World Economy: Potential Benefits and Costs and a Net Assessment', paper presented at a conference organized by the Instituto Affari Internazionali, Rome, 21–3 March 2002 (Available online).

[59] Kennan, *Memoirs*, 335.

[60] Ibid., 337.

by the former in order to bury its Nazi past, and by the latter to recover its role as a great power—soon complemented the American condition. That condition on European cooperation was of historic significance, for it would eventually lead through successive periodic steps to the formation of the EU. In supporting the development of the common market in Europe, the US chose to ignore the application of the 'most favoured nation' principle of GATT. In this fashion, 'Reversing its earlier commitment to global multilateralism and nondiscrimination, the United States promoted the creation of a preference area in Western Europe which discriminated against American goods.'[61]

A Marshall Plan was also mooted for Japan, 'the sole great potential military–industrial arsenal of the Far East'[62], but the proposal did not reach the fruition stage. Instead, the Occupation authorities in Japan changed economic policy to launch Japan on a course of economic recovery in place of the earlier path of economic punishment. Kennan's role in that policy change was crucial, and he has been referred to as 'the father of reverse-course policy.'[63] Fortuitously, but more critically, Japan found in the Korean War (1950) the functional equivalent to the Marshall Plan as the US made Japan a base for the massive procurement of supplies for the war. Moreover, 'With the advent of Korean hostilities, every question about reparations, the break-up of industrial combines, and trade and production policies was resolved in Japan's favour.'[64] Besides, to aid the recovery of Europe and Japan, the US, as befitting its leadership role as hegemon, opened its own markets to labour-intensive imports from them without insisting, in a selective deviation from GATT, on reciprocity. Spurred by American economic aid and military expenditures (on the stationing of troops, and on war in Korea and Vietnam) and by

[61] Gilpin, *US Power and the Multinational Corporation*, 108.

[62] Kennan, *Memoirs*, 374.

[63] Miscamble, *George F. Kennan*, 267; see also Mayers, *George Kennan*, 138. As Kennan himself noted: 'My own visit, the talk with General MacArthur, and the directives that finally emanated from Washington represented in their entirety a major contribution to the change in occupational policy that was carried out in late 1948 and in 1949; and I consider my part in bringing about this change to have been, after the Marshall Plan, the most significant constructive contribution I was ever able to make in government.' Kennan, *Memoirs*, 393.

[64] Mayers, *George Kennan*, 169.

the opening of American markets to their imports, Europe and Japan rose Phoenix-like as major economic powers. At the same time, these economic powers were highly integrated with the American economy, thus leading directly to the manifest phenomenon of 'triadization' in the world economy.

Summary

In brief, the contemporary economic globalization and its truncated nature have their roots in geopolitics during and after World War II. Fundamentally, the economic and military power of the US originally created, and has subsequently sustained, the American-dominated world economic order, in respect of both world trade and international finance. Economics and politics, at the global level, have been linked processes, and globalization needs to be assessed in the context of geopolitics and not simply taken to be an economics-driven process. The 'triad' as a dominating feature of present-day globalization is directly traceable to the geopolitical reshaping of the world as a result of post-war American strategic policy. Contemporary configurations in the world economy thus have strategic origins.

Chapter 6

FROM HEGEMONY TO EMPIRE
The Diffusion and Concentration of Power

The radically new distribution of power at the end of World War II resulted in the installation of a new world economic and political order. In its fundamentals, the new world order reflected the preferences of the US, the emergent hegemonic power. Much of it had been conceptualized, negotiated, and agreed upon during the course of the war itself, especially in its later stages, when the Allies were abjectly dependent on the US, militarily and economically.

No distribution of power ever remains constant over time, however. In more than half a century following the end of the war, it saw several substantial shifts. The changes in the power configuration, in turn, had an impact on the international economic and political order. The purpose of this chapter is to examine the changes in the distribution of power and to see how they affected the economic and political order. In brief, the argument is that there has been both the diffusion of power as well as the increased concentration of power. The diffusion has resulted in challenges to American hegemony and the world order that it has sustained. On the other hand, the increased concentration of power in the US has led to a virtual American empire that decisively shapes the globalization process.

The New Post-War World Political Order

In the political sphere, the new world order following the end of World War II comprised the institutional complex of the United Nations system. Its chief organs were two: One, the UN Security Council which, with its five permanent (P-5) members having veto power, was the executive body mandated to keep the peace in the world.

Two, the UN General Assembly, with the sovereign states represented as equal members, which was the deliberative body to debate the various issues that were important to the world but was otherwise largely powerless to determine policy. The smooth operation of the UN system, particularly the UN Security Council as the custodian of world order, was premised on cooperation among the Big Five. However, with the binding glue holding the Allied powers gone after the defeat of the Axis powers, the wartime alliance split. Instead, there arose a *bipolar* international system in which the two poles—with the superpowers of the US and the Soviet Union leading their respective 'Western' and 'Eastern' blocs—lay outside Europe, which until the war had been the centre and master of world politics.

As the weaker party, the Soviet Union increasingly employed its veto in the Security Council to forestall actions against it that were often initiated by the US in the pursuit of its policy of containment. At the same time, with Europe devastated by the war and divided between the two blocs, the Western bloc felt itself to be threatened by the vast Soviet military presence in the heart of Europe. It therefore organized itself in 1949 into a military alliance, the North Atlantic Treaty Organization (NATO), led by the US and essentially dependent on it. The Soviet Union countered with a military alliance of its own, known as the Warsaw Pact, comprising the states under its occupation or control. From that point on, for much of the remainder of the twentieth century, the political-cum-military conflict between the two blocs became the defining axis of world politics, subordinating almost all other issues to this central conflict. The centrality of this proposition to international politics can hardly be exaggerated.

In the bipolar conflict, notwithstanding the fact that the US and the Soviet Union were both extraordinarily mighty military powers, wielding vast nuclear arsenals—hence, the bipolarity—the Soviet Union was much the weaker power, because it was, unlike the US, an incomplete power. Not only was it not competitive economically in the area of hard power, but it was also weak in soft power. Besides, the Soviet Union was essentially a regional power, albeit a big regional power, dominant only in the region that it physically controlled with its military presence. On the other hand, much of the world outside this region—a region that largely coincided with Mackinder's Heartland—was within the orbit of the US, either through military alliances or economic dependence. After 1949, when China, after its successful revolution, joined the Soviet bloc, the Soviet Union seemed to be a more potent threat, especially following the Korean War in 1950. However, about a decade later, China had defected from the bloc and had started its own rivalry with the Soviet Union, ideologically and politically, especially in the underdeveloped regions of Asia and Africa. The Soviet bloc was weakened immensely as a result, but the Soviet Union, as one of the two superpowers, remained critical to the central balance of power in the world.

With decolonization in the 1950s and 1960s, many of the newly independent states, especially those that came to constitute the non-aligned bloc, found common cause with the Soviet Union over issues that were important to them. But these states were lacking in power. As one prime minister of Pakistan expressed it mockingly in reference to them in the mid-1950s on the occasion of the Suez crisis, zero plus zero plus zero equals zero. Moreover, despite their frequent rhetorical assertions of foreign policy independence, these states were integrated economically as the periphery, with the Western bloc as the core, and were dependent on the latter for trade and, especially, economic aid. Indeed, neo-colonialism formed a major theme in the dependency literature of the 1970s.

At the same time, the US was forthright about its readiness to deal sternly with these states through economic and military means, warning them, in Secretary of State John Foster Dulles' words, that the US regarded those states that were not with it as being, in essence, against it. The classic policy employed by the US in dealing with regional powers that proved obstreperous toward accepting American hegemony was to create regional balances of power against them. More broadly, the US employed, as the realist scholar George Liska delineated them, three major policies in handling regional powers. Foremost among them was the policy of regional *containment* of the primary regional power through the US aligning itself with the secondary regional powers. The second policy was that of *satellization,* under which the US turned regional powers into client states by rendering them economically dependent through aid. Finally, in some cases, there was the policy of *accommodation,* where the US devolved power to regional powers when they were agreeable to being cooperative with it.[1]

---

[1] George Liska, 'The Third World: Regional Systems and Global Order', in Robert E. Osgood *et al.* (eds) *Retreat From Empire* (Baltimore, MD: Johns Hopkins University Press, 1973), 326.

Because of the central bipolar conflict between the two superpowers and their respective blocs, the UN was in its executive function largely a permanently deadlocked body. When vital security interests were at stake for either superpower, including its allies, each chose to ignore the UN system and acted on its own. Thus, the Soviet Union acted as it chose fit at various times in regard to Poland, Hungary, and Czechoslovakia, just as the US did in respect of Guatemala, Vietnam, Grenada, Nicaragua, and Afghanistan. The UN was quite marginal to the actions and outcomes concerning the conflicts in these various states. The world was simply divided quite rigidly in political terms, though the extent of division waxed and waned according to whether or not a thaw temporarily developed between the two superpowers, or whether or not détente was in the air. The world was, in effect, bifurcated politically.

As a result, there was a sharp discrepancy between the formal world order in the shape of the UN system and the substantive world order. The latter was marked by the absence of a world order in the face of two alliance systems in confrontation, indeed at times in mortal combat (even if not directly), with each other. Security and stability in this sort of world order was a function, not of the UN system, but of bipolarity itself and nuclear deterrence through the MAD (mutual assured destruction) doctrine and the consequent constraints it placed on the two nuclear superpowers in the interest of their own survival. American hegemony was thus *partial* although extensive; it did not extend to the Soviet bloc, even though the US was the pre-eminent superpower within its orbit that comprised much of the world outside the Soviet bloc. In essence, the new so-called international order was a truncated one, encompassing only the Western alliance system and most of the decolonized world. It excluded the Soviet bloc, and its designation as being 'international' is simply a concession to the wide scope of its coverage and to linguistic ease of expression. The Soviet bloc lay outside it not only politically but also in economic terms. Notwithstanding all that, at times the two superpowers cooperated, indeed collaborated, as in the case of the Nuclear Non-Proliferation Treaty (NPT) in order to pre-empt challenge to their superior nuclear status.

The New Post-War International Economic Order

In the economic arena, the new liberal international economic order of American design, which has been more narrowly described as one of 'embedded liberalism', encompassed a tripod of institutions. Two of these were the Bretton Woods institutions, that is, the International Monetary Fund (IMF) and the International Bank for Reconstruction and Development (IBRD, more popularly referred to as the World Bank). The third one was the General Agreement on Tariffs and Trade (GATT), which came into being since the US did not wish to subscribe to an International Trade Organization because of concerns over compromising its national sovereignty. GATT proved useful in bringing about radical reductions in tariff rates among the advanced industrial countries, and in tremendously boosting international trade among them. Let it be noted, however, that the Soviet bloc lay outside this economic order. Not only that, it was subjected to, as it were, economic warfare by the US and its allies through a sophisticated system of controls and international regimes in order to thwart its economic and technological development in the cause of containment.[2]

The IMF provided overall monetary stability for almost a quarter-century through its fixed exchange rate regime. For a considerable period, the US was, because of its predominant economic and financial muscle, able to have the IMF function pretty much in accordance with its own preferences. Indeed, 'the US basically ran things differently from how the rules dictated.'[3] It forced currency devaluations in 1949 as a condition for providing Marshall Plan aid. The intent was benign, however; it was to enable the European countries to earn more dollars by making the purchase of their goods more attractive to Americans. At the same time, because of the poor economic condition of Europe following World War II, the provision on removal of capital controls included in the IMF charter was not applied until after 1958 when the economic situation had become more stabilized.

With the establishment of the IMF, the dollar became the international currency of choice. Because of 'the privileges associated with being the world's banker', the US could afford to run up current account deficits since all it had to do was to simply pay for them with its domestic currency over which it had national control. As the

[2] Michael Mastanduno, *Economic Containment: CoCom and the Politics of East–West Trade* (Ithaca, NY: Cornell University Press, 1992).
[3] Mark R. Brawley, *Turning Points*, 296.

world's banker, 'the United States printed dollars rather freely to finance its political and economic position overseas.'[4] This privileged position was one that, not unexpectedly, 'the US learned to like'.[5] Concomitantly, the European central banks built up their foreign exchange reserves with their dollar accumulations rather than cashing them for gold from the US. In turn, their dollar holdings became a means of exchange for trade and foreign investment. In due course, these Eurodollars, as they came to be known, piled up outside the US, and gave rise to the phenomenon of 'dollar overhang', which would later pose problems for the US.

Meanwhile, the World Bank acted on its mandate to provide loans to European countries for purposes of reconstruction. However, the real contribution to the reconstruction of the economies of Western Europe, the retooling of their industrial plant, and the push toward developing a common market among them, was made by the massive American economic aid under the Marshall Plan. In the case of Japan, the equivalent of the Marshall Plan was, apart from direct American economic aid, the American procurement of military supplies on a large scale from Japan for the Korean War in the early 1950s, and for the Vietnam War during the 1960s and early 1970s. The enormous American economic assistance plus Keynesian economic policies worked to restore economic health to the various countries of Western Europe and to Japan. With the heightening of economic growth in the 1950s and 1960s, the economies of these countries revived and prospered, and their foreign trade saw dramatic expansion. For a quarter of a century after 1948 in the post-war era, modern capitalism witnessed a period of remarkable and sustained economic growth, unmarred by any serious depression unlike every decade in the century prior to World War II. Shonfield characterized this long boom as 'the age of acceleration'.[6]

The Soviet bloc also advanced economically, displaying tremendous powers of economic recovery under totalitarian auspices. At the same time, the Soviet Union rapidly built its nuclear and missile capabilities to create symmetry with the US in the military arena, and thus make

---

[4] Robert Gilpin, *US Power and the Multinational Corporation*, 216.

[5] Brawley, *Turning Points*, 296.

[6] Andrew Shonfield, *Modern Capitalism: The Changing Balance of Public and Private Power* (London: Oxford University Press, 1965), chapter 1.

for a genuine bipolar system, at least in military terms. Indeed, for a brief period, the US was put on the defensive in the realm of military technology when the Soviets pioneered in sending a space satellite into orbit in 1957. The event stunned and traumatized the US at the time. There even developed, for some time, the belief that the Soviet Union, by virtue of its higher economic growth rates of 5 to 6 per cent during the 1950s and 1960s was destined to overtake and outclass the US. It was feared that the Soviets would thus make their own economic system a beacon for other countries, especially in the decolonized developing world. The Soviet Premier Nikita Khrushchev was brazen enough to proclaim, while visiting the US in 1959, that the Soviet Union would outstrip the US economically by 1970, or at the latest by 1980.[7] Earlier, in 1956, he had predicted the coming end of the capitalist system and American power by declaring to Western diplomats: 'Whether you like it or not, history is on our side. We will bury you.'[8] Significantly, the Soviet Union also displayed considerable adaptive capacity in adjusting to changing political circumstances by undertaking modification of its reigning ideology through propounding the doctrine of 'peaceful transition to socialism' in the developing world. Again, it demonstrated a readiness to compete economically with the much more industrially advanced West in the developing world through launching a programme of economic aid for development, and giving socialism a push there in the process. In this manner, competition developed between the two blocs for some time, at least until the growth of détente between the two superpowers (even if episodically), in order to attract the affections of developing countries through economic aid.

While the Soviet economic performance was impressive during the quarter century after World War II, it masked an Achilles heel. One part of its central weakness was a poor agriculture as a result of collectivization. The other related to its industry. The Soviet Union had, no doubt, demonstrated that it could do well in pushing *extensive* industrialization, where it could copy what had already been accomplished under capitalism, and that it could also innovate quite well in military technology where it poured in vast resources.

[7] Joseph S. Nye, Jr, *Bound to Lead: The Changing Nature of American Power* (New York: Basic Books, 1990), 116–19.

[8] William J. Thompson, *Khrushchev: A Political Life* (New York: St Martin's Press, 1995), 171.

However, its command economy proved to be weak at *intensive* industrialization through self-generated technological innovation and advance, which is the hallmark of the market economy as a result of the frenetic pace of competition among producers. Once the Soviet Union had pushed through the phase of economic reconstruction after the devastation inflicted on it by World War II, and had completed its extensive industrialization, economic stagnation set in and undermined it in its competition with the US.[9] Meanwhile, the excessive diversion of resources to military purposes, for reasons of national security in the rivalry with a much more advanced and well-endowed economic power, eventually proved counterproductive and weakened the Soviet Union economically. The ultimate result for the Soviet Union as 'a one-dimensional power'[10] was not just economic stagnation and falling behind in the rivalry, but political collapse and territorial break-up.

The Discontent with Hegemonic Leadership

The economic reconstruction and restoration of Western Europe and Japan, no doubt, meant the integration of the economies of Europe and Japan with the American economy in the context of a generally expanding world economy. Such integration necessarily followed from the fact that their economic revival took place within the overall framework of American hegemony and security management, as well as with American assistance by way of both direct financial aid and the deliberate and favoured opening of the American market to them. Thus was laid the basis of both post-war economic globalization and the predominance of the 'triad' of the US, the EU, and Japan within it. At the same time, that economic reconstruction and restoration meant a greater diffusion of power, even if within the constraints of American economic and military predominance. In turn, such diffusion of power, howsoever limited in relative terms compared to the overwhelming power of the US, resulted in some assertion of independence in foreign policy on the part of some of the European powers.

---

[9] The economic growth rate in the first half of the decade of the 1970s slowed down to 3.7 per cent, and in the second half to 2.7 per cent. One advisor to Soviet President Mikhail Gorbachev maintained that the rate was zero over the period from 1980 to 1985. Nye, *Bound to Lead*, 119.

[10] Nye, *Bound to Lead*, 127.

The first attempt at such assertion in 1956 by the former imperial powers, Britain and France, through a joint military operation in collaboration with Israel against Egypt over the management of the Suez Canal, however, ended in disaster. The US refused to come to their support, the Soviet Union threatened to rain missiles over these imperial powers unless they ended their aggression, while the developing world joined in unison to oppose the venture. The event called attention to the weakness of the former imperial powers in the absence of support from the US.

Still, France continued to assert itself as an independent actor in world affairs by developing its own nuclear deterrent, by refusing to integrate its military forces under the command of NATO, by cultivating relations with the Soviet Union, and by recognizing Communist China against the wishes of the US. France was also sceptical about the American willingness to risk its own security for the sake of that of Europe in its nuclear rivalry with the Soviet Union, and therefore went in for an independent nuclear deterrent of its own. Some of NATO's other partners were also dubious about the American nuclear strategy of massive retaliation, for its actual employment would mean the certain and instant incineration of Europe. To calm European fears, the US then changed to a strategy of flexible response. The US also took part in many discussions about developing a multilateral nuclear force to satisfy European demands about participation in the life-and-death security decisions about Europe. However, it is noteworthy that at no stage was the US willing to share the ultimate control over the nuclear button with its NATO partners.

The first real challenge to American hegemony from its alliance partners arose in the economic arena rather than in the security issue-area. The origins of the challenge lay in the American pursuit of an expansionary policy on account of both guns and butter at the same time. Even as it was prosecuting a massive expeditionary war in Vietnam in the 1960s, it was also engaged in an active interventionist social policy to build the Great Society after the vision of President Lyndon Johnson. The resulting fiscal profligacy created serious economic problems by way of rising inflation and mounting current account deficits. With the future stability of the dollar in doubt, there was increasing speculation on the dollar in the financial markets. As their economic situation weakened, the Americans grew less tolerant of their former economic wards in Europe and Japan who now seemed to have turned into potent economic competitors.

The subsequent unfolding of events made manifest the deep policy fissures that had developed between the US and its allies. America's allies wanted the US to devalue its currency, which the US refused to undertake because that would reflect adversely on the greatness of the US; devaluation, in American eyes, was something that was meant for poor or weak countries. Perhaps, a more weighty reason for turning down devaluation was that it would boost the dollar value of the Soviet Union's gold stock.[11] Instead, the US wanted the major European economic powers and Japan to revalue their currencies, which would have had the result of expanding American exports, and thus resolving the problem of its current account deficits. However, the allies proved unwilling to take that prescription. In the circumstance, the US stunned the world by acting unilaterally in 1971 to discard the Bretton Woods accord on fixed exchange rates, to break the link between the dollar and gold, and to impose a surcharge on imports. The surcharge was meant to coerce its alliance partners to revalue their currencies in line with American wishes.

These 'Nixon shocks' demonstrated that, despite the renowned American proclivity for multilateral bargaining and negotiated agreements, the US was not above unilateral action when the pursuit of its national interests warranted it. Indeed, it could be asserted that the earlier American preference for multilateral bargaining was (in large part) based on the assurance, even certainty, that the US would ultimately prevail on any issue because of the predominance of its power. It may also have been based on the calculation that the allies would factor in gratitude in their decisions for past American generosity in providing economic aid and military security.

It is not only that the American unilateral and coercive action exposed the deep fissures in policy that had arisen among the allies, but the build-up toward it was also revelatory of the hardened attitudes of the US toward its allies. Such attitudes were definitely quite removed from the normal expectations concerning the behaviour of a hegemonic leader. They seemed, too, to stem from changed American perceptions rather than being a consequence of any drastic shift in economic and military power. Behind the change in

---

[11] Michael Loriaux, 'Realism and Reconciliation: France, Germany, and the European Union', in Ethan B. Kapstein and Michael Mastanduno (eds), *Unipolar Politics*, 362.

perceptions lay the fact of American power having been frustrated at the hands of poor and ill-equipped Vietnamese peasants in the Vietnam War. After a careful review of the evidence, John Odell strongly disputes the notion that there was any sharp shift in American hegemony, which accordingly cannot serve as a plausible explanation for American behaviour. In regard to the security issue-area, he maintains:

> It was still the case in 1971 that no power in the world came close to rivaling the military strength of either superpower. America's allies remained clearly dependent on the United States for security. This dependence remained especially marked, in fact, for precisely that country from which Washington wanted the largest monetary adjustment—Japan. At the global military level, the power structure remained essentially the same as it had been since World War II.

As for the economic arena, Odell's assessment is not as strong but it is still firmly on the side of continued American hegemony:

> Economic capabilities did become somewhat more evenly distributed among capitalist industrial states over the post-war period. But the erosion of American dominance over the other major states by 1971 has been much exaggerated in the US. Not only did those states remain dependent on the US for military protection, but the system's economic structure also remained centred on an economic superpower.
>
> The United States alone controlled an extraordinary 39 per cent of the world's total productive capacity and spending power in 1950. The subsequent recovery of Western Europe and Japan increased their shares, but in 1970 the American share of world GNP was still 30 per cent. The European Community as a whole controlled 15 per cent, Japan 6 per cent....
>
> The critical dimension distinguishing the superpower from other leading economic powers was its relative self-sufficiency. In 1970, US exports plus imports were still only 8 per cent of GNP.... Each of America's major trading partners was much more dependent on the American market than was the US on that country's market.... In short, the extraordinary American position in the international economic power structure had eroded somewhat over the first post-war generation, but the amount of the decline hardly seems sufficient to explain the dramatic reversal of 1971.[12]

The purported decline in American hegemony at this time thus seems exaggerated. Nonetheless, despite this reality, American leaders had in 1971 started campaigning in favour of the line that a

[12] Odell, *US International Monetary Policy*, 210–14.

fundamental shift had taken place in the global structure of economic power in favour of Western Europe and Japan at the cost of the US. In accord with that line, the US believed that 'Europe and Japan had become much stronger since the 1940s, yet they continued to follow selfish policies, requiring the United States to bear disproportionate burdens for the international system. They ought to give more. The power shift was cited to justify American unilateralism and withdrawal from leading joint efforts. Americans, preoccupied and frustrated in Vietnam, found the view appealing.' Treasury Secretary John Connally was the most forceful spokesman for the position, holding other states responsible for America's predicament rather than its own policies:

> Much of the condition that we find ourselves in today is the result not of our actions but the actions of other nations who have strengthened their own position, and during the last decade both Germany and Japan have immeasurably strengthened their position.[13]

For Connally, protectionism by the European Community through its agricultural policy was particularly reprehensible as it hurt American farm exports. Contrary to the long-standing American support for European economic integration, there had by then developed serious doubts in the Nixon administration whether such integration was, in fact, in America's interest.[14] On the basis of interviews with high-level decision-makers, Odell states: 'In internal

---

[13] Ibid., 209, 247

[14] This may not have been such a new development at all. It is noteworthy that before Henry Kissinger joined the Nixon Administration, one of the themes that he articulated strongly concerned the unwillingness of the US to concede a measure of independence to Europe, especially in matters of nuclear planning. He underlined the American penchant for hegemony, and believed General de Gaulle to be justified in his charge to that effect. At the time, he held that notions such as 'multilateralism' and 'interdependence' to be simply a mask for attempting to retain American control. He believed, too, that, although the US formally approved of European unity, it was anxious to keep its special relations with specific European countries intact, while making sure that there was no challenge to its dominance in Europe, particularly in matters of defence. He further noted: 'A decade and a half of hegemony have accustomed us to believing that our views represent the general interest. The difficulty with which decisions are reached in our government produces temptations to turn Allied consultation into an effort to implement eventually American conceptions.' See Stephen R. Graubard, *Kissinger: Portrait of a Mind* (New York: W.W. Norton, 1974), 201, 206.

meetings during 1971, Connally was "vociferous about how the United States was getting the short end of the stick in trade matters". At one Cabinet-level meeting with the President, he delivered, according to an official who was present, "an unbelievable diatribe" against the European Community and Japan, implying that they were America's real enemies.' It is significant that after the 'Nixon shocks', Connally summarily told a group of American economists who had been invited by him for consultation: 'I appreciate your coming in today. And since you have shared [your thoughts] with me, I think I should give you an idea of where I am going. My basic approach is that the foreigners are out to screw us. Our job is to screw them first. Thank you, gentlemen.'[15]

It may well be objected that other American decision-makers did not all share Connally's views. But it is noteworthy and a sign of the temper of the times that the President partook of those views and that he took Connally's advice, rather than that of the others, on the path to pursue as regards Bretton Woods. The more significant aspect is that the US had the power, notwithstanding assessments about its relative decline, to carry out its preferences in the international arena. In the final analysis, using the leverage of the surcharge on imports, the US was able to have its alliance partners largely concur with its major demands through the Smithsonian Agreement in 1971. The new arrangement on the values of the different major currencies, within a wider band for the fixed rates under Bretton Woods, did not prove to be stable, however. The dollar underwent devaluation twice, but speculative pressure did not stop. The British pound, too, came under strong pressure; unable to defend its parity value, Britain finally let the pound float in 1972. Eventually, by 1973, the practice of fixed exchange rates had come to an end, with all currencies being put on the float.[16]

The Elusive/Illusive Decline of American Hegemony

The 'age of acceleration' during the 1950s and 1960s among the 'triad' had been fuelled not only by American aid and indulgence and Keynesian policies, but also by cheap oil from the Middle East. Then, suddenly, on 17 October 1973—for some, 'energy Pearl

---

[15] Odell, *US International Monetary Policy*, 248, 263.
[16] Brawley, *Turning Points*, 308.

Harbour day'[17]—in the midst of the Arab-Israeli war, the Arab members of the oil cartel of the Organization of the Petroleum Exporting Countries (OPEC) imposed an oil embargo on countries supporting Israel. Meanwhile, OPEC also hiked oil prices almost fourfold.

The OPEC 'oil price shocks' were a watershed in the post-war world economy; they shook the foundations of the world economy as it had evolved in the post-war period. They constituted a virtual economic earthquake, causing a mighty upheaval in the international economy. They threw the world economy into enormous turmoil, not only putting an end to the post-war phase of economic expansion in the advanced industrial economies, but also threatening their very economic stability. In the eyes of some observers, the oil price hike was 'the opening stage of a struggle for a new world order, a search for positions of strength in a global realignment, in which the weapons (backed, naturally, by the ultimate sanction of force) are food and fuel.'[18] For American political scientist John Ikenberry, 'Most important, American post-war leadership, already perceived to be on the wane, looked to have been dealt another, perhaps decisive, blow. An era was ending.'[19]

Through the 'oil price shocks', OPEC generated the deepest economic recession in the industrial countries since the 1930s, not only bringing an end to the 'age of acceleration' but also causing economic havoc by giving rise to both double-digit inflation and unemployment, or 'stagflation' as it was called.[20] The result was to shift the focus of decision-makers from tackling unemployment to inflation as 'the cardinal economic concern', with the industrial countries using exchange rate and trade policies 'to export inflation or—at minimum—to avoid importing inflation from the rest of the

[17] David Freeman, *Energy: The New Era* (New York: Vintage, 1974), 1, cited in G. John Ikenberry, *Reasons of State: Oil Politics and the Capacities of American Government* (Ithaca, NY: Cornell University Press, 1988), 3.

[18] Geoffrey Barraclough, 'Wealth and Power: The Politics of Food and Fuel', *New York Review of Books* (7 August 1975), 5, cited in Ikenberry, *Reasons of State*, 1.

[19] Ibid.

[20] C. Fred Bergsten, *Managing International Economic Interdependence: Selected Papers of C. Fred Bergsten, 1975–76* (Lexington, MA: Lexington Books, 1977), 25.

world'.[21] If the economic damage from the initial price shocks was not enough, about half a dozen years later there followed the second 'oil price shocks' in 1979, altogether raising the inflation-adjusted price of oil by 500 per cent. The shocks also resulted in massive transfers of revenue surpluses to the oil cartel states not only from the advanced industrial countries but also from the poor LDCs as well. In the single year of 1974, OPEC members saw a rise of $70 billion in their oil revenues; with the second 'oil price shocks', their oil revenues rose by some $180 billion.[22]

The oil price revolution sowed confusion in the advanced industrial countries about how it should be managed. It proved difficult to develop unity among them. On the one hand, the US wanted a multilateral approach to confront the oil cartel in order to reduce its power, and to bring down the price of oil. On the other hand, other industrial countries, such as France and Japan, were more anxious to develop oil security through working bilateral deals, and were afraid of provoking the OPEC countries.[23] Parenthetically, it needs to be acknowledged that the 'oil price shocks', no matter how painful they may have been to the US in absolute terms, placed it at an advantage in relative terms in respect of the European Community and Japan. It had not been too long ago that Connally had called them America's real enemies. The relative advantage to the US stemmed not simply from the greater relative self-reliance of the US in oil, its large oil reserves, and its political and military presence and influence in the Middle East. It also arose from the fact that American leadership was absolutely essential to the development of a common strategy to counter OPEC, and to manage the impact of the oil price shocks on the world economy.

Meanwhile, the success of the oil cartel in its confrontation with the developed countries became a source of inspiration for the developing countries in their effort to advance their own interests. In their quest for a better economic deal, the LDCs were influenced by the ideas of Raul Prebisch and his 'structuralist school'. Chief among these ideas was that the liberal international economic order had worked to the benefit of the industrial 'core' at the cost of the non-industrial 'periphery' through a secular decline in the terms of

[21] Ibid., 24.

[22] Ikenberry, *Reasons of State*, 3–4.

[23] Ibid., chapter 4.

trade for the latter. The LDCs also found the dependency theory to resonate with their concerns and conditions, especially in view of its central position that the development of the developed countries had been built directly on the foundations of underdevelopment of the underdeveloped countries.[24]

The LDCs now argued forcefully at the UN and its various organs that the developed countries had cheated them out of their future prosperity by cornering all the benefits of the post-war economic boom while rendering them economically marginalized. They pushed for the acceptance of a wide-ranging set of demands, which asked not only for increased economic aid but also for the restructuring of the market-based relations between the developed and less developed countries through a New International Economic Order (NIEO). Such restructuring would have entailed greater state intervention and authoritative allocation in the management of international economic relations, since excessive reliance on the Western-structured market had, in the view of the LDCs, allegedly worked only to the benefit of the developed countries. As such, of course, the NIEO charter of demands was incompatible with the proclaimed liberal ideological orientation and market-based interests of the US and most of the advanced industrial powers.[25]

While the developed countries were initially in doubt as to how to cope with the radical demands for a NIEO, they were able to stall the developing countries, and then to fend them off by vague assurances of increased aid and some marginal concessions. Eventually, the NIEO movement met with defeat at the hands of the industrial states. The LDCs failed in their attempt to lift themselves from being

[24] The literature on the dependency theory is vast. For some of the different trends in it, see John D. Cockcroft, Andre Gunder Frank and Dale L. Johnson, *Dependence and Underdevelopment: Latin America's Political Economy* (Garden City, NY: Anchor Books, 1992); Fernando Henrique Cardoso and Enzo Faletto, *Dependency and Development in Latin America* (Berkeley: University of California Press, 1978); and Samir Amin, *Accumulation on a World Scale: A Critique of the Theory of Underdevelopment* (New York: Monthly Review Press, 1974). For a comprehensive contemporaneous survey, see Gabriel Palma, 'Dependency: A Formal Theory of Underdevelopment or a Methodology in the Analysis of Concrete Situations of Underdevelopment', *World Development*, 6 (1978), 881–922.
[25] Stephen D. Krasner, *Structural Conflict: The Third World Against Global Liberalism* (Berkeley: University of California Press, 1985), chapter I.

objects to become subjects in international decision-making. On the one hand, the developed countries led by the US sternly refused to concede the NIEO movement's central demands. On the other hand, the movement fell victim to the disunity among the developing countries flowing from the economic diversification that had occurred among them because of economic and political change, which pitted oil exporters against oil importers and the more flourishing economies against the less advantaged.[26] At the same time, the advanced industrial countries were eventually able to adjust sufficiently to the oil price shocks, especially with OPEC members finding a common interest with them in depositing their vast petrodollar earnings with the financial institutions of the major economic powers. They were no longer terrified by the consequences of the oil price shocks, with OPEC looking more like a paper tiger to them. Meanwhile, the NIEO movement gradually faded away without much to show by way of achievement. The US-led coalition had triumphed.

More damaging for the developing countries was the debt crisis that overtook many of them in the 1980s, in considerable part as a consequence of the easy credit that the oil price revolution had made possible. The debt crisis led to a reassertion by the developed countries of their dominant economic role in international economic affairs. They now rushed in, through the international financial institutions (IFIs), to restructure the economies of the debt-ridden developing countries by way of imposing structural adjustment programmes (SAPs) on them. The decade of the 1980s saw scores of LDCs subject to the discipline of SAPs in their situation of financial distress, with the IFIs in effect lording over them as their *de facto* finance ministers. The process vividly illuminated the status of the LDCs as objects in the existing world order. The guiding doctrine of the SAPs was that of the 'Washington Consensus', developed among the US Treasury and the IFIs, which sought to create in the LDCs a common pattern of a liberalized and open market economy while shrinking the role of the state. Thus, those developing economies that had not already taken the liberal economic cure were yanked into a forced-march economic globalization.

[26] See Marianne H. Marchand, 'The Political Economy of North-South Relations', in Richard Stubbs and Geoffrey D. Underhill (eds), *Political Economy and the Changing Global Order* (Toronto: McClelland & Stewart, 1994), chapter 17.

Social Science and American Hegemony

Conceptual innovations and debates in the social sciences are often provoked by serious disturbances in the usual patterns of relations in human affairs. Until the collapse of the Bretton Woods fixed-rate regime and the oil price revolution in the early 1970s, *realism* had been the reigning paradigm in the study of international relations. The core principles of realism have been: (1) The international system, constituted by unitary and normally impermeable sovereign states, is an anarchic arena, placing states in perpetual conflict against each other. (2) With survival as their axiomatic goal, states accord primacy to security in the hierarchy of national goals, with other goals subordinated to it. (3) States necessarily build military power in order to assure their security. (4) They also build economic capabilities since these are a prerequisite for developing military capabilities, and in building them, they tend to be mercantilist in their orientation, and attempt to reduce their own dependence on others.

Notwithstanding the liberal international economic order instituted by the US in much of the world after World War II, the post-war international system as such, with its bipolarity, was dominated by security concerns flowing from the Cold War contest between the two power blocs. The Cuban missile crisis of 1962, however, chastened the chief antagonists in regard to the risks of nuclear war, and inclined them toward détente and even collaboration on nuclear non-proliferation. A sort of military stalemate developed between the two superpowers along with their alliance systems, even though violent skirmishes between their proxies in the periphery continued in their ongoing contest. Meanwhile, the two significant episodes in the early 1970s of the collapse of Bretton Woods and the oil price shocks, which were intensely economic in nature, suggested the evolution of the international system in a direction that seemed somewhat different from that posited by realism. In this context, two rather contrasting approaches or theories emerged to explain the new phase in the development of the international system. One was the *theory of complex interdependence*, while the other was the *hegemonic stability theory.*

The theory of complex interdependence, going under different names such as liberal institutionalism, liberalism, globalism or transnationalism, had as its point of departure, the increased economic interdependence that had developed among nations by the early

1970s, as a consequence of the operation of the liberal international economic order. It sought to delineate the political implications of this interdependence in an endeavour to replace the traditional state-centric view that realism represented. The theory's posture on the traditional perspective is well expressed in the title of Raymond Vernon's book *Sovereignty at Bay* and in Walter Wriston's *The Twilight of Sovereignty*. It is also expressed in such statements as: 'The nation-state is just about through as an economic unit' (Charles Kindleberger) and 'the nation-state is a very old-fashioned idea and badly adapted to serve the needs of our present complex world' (George Ball).[27]

More systematically, Sullivan underlined four decisive ways in which the new theory is said to have differed from realism in its perceptual universe. First, there has occurred the diminution in the role and function of the state in international affairs, following the rise of other governmental and non-governmental international organizations, particularly MNCs, which exercise leverage on internal politics as well as external relations of states. Moreover, states are no longer the unitary actors of old. Rather, they consist of large bureaucracies that are internally divided and subject to the influence not only of domestic forces but also external actors. In sum, the state's traditional role has been drastically reduced. Second, there has been a change in the nature of the dominant issues in international politics. Military–security issues have become downgraded in the face of the rising critical issues of population explosion, food security, and threats to the world's ecology. Being global in nature, these new issues cannot be addressed by any one nation alone or in alliance with a small group of nations, as was the case with military–security issues. On the contrary, they compel cooperation among states rather than rivalry as had been the pattern in the past. Third, the requirement of cooperation has been reinforced by the intense interdependence that has come to characterize the international system not only in economic areas but also in communications and transportation. Finally, the nature of military technology itself, with the development

[27] Raymond Vernon, *Sovereignty at Bay: The Multinational Spread of US Enterprises* (New York: Basic Books, 1971); Walter B. Wriston, *The Twilight of Sovereignty: How the Information Revolution is Transforming Our World* (New York: Scribners, 1992); and Robert Gilpin, *US Power and the Multinational Corporation*, 20, 220.

of nuclear weapons, places constraints on states in resorting to the traditional means of statecraft centring, in the final analysis, around war. In brief, these developments are said to have made the traditional state obsolete and realism outmoded.[28]

From the perspective of complex interdependence theory, it is apparent that the international system, and along with it the international economic order, was in the process of change at the beginning of the 1970s. What underlay the change? Drawing on realism, Robert Gilpin offered a theory of more ambitious scope by way of explanation,[29] which subsequently Robert Keohane christened as 'hegemonic stability theory'.[30] Gilpin contended that, as a new power achieves hegemony through war in the international system, it establishes a new international economic order. In recent history, Great Britain and the US had instituted liberal international economic orders because of the benefits that accrued to them:

> Great Britain and the United States created and enforced the rules of a liberal international economic order. British and American policies fostered free trade and freedom of capital movements. These great powers supplied the key currency and managed the international monetary system.... they assumed these responsibilities because it was profitable to do so. The benefits to them of a secure status quo, free trade, foreign investment, and a well-functioning international monetary system were greater than the associated costs. While bringing benefits to themselves, however, the policies of the hegemonic powers were also beneficial to those other states that desired to and could take advantage of the international political and economic status quo.[31]

In other words, the existence of a stable world economic order was a function of the benefits exceeding costs for the hegemonic power and of the continuing adequate supply of international public goods in the shape of security and economic welfare for the others. It was

---

[28] Michael P. Sullivan, *Power in Contemporary International Politics* (Columbia, SC: University of South Carolina Press, 1990), 9–11.

[29] Robert Gilpin, *US Power and the Multinational Corporation*; and Robert Gilpin, *War and Change in World Politics*.

[30] Robert Keohane, 'The Theory of Hegemonic Stability and Change in International Economic Regimes, 1967–1977', in Ole R. Holsti *et al.* (eds), *Changes in the International System* (Boulder, CO: Westview Press, 1980), 131–62.

[31] Gilpin, *War and Change in World Politics*, 145

Gilpin's contention, however, that over time, for certain sound economic and political reasons, 'there is a tendency for the economic costs of maintaining the international status quo to rise faster than the financial capacity of the dominant power to support its position and the status quo.' This development is a necessary accompaniment of the redistribution of power in the international system that inevitably takes place because of the differential rates of economic growth among the various powers. As a consequence, there arises a disequilibrium in the international system, that is, there develops a 'disjuncture among the components of the system'. The combination of change in the international distribution of power and continuance of the extant world economic framework makes for a serious disequilibrium:

> From the perspective of dominant powers, the costs of maintaining the international status quo have increased, producing a serious discrepancy between one's power and one's commitments. From the perspective of rising powers, the perceived costs of changing the international system have declined relative to the potential benefits of doing so.

With some pessimism, Gilpin noted: 'Throughout history the primary means of resolving the disequilibrium between the structure of the international system and the redistribution of power has been war, more particularly, what we shall call a hegemonic war.'[32]

In this interpretation, then, the troubles manifest in the international economic order in the form of the collapse of Bretton Woods and the oil price revolution were a consequence of the decline of American power. In the larger scheme of things, they were part and parcel of change in the international system. They were likely to persist until such time as the US can either restore the equilibrium through a reassertion of its power, or there is a settling of accounts among the contending powers and a new hegemony emerges and installs another international economic order. Of course, nuclear weapons complicate the issue for the theory: nuclear deterrence will perhaps prevent rising powers from mounting a violent challenge, and it is more likely to favour the maintenance of the *status quo*.

Another set of scholars who subscribed to the theory of 'international regimes' was, however, not perturbed by the decline of American hegemony in relation to its possible implications for the international

---

[32] Ibid., 145, 156, 186–7, 197.

order, political or economic. They defined regimes as 'sets of implicit or explicit principles, norms, rules, and decision-making procedures around which actors' expectations converge in a given area of international relations'. These scholars could accept the position that hegemonic power may well be necessary for the creation of international institutions. But they believed that, once formed, such institutions come to be valued for the functions they perform for states, and accordingly, have the potential to persist even though the original hegemony responsible for their creation may have suffered decline.

For these scholars, international regimes were intervening variables between the basic causal variables (primarily the distribution of power) and outcomes or behaviour, but they have the potential for independent influence and persistence even after changes have occurred in the distribution of power. As they put it: 'A change in power distributions does not always imply a change in outcomes because regimes may function as intervening variables. Regimes may assume a life of their own, a life independent of the basic causal factors that led to their creation in the first place.' Looking back at the events of the 1970s, they were struck by the practical puzzle as to why things did not actually fall apart. Their stand was: 'Regimes offer one way to account for the persistence of behaviour and outcomes even though basic causal factors associated with political power have changed. Once regimes are established they assume a life of their own.'[33] They were inclined therefore to expect the persistence of the American-established international institutions even in the face of decline of American hegemony, especially in view of their assumption that states as rational actors and utility-maximizing actors would find such institutions designed for international cooperation to be fundamentally useful.

An inveterate sceptic concerning the theory of international regimes among the contributors to the classic symposium on the subject was Susan Strange, who simply dismissed the theory as one more in a series of typical American fads that will soon pass. She attributed the emergence of the theory to 'certain, somewhat subjective perceptions in many American minds', chief among them being that some external shocks combined with some internal

---

[33] Stephen D. Krasner (ed.), *International Regimes*, 2, 8, 357, 358; see also Robert Keohane, 'The Demand for International Regimes', in ibid., 141–71.

problems such as Watergate 'had accelerated a serious decline in American power'. More substantively but iconoclastically, she suggested that America's nonterritorial imperialism, even if unacknowledged as such, was fully intact, and that the impact of the shocks had patently been overrated. Further, she argued that to non-American eyes 'there is something quite exaggerated in the weeping and wailing and wringing of American hands' over the alleged decline of American power. Instead, she maintained: 'In a broad, structuralist view ... of the structures of global security, of a global credit system, of the global welfare system (i.e.; aid and other resource transfers), and the global knowledge and communications system, there seems far less sign of a falling-off in American power.' She failed to see any 'significant change in the distribution of military or economic power to the favour of other states.'[34] In this view, then, there was really no puzzle to explain about things not falling apart in the 1970s; simply, no significant decline in American hegemony had taken place.

The basic position of Susan Strange found support in the work of Joseph Nye, a scholar with considerable experience as a high-level official in the Departments of Defence and State. In a book significantly titled *Bound to Lead*, Nye argued in 1990, when the Soviet Union was still intact, that the US had no challenger to speak of in its combination of 'hard power' (economic and military capabilities) and 'soft power' (cultural attraction and prestige). He acknowledged that there had been some change in the power position of the US, but he thought it was 'misleading' to describe it as American decline. Rather, this was a natural consequence of the diffusion of power from the highly unusual asymmetrical power situation that prevailed at the end of World War II. Once the 'World War II effect' had worked itself out in the international system by 1973, there was little change during the subsequent decade and a half. He thought the apparent decline after 1945 had been 'often exaggerated by comparison with a mythical past'. On the contrary, he maintained that 'no country is at this time well positioned to challenge the United States for global leadership.' Systematically comparing the great powers on the criteria of basic, military,

[34] Susan Strange, 'Cave! Hic Dragones: A Critique of Regime Analysis', in Krasner (ed.), *International Regimes*, 337–54. See also Strange, 'The Future of the American Empire', *Journal of International Affairs*, 42 (Fall 1988); and Strange, *States and Markets* (New York: Basil Blackwell, 1988).

economic, and technological power resources, he concluded: 'only one country ranks above the others on all four dimensions—the United States.' He posited that 'the United States remains the largest and richest power with the greatest capacity to shape the future' and that 'American leadership remains essential to the future world order'.[35]

It may well be that, while no doubt justified on the basis of sheer hard data, Nye's high confidence in American power also reflected the change in perceptions that had occurred during the decade of the 1980s. Before then, a series of developments had induced a mood of great concern, if not despair: the external economic problems of the US that had led to the collapse of the Bretton Woods regime, the oil price revolution, the military defeat in Vietnam, the clamour of the LDCs for a NIEO, the Islamic revolution in Iran in 1979, which not only reduced American power in the region, but also heaped humiliation on the US through holding large numbers of its officials hostage for over a year, and the Soviet intervention in Afghanistan the same year.

The decade of the 1980s, however, marked a reassertion of American power under the Reagan Administration, which, in a clear rebuff to the school of complex interdependence and liberal institutionalism, apotheosized national security and military power. Five years in a row, the Reagan Administration successively increased the defence budget; it readily took on the Soviets in Afghanistan through aiding the Islamic forces and succeeding in driving them out; it downgraded arms control and instead threatened the Soviets with arms escalation through developing the technology for anti-missile defence or 'star wars'; it unilaterally engaged in military interventions in Grenada and Libya; it undertook covert operations against radical regimes; and it repulsed the NIEO movement and instead asked the LDCs to take the cold shower of structural adjustment. Meanwhile, the Soviet Union was economically stagnant and, focusing on internal reform, had under Gorbachev defensively switched to a foreign policy course of moderation that brought an end to the Cold War. In the face of this new situation, it would have been difficult to have still maintained the thesis of the decline of American hegemony at the end of the 1980s. The US had been spectacularly successful in bringing an end to the turmoil of the 1970s. It had also demonstrated continued American capacity, notwithstanding much American unilateralism during the period, for

---

[35] Nye, *Bound to Lead*, 21, 110, 259, 261.

adaptation and institutional creativity in the shape of the Group of Seven (G-7) of the top industrial democracies for the multilateral management of the international economy.

The Collapse of the Soviet Bloc and the Rise of the American Empire

About a decade-and-a-half before the end of the twentieth century, the Soviet Union led by Mikhail Gorbachev started on a course of internal political and economic reforms to reverse the decline resulting from economic stagnation 'in order to preserve its position in the world'.[36] However, the reforms spun out of control and the Soviet bloc was soon faced with political unrest and rebellion among its members, and was on the road to disintegration. By the end of 1989, East Germany had defected from the bloc, and had become part of a new unified Germany. Then, in 1991, the Soviet Union itself began to unravel as the communist regime under Gorbachev was overthrown, and it was reduced to the rump of the Russian Federation with the other republics becoming independent sovereign entities. With Boris Yeltsin in charge, Russia made a dramatic switch from communism and the command economy to political democracy and a market economy—as did the other members of the former Soviet bloc and the former republics of the Soviet Union, even if often only formally and not substantively. Russia was now desperately and fawningly eager to join the West as a junior partner.

In a broad sense, these events represented a remarkable triumph of the West. Democracy and the market system as the central values of the modern West had triumphed over totalitarianism and communism. In Fukuyama's view, the events marked the end of history in the sense that all modern alternatives to liberalism in its political and economic form had met with utter failure.[37] In a more narrow sense, the events manifested a triumph of the US, which had for nearly four-and-a-half decades led the West and implacably stuck to the policy of containment, with the ultimate aim of squeezing the Soviet regime so as to bring it to its knees. No doubt, the Soviet

---

[36] Kenneth N. Waltz, 'Structural Realism after the Cold War', in G. John Ikenberry (ed.), *America Unrivaled: The Future of the Balance of Power* (Ithaca, NY: Cornell University Press, 2002), 65.

[37] Francis Fukuyama, *The End of History and the Last Man*.

Union had, for some time, been suffering from internal decay. However, more recently, the US had under President Ronald Reagan determinedly followed a deliberate policy course to drive the Soviet Union into economic collapse by forcing it to match the acceleration of military spending by the US, or to concede supremacy in the rivalry. The US succeeded admirably in this aim, forcing both the collapse of the Soviet Union and winning supremacy.

In the process, the US brought an end to the bipolar system and created instead a unipolar system in which it emerged as the only superpower. The collapse of the Soviet Union had been preceded by the victory of the American-led Western alliance in the Gulf War against Iraq in 1991. The US now stood as a power colossus across the entire planet, dominating the world as no imperial power had ever done before. American hegemony became truly global for the first time in history.

China had become a *de facto* ally of the US as far back as the early 1970s, and during the 1980s its economy became interdependent with the American economy. With the collapse of the Soviet bloc and the Soviet Union, and with its former members and republics opting for liberal democracy and the market economy, economic globalization that had developed under American hegemony became worldwide in scope. It should be no surprise that it is precisely in the 1990s that globalization first saw a massive surge in the consciousness of the academia and the public. Economic globalization, in the true sense of the word, though still undoubtedly truncated, followed unipolarity and the emergence of the US as the sole superpower.

As the power position of the US expanded, so did its aims. The draft Defence Guidance Policy Paper in 1992 under President George Bush (senior), who had presided over the demise of the Soviet bloc and the Soviet Union, and over the victory in Iraq, asserted:

> Our first objective is to prevent the re-emergence of a new rival, either on the territory of the former Soviet Union or elsewhere.... This is a dominant consideration ... and requires that we endeavour to prevent any hostile power from dominating a region whose resources would, under consolidated control, be sufficient to generate global power.... Our strategy must now refocus on precluding the emergence of any potential future global competitor.[38]

---

[38] Cited in Barry R. Posen and Andrew L. Ross, 'Competing Visions for US Grand Strategy', *International Security*, 21 (Winter 1996–7), 5–53. For the text, see *New York Times*, 8 March 1992.

Following the lead of the guidance paper, one American scholar demanded, more colourfully, that the US 'be the global hegemon of the regional hegemons, the boss of all the bosses'.[39] The great triumph and the grand vision, however, did not win Bush re-election to the presidency, with the state of the economy proving a handicap for him.

Under President Bill Clinton (1993–2001), attention shifted to the economy as a 'peace dividend' and the US saw almost a decade of unprecedented economic growth and prosperity, with information technology serving as the leading sector. Meanwhile, Japan, which had been seen as a serious economic rival and threat, went into an economic crisis of long duration. Still, fearing competition from Japan, Europe, and the newly industrializing economies, the US also increasingly turned protectionist, often at the behest of organized labour. Instead of advancing the liberal international economic order on a broad multilateral basis, the US now seemed inclined toward a mercantilist policy. This policy was evident not only in terms of pushing for 'managed trade', but also of building a regional economic bloc of its own, first in the form of a Free Trade Area with Canada (FTA) and then a larger North America Free Trade Area (NAFTA) that additionally included Mexico. The larger NAFTA may have had as one of its goals to tie in Mexico permanently to liberalism, but it also aimed partly to rival the growing economic power of an expanded EU, and partly to serve as a protectionist device against Japan. The US hoped to later expand NAFTA into a much larger Free Trade Area of the Americas (FTAA). In this fashion, the US has been complicit in moving the world economy in a direction that contains the potential for fragmentation of that economy.[40]

At the same time, as the sole superpower in a unipolar system, the US perceived itself—and had no hesitation in so declaring—as the

[39] James Kurth, cited in Posen and Ross, 'Competing Visions', 36.

[40] On the pros and cons of regional economic blocs, see Donald Barry and Ronald C. Keith (eds), *Regionalism, Multilateralism, and the Politics of Global Trade* (Vancouver: UBC Press, 1999); Jagdish Bhagwati and Anne O. Krueger, *The Dangerous Drift to Preferential Trade Agreements* (Washington, DC: AEI Press, 1995); Jeffrey A. Frankel (ed.), *Regionalization of the World Economy* (Chicago: University of Chicago Press, 1998); Takatoshi Ito and Anne O. Krueger (eds), *Regionalism versus Multilateral Trade Arrangements* (Chicago: University of Chicago Press, 1997); and Arvind Panagariya, *Regionalism in Trade Policy: Essays on Preferential Trading* (Singapore: World Scientific Publishing, 1999).

only 'indispensable nation' in the world.[41] As such, it demonstrated its determination to shape the strategic architecture of the world, and accordingly proceeded to enlarge NATO to encompass several of the earlier Warsaw Pact members, and thus to take NATO to the gates of Russia as if to encircle it. In 1999, Poland, Hungary, and the Czech Republic were admitted into NATO, while in 2004 another seven countries (Bulgaria, Estonia, Latvia, Lithuania, Romania, Slovakia, and Slovenia) joined the organization, expanding the alliance's membership to 26.

The Turn to Unilateralism

The successor administration of George W. Bush (junior) came to power in 2001 with an exceedingly unilateralist outlook, springing from its consciousness of the awesome power of the US against the background of the disintegration of the Soviet Union and the decade-long economic prosperity of the US during the 1990s. The Bush Administration believed in the assertion of American power around the globe, and a readiness to take on all challengers. It was deeply unilateralist and aggressively muscular in its military posture. As one reporter put it: 'It is not isolationist but unilateralist, unashamed of using military power.'[42] Echoes of the draft Defence Guidance Policy Paper of 1992 were evident in the National Security Strategy document, issued a decade later in 2002:

> We must build and maintain our defences beyond challenge.... Through our willingness to use force in our defence and in defence of others, the United States demonstrates its resolve to maintain a balance of power that favours freedom.... The United States must and will maintain the capability to defeat any attempt by an enemy—whether a state or non-state actor—to impose its will on the United States, our allies, or our friends. We will maintain the forces sufficient to support our obligations, and to defend freedom. Our forces will be strong enough to dissuade potential adversaries

---

[41] In defence of raining Cruise missiles on Iraq, Secretary of State Madeleine Albright stated in February 1998: 'If v.e have to use force, it is because we are America. We are the indispensable nation. We stand tall. We see farther into the future.' Cited in Chalmers Johnson, *Blowback: The Costs and Consequences of American Empire* (New York: Henry Holt, 2004), 217.

[42] Stephen Fidler, 'Between Two Camps', *Financial Times*, 14 February 2001, cited in Ikenberry (ed.), *America Unrivaled*, 302.

from pursuing a military build-up in hopes of surpassing, or equaling, the power of the United States.[43]

The US under the Bush Administration seemed to have little faith in multilateralism any longer. It was against subscribing to, or ratifying of, a whole series of international agreements or accords— the Kyoto Protocol on gas emissions, the International Criminal Court, the Germ Weapons Ban, the Trade in Light Arms Treaty, and the CTBT (designed to bar nuclear tests). It also favoured rescinding the ABM treaty with Moscow in order to feel free to build an anti-missile defence, and in the end it was able to coerce Russia to agree to that course.

However, the US and the Bush Administration suffered a severe blow to their collective prestige and psyche with the 9/11 terrorist attacks on the Twin Towers in New York and the Pentagon in Washington on 11 September 2001—the Pearl Harbour of 2001— which killed some 3,000 people. The Administration responded with great determination and resolve. What is impressive about this response is that, as against the prognostications of the enthusiasts of globalization, it made patently clear that geopolitics had not been eclipsed by the international economy. Rather, it made manifest that globalization was no self-driven and economically autonomous process, but operated within the overarching framework of a geopolitical architecture as determined by the most powerful state on the globe. The response also made it abundantly evident that the economy had not reduced the supremacy of the state.[44] Economic interdependence constrained little the power of the American state when its security and that of its citizens were at stake. The American state responded to the challenge comprehensively and aggressively. Controls were quickly introduced in regard to international transactions in finance, immigration, and air and surface transportation, even at the expense of civil liberties, in order to counter the threat of

[43] President of the United States, *The National Security Strategy of the United States of America* (Washington, DC: The White House, September 2002), 29–30.

[44] An effective rebuttal to the thesis of the decline of the state in the face of economic globalization is provided in Michael Mann, 'Has Globalization Ended the Rise and Rise of the Nation-State?', in T.V. Paul and John A. Hall (eds), *International Order and the Future of World Politics* (Cambridge: Cambridge University Press, 1999), chapter 12.

terrorism. And the US was able to pressure most other states to fall in line. The US proved to be a *hard* state when it came to security.

In matters of security, war has historically been the *ultima ratio* in the relations among states, and the Bush Administration was ready to carry the war to states that harboured or aided terrorists. The first target was Afghanistan, where the extremist group Taliban was in power and gave sanctuary to the al-Qaeda terrorists. Where international cooperation was forthcoming as in this case, because of the sympathy for the US that the 9/11 attacks had evoked in many countries, the US took to a multilateral course, rallying NATO and many other countries to its cause. The Taliban regime was overthrown in short order, though the longer-term task of reconstruction of the economy and state has proved to be daunting. However, in other cases like Iraq in 2003, where the US got little support at multilateral institutions, such as the United Nations or NATO, or from major allies, such as France and Germany, it acted unilaterally in defiance of the UN, and at the cost of alienation of long-standing allies. It mattered little to the US if the UN or NATO were not forthcoming with support for its chosen course. The US proceeded regardless, as if UN and NATO were irrelevant. Nor did it show any compunction in resorting to the classic imperial policy of divide and rule, setting 'new Europe' against 'old Europe', or one set of allies against another set. This new approach to Europe by the US has been termed 'disaggregation',[45] where the US picks and chooses its allies in 'coalitions of the willing', depending on the occasion. Equally, the Bush Administration brought forward new doctrines, such as pre-emptive war, in pursuit of its unilateralist course.

These features of the new American posture did not emerge in the heat of the relentless pursuit of the objective to attack and overthrow the regime in Iraq. Rather, they were the consequence of a deliberate strategy that had been planned far ahead, and of a mindset that the decision-makers brought with them, even before they entered office. The National Security Strategy document issued in September 2002 had warned:

> The United States possesses unprecedented—and unequaled—strength and influence in the world.... While the United States will constantly strive to enlist the support of the international community, we will not hesitate to

[45] John Vinocur, 'After the Iraq War: A New Balancing Act in US–European Relations', *International Herald Tribune* Online, 13 May 2003.

act alone, if necessary, to exercise our right of self-defence by acting
pre-emptively.... The United States has long maintained the option of
pre-emptive actions to counter a sufficient threat to our national security....
To forestall or prevent such hostile acts by our adversaries, the United States
will, if necessary, act pre-emptively.[46]

When the US decided to attack Iraq, those who had consistently
opposed this course, such as France, Russia, and China among the
P-5, plus Germany, could only stand by helplessly and watch the
events unfold, given the stupendous power of the US. At the same
time, American actions left its longtime allies, France and Germany,
deeply wounded at the dismissive treatment meted out to them by
the US. Of course, the dazzling and swift success of the American
armed forces in subduing the Iraqi military, with their heavy
reliance—following the 'Revolution in Military Affairs' orientation—
on modern technology, reinforced further the image of the awesome
nature of power of the US. American power was simply overwhelming
in its sheer scale, sophistication, and 'shock and awe' tactics.
Regardless of the rather insurmountable problems subsequently
encountered in restoring stability and normalcy, the victory in Iraq
further strengthened the realization that was already obvious to most,
that no power or combination of powers in the world was presently
in a position to challenge the US.

Cooperation and Contention under the American Empire

The re-emergence of Europe and Japan under American auspices as
major economic players on the world scene had brought in its train
some adjustment in the relations between the US and the other two
constituents of the triad. The US had accommodated several of the
European powers and Japan in the management of the world economy,
particularly following the economic turmoil in the wake of the OPEC
oil price shocks of the 1970s. The G-7, as an exclusive club of the
principal developed economies, has been the visible apex symbol of
cooperation among the triad in global economic management. The
same group of powers, dominating in combination as it does the
international financial institutions (IMF and World Bank), has

---

[46] President of the United States, *The National Security Strategy of the
United States of America*, 1, 6, 15.

promoted a forced-march globalization in the developing world through structural adjustment programmes based on the Washington Consensus. The considerable degree of cooperation evident among the G-7 members in the management of the world economy is, no doubt, a reflection of a certain commonality of interests among them in regard to the rest of the world. These interests are not just economic, however, for the same powers are also embedded in a far-flung military alliance system under the hegemony of the US. Indeed, some see in this phenomenon, which combines active cooperation in the economic and military realms, the development of *a new type of state* encompassing these powers in the age of globalization.

In a work that is an unabashed celebration of such a state, Martin Shaw refers to the new type of state as the 'global-Western state' or 'globalized Western state-conglomerate', comprising the NATO powers, Japan and Australasia. It is this state's force-backed dominance that forms, for Shaw, the ordering framework within which the entire present-day international system functions. Drawing on Michael Mann's definition of the state, he takes the Western global state to be 'an integrated authoritative organization of violence which includes a large number of both functionally defined states and international interstate organizations.' It is one that 'functions as a single centre of military state power in relation to other centres'. Holding this state as benign and rejecting the epithet of imperialist for its dominance over the world, Shaw views negatively all other types of existing states, perversely calling most of the well-known ones as 'quasi-imperial nation-states' (China, Russia, India); the remainder are dismissed as 'new, proto- and quasi-states'. Under the undisputed leadership of the US, he declares, 'the Western state has ever greater worldwide influence, resting fundamentally on the unrivalled economic, military and infrastructural power which it can mobilize:' 'An increasingly integrated West finds itself in a position of inescapable dominance and hence leadership. It is irrevocably implicated in the development of a global layer of state institutions, which both entrench but also extend Western dominance.' Under the guise of these institutions, including those of the United Nations, and other ad hoc coalitions, the Western global state 'has attempted to police the relations of nation-states and new states worldwide, intervening both politically and militarily in regions of crises'. Altogether evading questions of inequality and redistribution in an economically divided world, Shaw mandates to this Western global state the political task of extending the 'global-democratic revolution' to the rest of the world.[47]

Essentially a similar position has been taken in a highly controversial article in 2002 by Robert Cooper, a key adviser to Prime Minister Tony Blair on foreign policy. In that article, Cooper distinguishes between three types of states: (1) post-modern, comprising the North Atlantic area and Japan; (2) modern, such as China and India; and (3) pre-modern, consisting of failed states, such as Somalia or Afghanistan. He assumes a unity or solidarity among the developed states and, therefore, a corresponding obligation of a new collective imperialism in relation to the rest of the world. This imperialism is taken to be order-endowing for the failed states while it behaves according to double standards in relation to the modern states, undeterred by traditional notions of sovereignty and non-interference:

> Among ourselves, we operate on the basis of laws and open cooperative security. But, when dealing with old-fashioned states outside the postmodern continent of Europe, we need to revert to the rougher methods of an earlier era—force, pre-emptive attack, deception, whatever is necessary to deal with those who still live in the nineteenth century world of every state for itself. Among ourselves, we keep the law but when we are operating in the jungle, we must also use the laws of the jungle.[48]

Subsequently, in 2004, Tony Blair himself directly supported changing international law to allow military action in the developing world, essentially by the West, not only pre-emptively to ward off possible threats to national security but also more broadly to advance human rights.[49]

Notwithstanding the considerable degree of cooperation among the members of the triad that is evident in the system of American-dominated military alliances and coalitions, there exist nonetheless also distinct fault-lines for potential conflict. One such fault-line is

---

[47] Martin Shaw, *Theory of the Global State: Globality as Unfinished Revolution* (Cambridge: Cambridge University Press, 2000), 199–200, 241, 244, 254, 268, 269.

[48] Robert Cooper, 'Why We Still Need Empires', *The Observer*, Sunday, 7 April 2002.

[49] Tony Blair, 'A Global Threat Needs a Global Response', *The Guardian* Online, 6 March 2004. See also Hasan Suroor, 'Blair Advocates Pre-emptive Strikes', *The Hindu* Online, 7 March 2004; and Rashmee Z. Ahmed, 'Beware, the Raj is Retro-chic', *Times of India* Online, 7 March 2004.

the formation of preferential trading blocs by the leading members of the triad—another indicator of the truncated nature of contemporary globalization over and above the divide between the developed and developing worlds. There is considerable irony in the fact that the US during World War II had been in the forefront of multilateralism, determined to dismantle the Commonwealth preferential trading area. But now it had no qualms, when it suited its interests, in moving to the establishment of a regional economic bloc of its own.

The Developing Antagonism with Europe

Meanwhile, Western Europe has since 1 January 1993 become integrated into a giant common market known as the EU that rivals the economic power of the US or NAFTA. With the subsequent expansion of membership to include countries from the former Soviet bloc, the EU is likely to become an even more formidable economic power. It now also has its own common currency, the Euro, which competes with the dollar in the world as a reserve currency. In due course, when it carves out an independent defence and foreign policy identity, it is likely to develop its own geopolitical ambitions, separate from, and perhaps in opposition to, the US.[50]

Omens on this score are already manifest. President Jacques Chirac of France declared in 1999: 'The European Union itself [must] become a major pole of international equilibrium, endowing itself with the instruments of a true power.'[51] Since at least the late 1990s, France has been in the forefront of the movement to reshape the world into a multipolar system. Such a strategy can be taken to be a form of *containment* aimed against the US, whose overwhelming power has been seen as dangerous for the independence and security of other actors in the international system. Laying stress on the status of the US as a 'hyper-power', the then French Foreign Minister Hubert Védrine highlighted the exceptional position of 'the US, which is the only and unique hyper-power. It is predominant in all fields:

---

[50] On the growing global role of the EU, see Carolyn Rhodes (ed.), *The European Union in the World Community* (Boulder, CO: Lynne Reinner, 1998).

[51] Cited in Charles Kupchan, 'Hollow Hegemony or Stable Multipolarity?', in Ikenberry (ed.), *America Unrivaled*, 72.

economic, technological, military, monetary, linguistic, and cultural. This situation is without precedent: what earlier empire has subjugated the entire world, including its adversaries.'[52] It would be unrealistic to assume that such French views and related activities, at times, in collaboration with Germany, were not a cause of concern in Washington.[53]

However, the EU, as a possible counterweight to the US presently suffers from a grievous infirmity in not having forged itself into a cohesive federal polity with its own common foreign and defence foreign policy. The US can, therefore, perhaps take a more or less relaxed view about any challenge to its hegemony from Europe. This is especially indicated in view of its own unprecedented military power, its military enthralment of Europe through NATO, and the presence of American Trojan Horses inside the EU, most prominently Great Britain, but now additionally Italy and Poland. Still, in the economic arena, a number of disputes have marked the relations between the US and the EU members, particularly in the area of agriculture, aircraft manufacture, and telecommunications.

The potential for increased tensions between the US and the EU, or at least a part of it, was laid bare in early 2003 in the dispute over the American plans to attack Iraq. France and Germany (along with Russia) were strongly opposed to such plans and felt that the US was acting as a bullying and unilateralist power in attempting to coerce the UN Security Council to endorse them. Indeed, the quarrel over Iraq marked a watershed in the relations between Europe and the US in which it demonstrated that 'the Europeans are no longer

[52] Hubert Védrine, *Les Cartes de la France a l'heure de la Mondialization* (Paris: Fayard, 2000), 9.

[53] Note, for example, the column by William Pfaff, 'Seeing Mortal Danger in a Superpower Europe', *International Herald Tribune* Online, 3 July 2003. Pfaff says, in part: 'A prominent theme of neoconservative writing and television talk is that a Franco-German-dominated European Union, rebuilt according to the new Giscardian constitution currently under debate, threatens to become "superpower Europe" and a mortal danger to the United States. The New Republic, an influential Washington weekly has just announced that "America must wake up!" to the danger from an expanded and united Europe and the newly strengthened European currency, the Euro.' The fundamentally different orientations of the US and Europe to power, politics, and war are discussed in Robert Kagan, *Of Paradise and Power: America and Europe in the New World Order* (New York: Knopf, 2003).

docile allies'. It also made apparent the conflicting aims of the two contending parties, for most thinking Europeans 'want what the French want: a Europe with an independent policy, exercising an equal influence on international affairs, probably through political and economic means, rather than military means. That is just what the United States does not want'.[54] The US was so incensed at having been opposed by its European allies that, even after its military victory in the Iraq war, it proved to be unforgiving. In a sentiment that could as well have been expressed by John Foster Dulles, Secretary of State Colin Powell explicitly stated in relation to France's behaviour: 'You take note of those who disagree with you and try to find out why, and, if it's appropriate, to draw some conclusions, and consequences follow those conclusions. That's the way it is.'[55] As one commentator underlined:

> This American administration does not accept an alliance relationship that is not one of domination and subordination. This is what the 'punishment' of France, Germany and Belgium is all about.... The Bush government has made a radical break with major assumptions and practices of post-war American foreign policy, on which the Atlantic alliance was founded.... This American government, in the Iraq war's aftermath, is intoxicated with notions of American omnipotence and unaccountability.[56]

More broadly, the same commentator maintained:

> Put simply, the Bush administration envisages a world run by the United States, backed by as many states as will sign on to support it but not interfere. Its stated intention is to maintain an overwhelming military advantage and do its level best to prevent other states from creating nuclear or other deterrent systems.... It doesn't want any government in a position to check it through international institutions or legal opposition, which is why the United Nations has to go. Otherwise, the only obstacles to neoconservative Washington's freedom of action (other than Chinese and Russian nuclear forces) would be Europe's economic power and potential political unity, and even there the American advantage is large, although not decisive.[57]

[54] William Pfaff, 'Europe will Follow France: A Contest of Identities', *International Herald Tribune* Online, 22 May 2003.

[55] Vaiju Naravane, 'The Surrender', *The Hindu* Online, 28 May 2003.

[56] William Pfaff, 'Europe Can Gently Check America', *International Herald Tribune* Online, 2 May 2003.

[57] William Pfaff, 'Bush's New Global Order Will Generate Resistance', ibid., 17 April 2003.

It is intriguing that American behaviour in the early years of the twenty-first century, marked by a muscular unilateralism while trashing multilateralism and disagreeing allies, runs counter to a major thesis in American political science about the 'benign hegemony' of the US. That thesis was essentially about American exceptionalism among hegemons due to a trinity of factors. These were: (1) America's institutions being based on the rule of law, which made for predictable and cooperative hegemonic behaviour; (2) its open and decentralized political process, which allowed foreign governments to have a 'voice' and thus influence the exercise of American power; and (3) its commitment to multilateralism.[58]

The basic flaw in the thesis stems from the fact that, even though it is based on American behaviour during the long Cold War, it fails to take into account the impact on that behaviour of the then prevailing overarching strategic conflict of the US with the Soviet Union. That conflict provided the incentive for the US to exercise restraint and be accommodative toward its allies and abide by multilateralism. The explanation, then, for the benign hegemony lay not in characteristics particular to the US, but in the overall strategic situation. Once the strategic conflict was gone with the collapse of the Soviet Union and the American economy had given a strong decade-long performance, the natural tendency of 'unrivalled power' to bullying and unilateralism, never fully absent earlier, asserted itself. American power is unrestrained since it dwarfs the power of the rest of the world, making it costly for others to countervail, jointly or severally. The only possible constraint in this circumstance can emerge from possible domestic recoil as a result of 'imperial overstretch'[59] that imposes economic and human costs that are unacceptable to the American public.[60] If that occurs, it may perhaps provide some scope for other powers to shift the world in a multipolar direction. American

---

[58] Ikenberry (ed.), *America Unrivaled*, 1–26, 284–310; Ikenberry, *After Victory: Institutions, Strategic Restraint, and the Rebuilding of Order After Major Wars* (Princeton: Princeton University Press, 2001); and Ikenberry, 'Liberal Hegemony and the Future of American Post-War Order', in T.V. Paul and John A. Hall (eds), *International Order and the Future of World Politics*, 123–45.

[59] Paul Kennedy, *The Rise and Fall of Great Powers*.

[60] Kupchan, 'Hollow Hegemony or Stable Multipolarity?', 68–97.

power, while unprecedented, is not limitless. Even Iraq, notwithstanding the technological brilliance of the American victory in the war, subsequently demonstrated that the US needed help from other powers to stabilize the situation on the ground.

The Tension with Japan

Unlike Europe, Japan has not provided any strong reason to invite American fury. However, such was not the case earlier. Interestingly, before Japan went into a long recession in the early 1990s, the US and the EU members felt threatened by market competition from Japan, and their protectionist inclinations and activities were directed against it. At that time, one of America's foremost intellectuals, Samuel P. Huntington, gave stark expression to the perceived economic threat from Japan.

Favourably quoting the statement 'economics is the continuation of war by other means', Huntington made a shrill case for the continued economic primacy of the US in the world, which was taken to be under siege by Japan through a deliberate strategy of economic warfare. 'Japan,' he said, 'has accepted all the assumptions of realism but applied them purely in the economic realm.... Japanese strategy is a strategy of economic warfare.... Japanese strategy, behaviour, and declarations, all posit the existence of an economic Cold War between Japan and the United States.' The consequences for the US of this new Cold War were considered very serious and potentially dangerous, given the increasing American dependence on Japan for technology and money, and as well the rising Japanese penetration not only of the American economy but also of its polity and society. Huntington then asked for decisive measures for the US to triumph in this economic Cold War much as it had done in the strategic Cold War with the Soviet Union.[61] Such a stand is not of mere intellectual

[61] Samuel P. Huntington, 'Why International Primacy Matters', *International Security*, 17, 4 (1993), 68–83. An authoritative expert on East Asia, Chalmers Johnson, held a similar view. 'Japan', he said, 'is a mercantilist trading state... Japan assuredly has a grand strategy.... The essence of the strategy is to build in the Asia-Pacific region a new version of the Greater East Asia Co-Prosperity Sphere.' Cited in Ethan B. Kapstein, 'Does Unipolarity have a Future?', in Kapstein and Mastanduno (eds), *Unipolar Politics*, 477.

In Europe, one French prime minister, Edith Cresson, asserted: 'Japan is an adversary that doesn't play by the rules and has an absolute desire to conquer

interest, for the overall American reaction that it reflected was linked to economic policy of the US and the stern American attitude toward Japan in trade negotiations. Indeed, in pushing NAFTA, 'President Clinton argued that NAFTA would help American firms to compete better with their (excluded) Japanese competitors.'[62]

It is noteworthy that, even though Japan was a staunch military ally, more accurately an American military protectorate, the US vetoed Japan's participation in an East Asian Economic Group or an East Asian Economic Caucus, which had been proposed by Malaysia in the early 1990s. The US was opposed to any such regional economic bloc because it excluded the US, Australia, and New Zealand. The US feared that, in Grieco's words, it 'would promote closure of Asian markets to the United States, and would do so precisely because it would be decisively driven by Japan'. American officials were afraid that, without the US, it could 'develop into a protectionist bloc prone to shedding traditional values of open markets', for 'the obvious tendency would be to emulate the Japanese model of development through industrial policy, managed trade and mercantilism.'[63] It is a testimony to the power of the US and the vulnerability of Japan in the face of American pressure that the US was able to have an economic superpower such as Japan behave in accord with American preferences.

Presently, American power is too overwhelming to be defied by any power or grouping of powers. While it is not limitless, it lies within the capacity of the US to determine what shape politically the Middle East takes, and consequently what shape the world's oil economy takes. Similarly, the political, and therefore economic, fate of Northeast Asia

---

the world. You have to be naïve or blind not to recognize that.' She also stated: 'The Japanese have a strategy of world conquest. They have finished their job in the United States. Now they are about to devour Europe.' See Lester Thurow, *Head to Head: The Coming Economic Battle Among Japan, Europe, and America* (New York: William Morrow, 1992), 81.

[62] Jagdish Bhagwati, 'Bhagwati on Trade: Fast Track to Nowhere', *The Economist*, 18 October 1997, 21–3.

[63] Joseph M. Grieco, 'Realism and Regionalism: American Power and German and Japanese Institutional Strategies During and After the Cold War', in Ethan B. Kapstein and Michael Mastanduno (eds), *Unipolar Politics*, 319–53.

depends on American power and diplomacy backed by that power. More generally, the shape that economic globalization assumes is profoundly dependent on American will and power. Almost all powers see greater advantage in bandwagoning with the US, than in counterbalancing against it. While some may rhetorically sing the praises of multipolarity, they attempt at the same time to protect their economic and political interests by preserving or enhancing their bilateral relations with the US through engagement or alliance with it. A most instructive aspect of the struggle at the UN Security Council over the policy course on Iraq in early 2003 was the conspicuous passivity and silence of China, due no doubt to the dependence of its economy on the American market.

Summary and Conclusions

Both contemporary globalization and its truncated nature have been rooted in geopolitics during and after World War II. They have clearly been a function of American policies within the larger power framework of American hegemony that emerged at the end of the war. Since then, economic processes under the protective umbrella of American hegemony have made for considerable change in the distribution of power. The US share of the world product is now only about a quarter as compared to nearly half at the end of World War II. That outcome reflects the resurrection of the earlier major economic powers and the rise of some new ones. At one time, it may have seemed that some of these powers, particularly when merged together, may become economic and military challengers, or at the very least, place serious constraints on the exercise of American power around the globe. However, the collapse of the Soviet Union immeasurably enhanced the geopolitical position of the US as the hegemonic power across the globe in a largely unipolar system, so much so that the US is regarded not just as a superpower but a 'hyper-power', indeed an empire.[64]

---

[64] Direct territorial conquest or control is not necessary to constitute an empire. As Strange pointed out, the British empire was no less an empire when it was run by a commercial firm, nor when it encompassed princely states with internal autonomy. See Strange, 'Cave! Hic Dragones', 340. The issue is one of such predominance of power that it constrains the foreign policy autonomy of other states.

The international arena is a dynamic one, however, and no prediction about the future can therefore be made with any certainty. There nonetheless exist two polar views on the issue of American hegemony. One view takes the position that the power preponderance of the US is unique, unprecedented, and unrivalled in modern history, and that the American role is presently unchallengeable by any power or combination of powers.[65] Take defence expenditures in 2001. The US spent $322 billion as against a combined total of $178 billion by the other four members of the P-5 or $245 billion by these four plus Germany and Japan. Even if one took all 13 non-American states with defence expenditures of over $10 billion, their total comes to $346 billion out of the world total of $835 billion.[66] Besides, the US has an almost monopoly of military R&D spending, amounting to 80 per cent of the world total.[67] From this perspective, there will continue over the medium term a stable geopolitical environment for economic globalization, albeit under sole American domination.

The other view is that the rise of challengers is inevitable, and it will balance the contemporary hegemonic position of the US.[68] From the perspective of this second view, geopolitics is constantly in flux and geopolitical conflict is a continuous feature of the global scene, and it can turn out to be a disruptive force for economic globalization. Accordingly, globalization rests on more shaky grounds than is often believed by those who focus only on the attacks on it for reasons of social justice or protecting the environment. The march of globalization is thus not immutable. The world economy can easily fragment once again, along the fault-lines already etched by the existing regional economic blocs.

However, no serious challengers to American hegemony are visible on the horizon at this time. Still, the US finds itself at the beginning of the twenty-first century increasingly confronted by awesome challenges, where the use of modern unconventional weaponry in

[65] William C. Wohlforth, 'The Stability of a Unipolar World', *International Security*, 24, 1 (Summer 1999), 5–39.

[66] Based on data in *The Military Balance 2002–2003*, 332–7, Table 26.

[67] Ikenberry (ed.), *America Unrivaled*, 1–2.

[68] Christopher Layne, 'The Unipolar Illusion: Why New Great Powers Will Rise', *International Security*, vol. 17, no. 4 (1993), 5–51; and Kenneth N. Waltz, 'The Emerging Structure of International Politics', *International Security*, 18, 2 (1993), 44–79.

asymmetric conflicts threatens its homeland security, its economic health, and its interests overseas. Whatever the final denouement in relation to these challenges, for now the towering feature of the geopolitical landscape is the overwhelming power of the US to shape, for good or ill, the world's economic and political order. Other nations, even the most powerful ones, have therefore to work in the interstices of that power, not counter to it. The choice for many is restricted simply to bandwagoning with the US or engaging with it, not counterbalancing it. Economic globalization is likely to evolve within the same constraints, not independent of them.

Part III
Development

Chapter 7

OVERCOMING TRUNCATEDNESS
Harnessing Globalization for Development

Truncated globalization underlines the fundamental division between the rich and poor countries, between the developed and less developed countries. Superficially, that division of the world makes the opposition to globalization understandable, or at least one strand of the opposition that is based on the claim of globalization having allegedly made the rich richer and the poor poorer. There can be no doubt that globalization has a wide-ranging impact on economy, society, and polity, just as modernization or industrialization was earlier considered to have. Indeed, globalization is but another incarnation of modernization, now raised to world scale. Assessing the precise nature of its manifold impact would require a separate and substantial study. The focus here, however, is a more narrow one: to evaluate the result of the integration of the less developed or low income countries into the world economy on overall national development, as measured by per capita GDP.

Globalization and Economic Growth

As the queen of the social sciences, economics as a discipline has strong claims to being the closest to the rigour and standards of the physical sciences. In reality, however, on major issues, economists tend to be divided by disputes no less than the other social sciences. This is true as well in relation to the issue of the merits or otherwise of international integration or national openness to the world economy for economic growth. There is nonetheless a considerable degree of consensus among mainstream economists and international financial institutions, on the basis of both theory and econometric studies, that integration or openness is beneficial for economic growth and therefore, for mass welfare. The fictional account by the eminent economist Dani Rodrik about the visiting Martian's initial conclusion on this issue, from a first quick review of the current economics literature, is testimony to this consensus.[1] Interestingly, the World Bank states matter-of-factly: 'The relationship between openness and growth appears robust.'[2]

As a thoughtful critic of globalization, Rodrik raises a fundamental question, however, as to whether correlation is cause in respect of the relationship between openness and growth. Indeed, he suggests that the line of causality may well run the other way, from growth to openness. Further, concluding from his own empirical analysis, quantitative and qualitative, he rightly underlines the critical importance, not of openness or exports, but of working out viable overall national strategies for economic growth. He demands that national leaders, in working out such strategies, focus principally on capital investment, both in physical plant and infrastructure, as well as on human capabilities. Importantly, he urges, and justifiably so, that development requires good governance, and therefore effective institutions for conflict resolution need to be established.[3] This

---

[1] Dani Rodrik, *The New Global Economy and Developing Countries: Making Openness Work* (Washington, DC: Overseas Development Council, 1999), 136.

[2] World Bank, *Rethinking the East Asian Miracle*, (eds) Joseph E. Stiglitz and Shahid Yusuf (New York: Oxford University Press, 2001), 34. This assessment is based on: (1) Jeffrey D. Sachs and Andrew Warner, 'Economic Reform and the Process of Global Integration', *Brookings Papers on Economic Activity*, No. 1 (1995), 1–118; (2) Sebastian Edwards, 'How Effective are Capital Controls?', *Journal of Economic Perspectives*, 13, 9 (1999), 65–84; (3) Jeffrey Frankel and David Roemer, 'Does Trade Cause Growth?', *American Economic Review*, 89, 3 (1999), 379–99; and (4) Douglas A. Irwin and Mario Tervio, 'Does Trade Raise Income? Evidence from the Twentieth Century', National Bureau of Economic Research Working Paper W7745 (Cambridge, MA: June 2000). Note that the World Bank, on a reassessment of the issue, adds: 'the balance has shifted between exports and imports as sources of growth.' To the previous studies listed, we may add the study by David Dollar and Aart Kraay, 'Spreading the Wealth', 120–33.

[3] Rodrik, *The New Global Economy and Developing Countries*, 12–19, 136–7.

recommendation is in line with the point made by economist Hla Myint that the success of export-oriented policies depends on the adoption of the appropriate 'open' domestic policies.[4]

Meritorious as Rodrik's point is about national strategy, with capital investment as its principal component, it does not resolve the question concerning openness, however. For, it is precisely the issue in regard to capital investment as to whether it should be in sectors that are outward-oriented as in an export-propelled growth strategy, or it should be inward-oriented as in import-substitution industrialization. The key concern here has to be as to what kind of orientation to the world economy would make for greater productivity of capital, and for better incentives for producers. Moreover, there is the critical issue for capital-deficient countries as to whether openness would additionally help them precisely by bringing in foreign capital for investment, which would otherwise not take place.

In his own quantitative analysis, Rodrik did find a high degree of correlation between economic success and openness among the 25 fastest-growing developing countries over the 1975–94 period, and he maintains: 'In this sense, increased export orientation has been a hallmark of practically all successful countries.' However, he asserts that 'the reverse is not true in general'. For, when he took the 25 LDCs with the highest export-GDP ratio increases, Rodrik discovered that about half of the countries showed only nominal growth, less than one per cent of GDP per capita, with five of them 'having experienced *negative* growth'. He therefore concludes: 'In practice, the links between openness and economic growth tend to be weak, and to be contingent on the presence of complementary policies and institutions.'[5]

If one puts export fetishism for its own sake aside, it is clear that integration into the international economy is by itself no panacea for economic growth. Fundamentally, economic growth is the result of many factors. It would be difficult, indeed, to isolate any one factor as alone being the determinant of growth. Even if we suspend disbelief

[4] Hla Myint, 'Inward and Outward-Looking Countries Revisited: The Case of Indonesia', *Bulletin of Indonesian Economic Studies*, 20, 2 (August 1984), 41–2, cited in William E. James, Seiji Naya, and Gerald M. Meier, *Asian Development: Economic Success and Policy Lessons* (Madison, WI: University of Wisconsin Press, 1989), 213.

[5] Rodrik, *The New Global Economy*, 33, 137.

for a moment and grant that the export-oriented growth strategy is more conducive to growth, its viability would nonetheless be crucially dependent on two other essential factors. One of them pertains to the capacity of the state to make the necessary social and political adjustments domestically to assure macroeconomic stability, to mobilize resources for investment, and to take advantage of the opportunities that the international economy may offer. Growth can certainly be wrecked by economic mismanagement by irresponsible decision-makers or by societal rigidities, especially in the face of disturbances from the global economy.

The other important factor concerns the requirement of an international economy that is favourable to fruitful economic participation by LDC economies. However, it is not within the power of decision-makers in the LDCs to will such an international economic order, at least in the short and medium terms that are relevant to policy-making. It would be quixotic, indeed, on their part to even expect to do so, though that has not prevented many of them from frequently acting in that fashion. Rather, they have to perforce function within the constraints of the international economic order that has been geopolitically shaped by the powerful states. There are stringent limits to any effort by the LDCs in *balancing* the powerful states to create an international economy that would be more conducive to their own participation. What is, however, possible for decision-makers in the LDCs, as considerable historical experience suggests, is a readiness to seize the opportunities as and when they arise, especially in the geopolitical arena, where at times *bandwagoning* may be a more handy strategy.

Investigating the Issue

Given the multiplicity of factors involved in economic growth, the issue of whether or not openness is cause or effect of growth cannot be satisfactorily resolved through econometric studies alone. The alternative case-study approach involving the investigation of a few selected countries perhaps holds greater promise. One could, for example, choose a few countries that have displayed success in their combination of openness and economic growth, and then attempt to determine whether growth followed or preceded the shift to openness.

That is the procedure that is employed here in the hope that it could shed some light on the issue, especially since the other variables would then remain largely the same for a given country. Mind you, these other variables are not unimportant, however. Quite the contrary, as will become apparent further along in this study. Chief among these variables are: whether the state was faced with an economic crisis or not; whether the state was hard or soft in nature in relation to society; whether the geopolitical situation was favourable or not for the shift to openness; whether the international economy was in an expansionary phase or not to accommodate increased exports; and whether the exports are manufactures or raw materials.

It should be noted that the pertinent issue at hand is whether higher economic growth was preceded by a shift to an export-oriented growth strategy, not whether government expanded or diminished its role in the economy. A commitment to export orientation is not necessarily equivalent to a reduction in the role of the government. Rather, the discussion here proceeds on the assumption that export promotion requires an activist state, not a passive state as envisioned in neoclassical economics.

Earlier, pointing to the phenomenon of 'triadization', this study has underlined the truncated nature of globalization. That assessment of the nature of globalization was based on taking into account the concentration of trade and capital flows around the turn of the millennium. Such a *synchronic* analysis as a snapshot of the situation at a given cross-section of time, however, provides only a static and limited view. It does not alert us to the tendencies that may exist in a given situation, whether by way of reinforcement or attenuation. For that, a *diachronic* analysis that examines the situation over a period of time is necessary.

Notwithstanding the decided concentration that has been shown to be manifest in trade and capital flows, the picture is not uniform throughout the global economy. Particularly noteworthy is the set of countries lying in the geographic arc stretching across the East–Southeast Asian region from Japan down to Indonesia. Most of these countries have shown considerable economic dynamism over the last third of the twentieth century that contradicts the image of the marginalization of the developing world and polarization of the world economy. It is the economic performance of these countries that forms the subject of investigation here.

The investigation focuses on countries that have populations of over 10 million, and therefore excludes political entities such as Singapore and Hong Kong that are the size of big cities. Also excluded are countries that have until recently been in continual political turmoil, such as Laos and Cambodia, or where there is lack of adequate data over a longer period of time, as in the case of Vietnam. This selection process gives us the following eight major countries in the region: Japan, Korea, China, Taiwan, Thailand, Philippines, Malaysia, and Indonesia. Two other major countries lying to the west of this set have been included for purposes of comparison: India and Pakistan. There are, then, 10 countries in all for examination. This may seem like a small number, but these countries account for roughly half of the world's total population of over six billion.

Around 1950, except for Japan, these countries constituted a rather homogenous set as low-income agricultural, subsistence economies, with more or less the same standard of living, their per capita income ranging by and large between 500 and 1,000 international (1990) dollars with the exception of Malaysia (see Table 7.1). Perhaps, it may seem somewhat unfair to include Japan at all in this set. For, before World War II, it was one of the major industrial powers of the world, and it was strong enough to dominate militarily the East Asia region and challenge the US to a mortal combat; its poor post-war economic condition was clearly a consequence of wartime destruction. However, Japan is important for consideration here because of the model that it provided for the rest of the region, and its own subsequent role in the development of the region. It is important as well for revealing how geopolitical developments are intimately implicated in economic growth, a feature that appears over and over again in the region.

In any case, despite the initial homogeneity that is apparent among most of the countries in the set, the beginning of the twenty-first century forcefully demonstrates the drastic heterogeneity that has come to characterize this group of countries. The World Bank differentiates among countries on the basis of their 2001 GNI (gross national income) per capita as high income ($9,206 or more), upper middle income ($2,976–9,205), lower middle ($746–2,975), and low income ($745 or less). Using these criteria, we find that Japan ($35,990), Korea ($9,400), and Taiwan ($12,876) are now high income countries, Malaysia ($3,640) stands alone as an upper middle income country, and China ($890), the Philippines ($1,050), Thailand ($1,970), and (controversially) Indonesia ($680) have become lower middle income countries. However, India ($460) and Pakistan ($420)

Table 7.1: GDP Per Capita (Constant 1995 US$) [except for 1950]

	1950*	1960	1965	1970	1975	1980	1985	1990	1995	2000
Japan	1,926	8,399	12,501	20,465	23,820	28,295	32,172	39,955	42,185	44,830
Korea	770	1,324	1,547	2,282	3,022	3,910	5,322	7,967	10,873	13,062
Taiwan#	936	145	206	362	845	2,348	3,243	7,918	12,488	13,985
Thailand	817	464	566	752	859	1,117	1,330	1,998	2,871	2,804
Philippines	1,070	724	801	888	998	1,172	974	1,090	1,084	1,167
Malaysia	1,559	975	1,164	1,370	1,712	2,297	2,586	3,104	4,310	4,796
Indonesia	840	248	246	297	384	503	601	776	1,042	993
China	439	111	106	119	137	167	260	349	581	824
India	619	182	194	211	217	226	263	323	380	459
Pakistan	643	180	225	274	274	317	384	447	500	516

* 1990 International $ (PPP)   # The figures are at market prices for 1960 and after.

Source: The figures for 1950 are from Angus Maddison, *The World Economy: A Millenial Perspective* (Paris: OECD, 2001). Except for Taiwan, the other figures from 1960 to 2000 are from World Development Indicators (WDI); WDI does not provide data before 1960 or for Taiwan. The figures for Taiwan are for national income per capita in US$ at market prices for 1960 to 1975, and are for GDP per capita in US$ at market prices for 1980 to 2000. They are based on *Statistical Yearbook of the Republic of China 1976*, 339, and *Statistical Yearbook of the Republic of China 2001*, 151.

Table 7.2: GDP Growth Rates (Five-Year Averages)

	1961–65	1966–70	1971–5	1976–80	1981–5	1986–90	1991–5	1996–2000
Japan	9.38	11.56	4.60	4.39	3.29	4.91	1.41	1.47
Korea	5.94	10.56	7.94	7.04	7.83	9.50	7.47	4.82
Taiwan	8.90	9.30	9.00	10.62	6.74	9.17	7.12	5.73
Thailand	7.18	9.16	5.77	8.00	5.45	10.34	8.66	0.44
Philippines	5.23	4.62	5.79	6.07	-1.14	4.75	2.19	3.57
Malaysia	6.88	6.11	7.19	8.55	5.15	6.91	9.47	4.87
Indonesia	2.03	3.44	7.82	7.93	5.67	7.14	7.87	0.97
China	1.87	5.47	5.21	5.49	10.80	7.70	12.07	8.24
India	3.66	4.12	2.91	3.22	5.38	6.36	5.21	4.85
Pakistan	7.43	7.06	3.22	6.23	6.78	5.80	4.84	3.10

Source: World Development Indicators (WDI). The figures for Taiwan are based on data in the *Statistical Yearbook of the Republic of China 1976*, 338; *Statistical Yearbook of the Republic of China 1987*, 98; and *Statistical Yearbook of the Republic of China 2001*, 151.

continue to remain low income countries even though they have certainly seen considerable economic growth.[6]

The variant outcomes among these countries raise the important question as to the factors that are responsible for the differential performance in economic growth over half a century. The focus here, however, is on the issue of whether openness to the world economy has played a role in the aforesaid variant outcomes, specifically whether improved economic performance preceded or followed the shift to openness. The subsequent five chapters explore this issue in respect of these 10 countries, and they also address the question of whether the international economy was open—and under what circumstances—to the specific countries so as to provide an opportunity for exports.

---

[6] World Bank, *World Development Report 2003*, 243. The *Report* itself classifies Indonesia as a low income country since its GNI per capita in 2001 was $680. On the consideration that this is a direct consequence of the financial crisis that struck East Asia in 1997 and the political crisis that ensued in the country as a result, Indonesia has been retained here as a lower middle income country. Note that the World Bank does not provide data on Taiwan; the source for its figure is 'Key Economic and Social Indicators' at the website of the government of Taiwan.

Chapter 8

THE ORIGINAL ASIAN TIGERS
Japan, Taiwan, and South Korea

Japan, Taiwan, and South Korea were the first of the large 'Asian Tigers'. Japan was, of course, the leader of the pack. But it was more than that. It came to serve as the model that the other two states self-consciously emulated. Japan's role in the development of South Korea and Taiwan, however, extends back in time and encompasses a period of 'preparation' before World War II in these two states, a task that Western imperial powers claimed to have undertaken in their colonies but failed to pursue. Indeed, in view of the linkages among the three countries, some refer to a 'Northeast Asian political economy'.[1] This chapter therefore treats the economic performance of these countries together.

Japan

Japan was the first 'economic miracle' of the post-war period. Its economic performance in the two decades of the 1950s and 1960s was simply spectacular. During that period, Japan's economy sped past one rival GNP milepost after another, leaving behind China in 1961, the UK in 1962, France in 1963, and West Germany in 1966. After the late 1960s only the economies of the US and USSR remained to be overtaken. Given its new exalted economic status, Japan was admitted to the OECD as a member in 1964.

---

[1] Bruce Cumings, 'The Origins and Development of the Northeast Asian Political Economy: Industrial Sectors, Product Cycles, and Political Consequences', in Frederic C. Deyo (ed.) *The Political Economy of the New Asian Industrialism* (Ithaca, NY: Cornell University Press, 1987), 44–83.

So impressed was Herman Kahn by Japan's high-speed economic growth that he wrote as early as 1970 a book entitled *The Emerging Japanese Superstate,* and predicted that the turn of the millennium would see Japan 'possessing the largest gross national product in the world'.[2] Such long-term prophecies rarely turn out to be accurate in human affairs, but by the early 1970s Japan had already become an economic superpower, and in 1980 it emerged as number two among the world's economies.[3] Its rate of growth had been an unrivalled average of 11 per cent over the period from 1952 to 1973 even as its share of world trade quadrupled from some two per cent to around eight per cent.[4] Chalmers Johnson maintained that from 1946 to 1976, Japan's economy multiplied 55 times, accounting at the end for 'about 10 per cent of the world's economic activity though occupying only 0.3 per cent of the world's surface and supporting about 3 per cent of the world's population'.[5] By any measure, it was a stunning performance, richly deserving the epithet of a miracle. How did this miracle come to occur?

The Developmental State

In his magisterial work on Japan's Ministry of International Trade and Industry (MITI), Johnson apotheosized 'the developmental state' as the key to Japan's astonishing economic performance, eschewing in the process cultural and neoclassical explanations among others. The developmental state has economic growth as its fundamental priority and overriding goal, which then frames and disciplines all national policy and activity. Development constitutes the *hegemonic project*[6] of the state, hence the very characterization as the developmental

---

[2] Herman Kahn, *The Emerging Japanese Superstate: Challenge and Response* (Englewood Cliffs, NJ: Prentice-Hall, 1970), 2.

[3] Bruce Cumings, 'The Origins and Development of the Northeast Asian Political Economy', 44–83.

[4] T.J. Pempel, 'The Developmental Regime in a Changing World Economy', in Meredith Woo-Cumings (ed.), *The Developmental State* (Ithaca, NY: Cornell University Press, 1999), 137–81.

[5] Chalmers Johnson, *MITI and the Japanese Miracle: The Growth of Industrial Policy, 1925–1975* (Stanford, CA: Stanford University Press, 1982), 6.

[6] Bob Jessop, 'Accumulation Strategies, State Forms, and Hegemonic Projects', *Kapitalistate*, 10/11 (1983), 89–101, cited in Pempel, 'The Developmental Regime in a Changing World Economy', 160.

state. The state's focus is on savings and production as against consumption and distribution. Beyond the encompassing goal, the Japanese model of the developmental state structurally comprised four important elements.

The first of these elements was a small cohesive bureaucracy consisting of 'the best managerial talent available in the system', which was endowed with the duty to formulate and execute an industrial policy for rapid development.The second element was that of a political system that gave the said bureaucracy adequate scope to function and exercise initiative in the management of the economy, with the other branches of the government primarily serving to deflect pressures from interest groups so as to safeguard the priority for development. The developmental state 'covertly separates reigning and ruling: the politicians reign and the bureaucrats rule'. The secret to its success is the capacity of the politicians 'to create space for bureaucratic initiative unconstrained by political power' and to perform 'safety-valve' functions when the policies of the bureaucracy result in antagonizing sections of the public.The third element was the adoption of 'market-conforming methods' of state intervention for fostering industry, and thus 'to avoid the deadening hand of state control and the inefficiency, loss of incentives, corruption, and bureaucratism that it generates'.This particular element distinguishes the developmental state from the largely regulatory state of the US, and the command and control economy of the USSR. Chief among the market-conforming methods of state intervention in the basically private economy is 'administrative guidance', marked characteristically by state–industry cooperation rather than conflict. The fourth and final element was 'a pilot organization' like the Japanese MITI, mandated to develop and implement industrial policy. MITI was endowed with sufficient control over finance for industry, think-tank functions, and a mix of powers that would make it effective without becoming too powerful.[7]

Authoritarianism and the Developmental State

It is noteworthy that not only the state as such but its particular type figures centrally in Johnson's model. Johnson himself recognized that, while Japan was formally a democracy under the

[7] Johnson, *MITI*, 305–24; see also Chalmers Johnson, 'The Developmental State: Odyssey of a Concept', in Woo-Cumings (ed.), *The Developmental State*, 32–60.

Occupation-imposed constitution, the bureaucracy had a great deal of autonomy in the making and executing of policy for economic growth, which was the overarching and system-determining goal of the state. Loosely considered, the developmental state is politically a variant of the 'bureaucratic-authoritarian' state. For his recognition of that state's superior effectiveness as an instrument for economic growth, Johnson was criticized that his 'book came dangerously close to a defence of fascism'. Johnson himself acknowledges that the Japanese state during the first several post-war decades was one of 'soft authoritarianism' and that 'administrative guidance' was 'a euphemism for governmental orders'.[8] While denying, even if somewhat unconvincingly, 'any necessary connection between authoritarianism and the developmental state',[9] he admits to the presence of some kind of elective affinity between the two features.[10]

From the perspective of the requirements for economic development, it is clear nonetheless that Japan's high-speed growth took place under the auspices of a hard or strong, or even authoritarian (albeit soft authoritarian), state. That does not mean, however, that the Japanese state was without legitimacy, for the special characteristic of the Japanese state–society relationship for over a century since the Meiji Restoration in 1868 has been a fairly generalized consensus over the hegemonic project of 'catch-up' industrialization. That consensus has, in turn, been founded—in a pattern very distinct from most LDCs—on a mono-ethnic nation conceived as a single family. Certainly, Woo-Cumings is apt in concluding: 'the power of the developmental state grows both out of the barrel of the gun and its ability to convince the population of its political, economic, and moral mandate.'[11]

Export Orientation and the External Environment

Beyond the lack of being fully explicit on the nature of the state and its ethnic base, Johnson's original model misses out on two other

[8] Chalmers Johnson, 'Political Institutions and Economic Performance: The Government-Business Relationship in Japan, South Korea, and Taiwan', in Deyo (ed.), *The Political Economy of the New Asian Industrialism*, 136–64.

[9] Johnson, 'The Developmental State', 52.

[10] Meredith Woo-Cumings, 'Introduction: Chalmers Johnson and the Politics of Nationalism and Development', in Woo-Cumings (ed.), *The Developmental State*, 20.

[11] Ibid., 20.

important elements. One relates to the nature of orientation of the developmental state to the world economy, or more broadly the world system. The notions of 'market-conforming methods' and 'administrative guidance' provide no inkling about the economic policy's primary thrust to boost exports. Johnson attempts to underplay the role of exports by arguing that 'Japan's growth did not depend nearly so much on exports as it did on the development of the domestic market.' Similarly, he maintains that 'Japan had a consistently lower dependency on exports and imports as a percentage of GNP at constant prices than France, Germany, Italy, Britain, and OECD Europe as a whole.'[12]

That argument, however, leaves unexplained why MITI would be so intolerant of old or obsolescing technology or industrial branches. Equally, it does not explain why Japan would readily exit from industries where it no longer had a competitive edge in world markets, a sure sign of an outward-oriented economy. The reality is that competition was conceptualized by MITI in terms of the world economy, and was addressed to penetrating foreign markets, more particularly the American market. Interestingly, William Borden, whose work focuses on Japan's economic policy during the 1947–55 period, when its economic model was set, states: 'Japan was truly a "workshop nation", which imported 70 per cent of its primary goods and exported 90 per cent of its manufactured goods.'[13] What, one may legitimately ask, is this if not dependence on exports?

Fundamentally, Japan's economic policy has been outward-oriented; it would be difficult to characterize it as inward-oriented. It is not sufficient to say that 'Japan, as a heavily populated resource-deficient country, has to export in order to pay for its vital imports.'[14] That purpose of exporting in order to pay for vital imports is no different from that in economies that are known to be export-driven ones. Johnson's argument does not enlighten us as to whether Japan's economic policy was inward-oriented or outward-oriented. In contrast, the position taken here, though not necessarily novel, is precisely that the distinctive characteristic of the Japanese goal-driven

[12] Johnson, *MITI*, 15–16.
[13] William S. Borden, *The Pacific Alliance*, 189.
[14] Johnson, *MITI*, 16.

model was that export-propelled growth was chosen over inward-orientation as the instrument for economic growth. It is not surprising that, for the same profound reason, Japan is held to be the exemplar of the 'trading state' in the post-war world.[15] In sum, Johnson tends to understate the importance of the choice Japan made in terms of its outward orientation to the world economy.

Related to the missing thrust for exports in the Johnson model, the other essential element that is absent in the model pertains to the nature of the external environment, more precisely the type that would be receptive to such exports. The thrust for exports can come to naught if the world economy is not ready to receive them. Imagine for a moment the counterfactual that Japan is ready to send out its exports, but the world is not willing to oblige by taking them. Critics are certainly justified in pointing out that 'Johnson's book consistently understates the contributions of world-system factors,' or that 'the developmental state is unthinkable apart from its relationship to the external world.'[16] To his credit, Johnson has since accepted this criticism.[17]

However, it is not merely a question of some already existent open world economy that Japan was shrewdly able to exploit. Johnson simplistically assumes that 'Japan profited enormously from the open trading system that developed throughout the world after World War II,' and he arbitrarily but misleadingly chooses his dates when he says that 'home demand led Japan's growth for the twenty years after 1955'.[18] In the process, he avoids grappling with the fundamental question of the influence of geopolitics by way of both conjuncture and purpose. In international politics, a distinction is at times made

[15] Richard Rosecrance, *The Rise of the Trading State* (New York: Basic Books, 1986).

[16] The citation is in Johnson, 'The Developmental State', 55; and Woo-Cumings, 'Introduction', 21.

[17] Johnson, 'The Developmental State', 55.

[18] Johnson, *MITI*, 15–16. Bhagwati makes a similar error in his reading of the prevailing trade regime: 'But it is indisputable that the Four Tigers rode to prosperity mainly on the back of an energetic commitment to an outward-oriented trade strategy, which enabled them to reap massive gains from trade in a world that offered expanding markets, thanks to the liberal international regime. Their prosperity then owed much to this regime.' Jagdish Bhagwati, *Political Economy and International Economics*, 476.

between 'low politics' and 'high politics', the former pertaining to economic issues, and the latter to strategic issues. In practical terms, it is difficult to compartmentalize the two in a hard and fast fashion, for high politics often determines the nature of low politics. Basically, the Johnson model profoundly neglects the geopolitical roots of the developmental state. What bears underlining here is that such a state was purposively constructed, nurtured, and sustained by the hegemonic power. The American Occupation as a hard state gave birth to the developmental state, even though the latter, of course, also had an earlier pre-war lineage. Further, the US as the superpower patron energetically endeavoured to work out policies as a matter of great urgency to enable Japan to flourish economically through exports to the world. The historical record is quite enlightening on this point.

Geopolitics and the Japanese Model

In early 1947, the US set out with great determination on a policy to contain the Soviet Union. In accord with that policy, it soon turned to 'reverse course' in Japan from punishment and reform to economic recovery. The switch to the goal of containing the Soviet bloc made it imperative for the US to prevent Japan as Asia's greatest industrial workshop from slipping out of American control and into the Soviet bloc. The denial of Japan's industrial capacity and potential to the Soviet bloc became a pivotal requirement, and it was turned into the fulcrum around which the entire American strategy in East Asia and Southeast Asia was designed. In short, the US made Japan the cornerstone of its containment strategy in Asia.

Because of the critical importance of Japan, it followed as a matter of course from that point on for the US to prevent the rest of East Asia and Southeast Asia from falling under Communist sway. That was precisely the underlying rationale for the 'domino theory', which subsequently found application in the American intervention in Vietnam. The security and prosperity of non-Communist East and Southeast Asia thus became inextricably linked with the security and prosperity of Japan. Both the Truman and Eisenhower administrations 'saw Asian policy as a whole, and viewed a precapitalist Southeast Asia, specifically Indo-China, as vital to preserve the Pacific alliance with Japan, which far outweighed the importance of any other nation in Asia.' Accordingly, 'Japan was the key to all Asian policy' and 'intervention in Southeast Asia was central to the success of policy in Japan'.[19]

As it made the policy shift, the US found that not only was Asia's principal industrial workshop lying idle, but that the Japanese economy was in extreme distress. It was reeling under rampant inflation (which was near 1,000 per cent within the first year of Occupation alone), severe food shortages, and massive unemployment. Besides, Japan faced a trade imbalance of more than $8 billion.[20] In this grim situation of virtual economic collapse, the Truman administration formulated a new agenda for the Occupation through NSC 13/2 in mid-1948. Making the economic recovery of Japan the 'prime objective', that directive called a halt to reparations and removed most of the restrictions that had been imposed on Japanese industry. The new directive required the authorities in Japan to provide raw materials and credit on a preferential basis to firms producing goods for export. For its part, the administration aided the effort by furnishing capital and raw materials to Japan.

Subsequently, President Truman appointed the Detroit banker Joseph Dodge to General MacArthur's staff to energize the process of economic recovery. Dodge went on to implement what today would be called an IMF stabilization package, based on what is referred to as the Washington Consensus. This was a far-reaching programme, focusing on deflation and austerity, but what is most noteworthy for our purpose here is the role accorded to exports in the package. Exports formed the centrepiece of the package, and in this fashion the policy on export promotion preceded, and did not follow economic recovery and high-speed growth. Indeed, that export-oriented package can be considered to constitute the real foundation of 'the developmental state'. This much emerges as emphatically clear from Michael Schaller's account:

> The so-called economic czar [Dodge] imposed budget and industrial policies that breathed new life into the *zaibatsu*, curbed inflation, drove down worker's living standards, limited the rights of unions to bargain and strike, and *aimed to restore Japan as an industrial exporter*…. During 1949 and early 1950, Dodge held to a rigorous programme of neo-classic economic policy designed to rationalize an inflation-driven economy operating at little more than two-thirds of its pre-war level. *He envisioned Japan as a*

[19] Borden, *The Pacific Alliance*, 16.
[20] Schaller, *The American Occupation of Japan*, 49, 97.

high-volume, low-cost exporter of consumer goods primarily to Asian markets. To reduce what he considered frivolous spending, he ordered major reductions in the public welfare budget, curtailment of business loans, and the firing of 2,50,000 government workers. These actions decreased domestic consumption and *shunted bank credit, foreign currency, and raw materials to large enterprises engaged in export production.*

In April 1949, Dodge and a now compliant SCAP encouraged the Japanese government to organize a Ministry of International Trade and Industry (MITI). Modelled on the wartime Munitions Ministry and staffed by many of that agency's veteran bureaucrats, MITI provided 'administrative guidance' to banks and corporations. It directed the flow of domestic credit, foreign currency, imported raw materials, and foreign technology to favoured companies that *produced primarily for the export market* and sold goods for hard currency. *Japan's government-guided, export-driven economy, later described as a 'capitalist development state' or, less charitably, 'Japan, Inc.', was nurtured by American directives.*[21]

Austerity may have been a necessary accompaniment of economic stabilization in the circumstance of triple-digit inflation, but it also had the conscious aim of aiding exports: 'By restricting the purchasing power of the Japanese people, Dodge sought to force producers to seek foreign outlets for their goods.' For Dodge, exports were essential to Japan's survival and prosperity, given the country's large population, its lack of adequate arable land, and its need to import the raw materials for industry. However, it was not simply a question of increasing production for exports, but one of adjusting the increased production to the challenge of international competition, especially since China and Manchuria were no longer available as markets. Dodge held up to Japan the spectre of a 'period of the most intense competition in international commerce. Japan's problem is to prepare itself now to engage in this intense world competition on an effective and self-sustaining basis. Japan cannot provide for itself as a high cost, low quality producer. Fundamentally, the stabilization programme is aimed at ensuring Japan an opportunity to meet this world trade problem.'[22]

In addition to the other measures, Dodge unified into a single exchange rate the thousands of exchange rates that existed for the

---

[21] Michael Schaller, *Altered States: The United States and Japan Since the Occupation* (New York: Oxford University Press, 1997), 17–18; [emphasis added]. See also Kawai, *Japan's American Interlude*, 141, 177–9.

[22] Borden, *The Pacific Alliance*, 92, 94.

yen. More importantly, the rate was deliberately set low at 360 yen to the dollar in order to aid exports and discourage exports. This rate remained unchanged until 1971.[23]

It is quite apparent that the events relating to the founding post-war economic policy for Japan proceeded in the following sequence: the monumental American decision to pursue a global strategy of containment against the Soviet Union → in pursuance of that strategy, the determination of the US to deny Japan's industrial capacity and potential to the Soviet bloc → the need for economic recovery and growth in Japan in order to prevent Japan from going into the Soviet orbit → the adoption of an export-driven economic policy to aid recovery and push economic growth.

The Search for Markets

Having decided on a policy of export-propelled economic growth for Japan, however, the US still faced the question as to what markets would be ready to receive the resulting exports. The US continued to grapple with this question for the next decade. Japan had before and during World War II forcibly integrated the economies of Korea, Manchuria, and Taiwan with its own economy in Northeast Asia. Indeed, it had pushed for establishing under its own hegemony a larger closed economic bloc in East and Southeast Asia called the 'Greater East Asian Co-Prosperity Sphere', an endeavour that brought it into conflict with Chinese nationalism and the Western powers. The effort eventually culminated in war between Japan and the US. Defeat in World War II put an end to that dream, even as Japan lost its colonized markets in Northeast Asia. In the wake of the 'reverse course' by the US, the critical question for the US was as to what should now replace those markets for Japan. The question became especially acute when China meanwhile in 1949 came under Communist rule after the Kuomintang government and its supporters fled to Taiwan. The Communist takeover in China posed two issues for the US: one, the extension to China of American containment of the Soviet bloc in order to safeguard American interests in Japan and East Asia, and, two, the implications of that policy in terms of the China–Japan trading relationship for a Japan eager to export and

---

[23] Cumings, 'The Origins and Development of the Northeast Asian Political Economy', 62; and Borden, *The Pacific Alliance*, 89, 94.

for a US anxious about such a relationship leading to a possible accommodation between Japan and China.

In its impatience to restore Japan to economic health, the US now began to entertain some radical thoughts. Kennan wondered how the 'Japanese are going to get along unless they again reopen some sort of empire to the South. Clearly we have got, if we are going to retain any hope of healthy civilization in the coming period, to achieve opening up of trade possibilities, commercial possibilities for Japan, on a scale very far greater than anything Japan knew before.' Similarly, a former Occupation official, Phillip Taylor, averred: 'We have got to get Japan back into, I am afraid, the old Co-Prosperity Sphere.'[24]

Japan was, however, not to be left unchecked in this endeavour, for that would have defeated the strategic purpose of keeping it in the American orbit in the first place. Instead, Kennan wanted the US to design a programme that would, of course, lead Japan to economic recovery, but one that would also bind it to the US after the end of the Occupation—a programme that would combine economic prosperity with political dependence. He required 'controls … foolproof enough and cleverly enough exercised really to have power over what Japan imports in the way of oil and other things' and thus 'we could have veto power over what she does'.[25] It is a testimony to the ingenuity of long-range American planning that Japan has over the last half-century turned out to be an *abnormal state*, which is both economically powerful and militarily and politically dependent on the US. The US was, no doubt, also helped in its planning by the Japanese political elite, which had been traumatized by defeat in war, and was therefore amenable to this arrangement.

Geopolitical Conjuncture and Japan's Recovery and Advance

To push Japan's economic recovery, some had already mooted an 'economic aid programme, similar to the Marshall Plan, for the Far East' and to link Japan's economy with Southeast Asia, both as a source of raw materials and a market for Japanese goods.[26] The matter

---

[24] Schaller, *The American Occupation of Japan,* 179. See also Cumings, 'The Origins and Development of the Northeast Asian Political Economy', 44–83.

[25] Ibid., 44–83.

[26] Schaller, *Altered States,* 18–19.

assumed greater urgency after the victory of the Communists in China in 1949, but it did not proceed far. It is uncertain whether the Dodge stabilization package would have helped in economic recovery in the short haul. Such packages need time to achieve their purposes, and they require the right external environment to be successful. At the time, the environment was hardly propitious: 'International economic conditions doomed the Dodge Plan from its inception. Foreign demand failed to absorb the surplus production created by the suppression of domestic demand.'[27] But the Dodge package established the policy framework that would have been useful over the longer term for boosting exports. In the immediate future, however, Japan was rescued by fortuitous events.

What helped the Japanese economic recovery at this juncture was intervention by geopolitical fate in the form of the Korean War in 1950, at which point the US turned Japan into a regional arsenal for its armed forces fighting in Korea. The American procurement policy of massive reliance on Japan for equipment and supplies was truly the equivalent for Japan of the Marshall Plan. It provided Japan an economic windfall of immense proportions, with US military procurement amounting to about 70 per cent of Japan's exports in the period from 1950 to 1952.[28] Military Keynesianism thus pulled Japan out of its desperate economic situation:

> In the summer of 1950, the Keynesian domestic multiplier effect rippled through the economy, as falling inventories stimulated production and employment, prompting the *Oriental Economist* to report that procurement and export orders created 'benefits to Japan's economy far beyond their actual face values'....The leap in production from the months of the Dodge Plan in 1949 to the war boom of 1950 to 1951 was so great, and the follow-up orders so large, that, in the words of British economist G.C. Allen, it 'swept the economy on to a new plane'. He concluded: 'It is scarcely possible to exaggerate the importance of these payments to Japan's economic recovery during the critical years after 1951.'[29]

The effects of the American procurement policy were more far-reaching for Japan than just boosting its exports and, therefore, its

---

[27] Borden, *The Pacific Alliance*, 98.
[28] Richard J. Samuels, *Rich Nation, Strong Army*, 133.
[29] Borden, *The Pacific Alliance*, 147, 221.

growth. The policy resulted not only in the rehabilitation of Japanese industry, but also in its modernization. Apart from the increased export earnings providing the capital for renovating Japan's industry, it brought in new technology and, with the guidance of American consultants, new management practices and quality-control techniques. As Schaller underlines, the 'massive defence procurements lifted Japanese industry from its post-war torpor. The war in Korea set the stage for Japan's economic "miracle".'[30] For the US, the Korean war 'permanently linked Japanese economic development to US military priorities in Asia',[31] and demonstrated 'the decisive and monumental role of military expenditures in overcoming the failure of economic aid to revive the world economy'.[32]

The American Occupation formally ended in 1952, but the Japanese offer to provide base rights to the US, with some 200,000 American troops in Japan, amounted, in Kataoka's words, 'to an invitation for continued US occupation'.[33] Instead of building itself militarily, Japan took to economic 'growthmanship'. In this, it had abiding help from the US, given the protracted American containment policy. The armistice in the Korean War in 1951 at first created anxiety in Japan over future American military procurement, but the US continued to acquire Japanese supplies at high levels even afterwards. Over the decade of 1952–62, the US military purchased about $6 billion worth of supplies.[34] Japan was also made the source of supplies for American foreign aid to third countries.

Besides, the US made serious efforts to secure Southeast Asia as a market for Japan, but found that, because of the underdeveloped nature of the region, it would be useful to Japan only over the longer term. The US successfully pushed Japan's entry into GATT in 1955,

[30] Schaller, *Altered States*, 30.

[31] Laura Hein, cited in Samuels, *'Rich Nation, Strong Army'*, 133.

[32] Borden, *The Pacific Alliance*, 190.

[33] Tetsuya Kataoka, *Waiting for A 'Pearl Harbour': Japan Debates Defence* (Stanford, CA: Hoover Institution Press, 1980), 14.

[34] Schaller, *Altered States*, 108. Borden states: 'Procurement still continued at the $500 million level in 1960, enabling Japan to add to her exchange reserves.' He adds: 'By 1964, military procurement alone reached $7.2 billion. Government transfers of dollars to Japan thus averaged $500 million per year for twenty years. By 1970 the Vietnam War and continued military expenditures in Japan pushed the military total near $10 billion.' Borden, *The Pacific Alliance*, 190, 220.

but to its dismay, it found its European partners unwilling to accommodate Japan on exports. Eleven members of GATT, including Great Britain, took recourse to the 'escape clause' in refusing most favoured nation status to Japan.[35] So much, then, for the liberal nature of the trading regime! Ultimately, the US as the patron hegemon allowed Japan, in the larger cause of containment, greater access to its own market, despite protests from domestic producers, and in this manner launched Japan on an irreversible course of export-propelled growth. The geopolitical foundations of the American receptivity to Japanese exports had been succinctly articulated in 1952 by a US government official:

> The most highly industrialized country in the Far East must remain outside the Soviet orbit if there is to be a free Asia, and to this end US policy should be directed by whatsoever means are necessary, military or economic, to assist in the establishment of political tranquillity and economic betterment in all of free Asia.... and until it is clear that Japan can stand firmly on its own feet, the United States must of necessity lend support, even to the extent of providing an unrestricted market for such Japanese goods as American consumers find attractive.[36]

The impact of American openness to Japanese exports was tremendous. As Schaller underlines, 'trade between Japan and the United States surged after 1955. That year Japan exported goods worth $449 million to the United States. By 1960, helped by tariff reductions from entry into GATT, exports more than doubled, to almost $1.1 billion. Japanese imports of American goods and raw materials increased from $772 million to $1.54 billion. This trade expansion contributed to Japan's accelerating growth, with its GNP rising at least 12 per cent in 1958, 1959, and 1960.' Japan was, no doubt, helped by the international trade boom that started in 1955, but the US occupied an immensely important and unique place in Japan's thrust for exports and, consequently, in its economic growth. As Pempel aptly points out:

[35] Borden, *The Pacific Alliance*, 187.

[36] Jerome Cohen, *Economic Problems of a Free Japan* (Princeton: Princeton University Center for International Studies, 1952), 89, cited in Eric Heginbotham and Richard J. Samuels, 'Mercantile Realism and Japanese Foreign Policy', in Ethan B. Kapstein and Michael Mastanduno (eds), *Unipolar Politics*, 187.

Virtually every follower of contemporary economic events knows that the United States is Japan's largest export market; generally, the United States took 30–35 per cent of Japan's exports for most of the post-war period. In contrast, Japan's number two market, most often South Korea but sometimes (West) Germany, rarely took more than 5 per cent of Japan's total exports. In short, the US market was consistently five and half to six times larger than Japan's number two outlet.[37]

In sum, the model of 'the developmental state' grossly understates the nature of the export-propelled growth of the Japanese economy and the role of the US in the Japanese miracle, and altogether neglects the strategic factors that underlay the American role in the growth of the Japanese economy. That role included laying the policy foundations for export-propelled growth, being the catalyst and host for Japan's military exports, and opening the American market to its non-military exports. This is not to say that the elements included in the model of the developmental state were not important but, rather, that their effectiveness has to be appreciated in the larger geopolitical context, which was critical to the economic performance of Japan.

Korea and Taiwan

Korea and Taiwan have, in their own right, made a miracle of their economies. Korea is classified as a high-income country, and in 1996 it became a member of OECD. Since Taiwan's per capita income is considerably higher than that of Korea's, were it not for geopolitical reasons, it, too, would have been classified by the World Bank as a high-income country, and also enrolled as a member of OECD.

Fast-Speed Growth

The two countries accomplished their economic miracles in dramatic fashion. In 1962, Taiwan with a per capita GNP of US$170 ranked 85 among the countries of the world, preceded by Zaire and followed by Congo (PR). A bare quarter-century later in 1986, it had, with a per capita income of $3,580, jumped to number 38, preceded by Greece and followed by Malta. Similarly, Korea with a per capita

---

[37] Schaller, *Altered States*, 108–9; and Pempel, 'The Developmental Regime in a Changing World Economy', 177.

income of $110, jumped from its rank of 99 in 1962 (placed between Sudan and Mauritania) to 44 in 1986 (between Surinam and Argentina) with an income of $2,372, leaving behind other newly industrializing countries (NICs) such as Mexico and Brazil.[38] Another decade and a half later, the two countries had again advanced rapidly in their rankings. The *World Development Report 2003* provides data on GNP per capita for 2001 for 133 political entities (including Hong Kong). On the basis of the data, Korea, with a per capita income of $9,400 would rank 26, preceded by Slovenia ($9,780) and followed by Saudi Arabia ($7,230), Argentina ($6,960), Uruguay ($5,670) and Mexico ($5,540). Taiwan, with a per capita income of $12,876 is not included in the World Bank's listing, but if it were, it would have ranked 23, with Spain ($14,860) ahead of it, and New Zealand ($12,380), Greece ($11,780), and Portugal ($10,670) making some of the rear.

Behind the rapid advance in rankings has lain fast-speed economic growth. Writing in the mid-1980s, Cumings averred as a broad estimate that 'since the onset of export-led growth in the mid-1960s the GNPs of both Taiwan and South Korea have grown by an average of about 10 per cent per year, with manufacturing expansion often doubling that figure.'[39] Table 7.2 provides more recent World Bank data for several countries on GDP growth rates. It is apparent that in the period between 1966 and 1995, which includes years of the OPEC oil price shocks, Korea's GDP annual growth rate was an average of 8.39 per cent. Taiwan's growth rate was only a shade higher at 8.66 per cent. Even at these slightly lower rates than 10 per cent, GDP would double in about 8.5 years. The lower performance during the 1996–2000 period is evidently related to the severe financial crisis that hit East and Southeast Asia in 1997 and persisted for several years thereafter.

Emulating the Japanese Model

The economic growth of Korea and Taiwan may be a miracle, but it is not altogether a mystery after what we have learned about Japan's

[38] Robert Wade, *Governing the Market: Economic Theory and the Role of Government in East Asian Industrialization* (Princeton: Princeton University Press, 1990), 34–5.

[39] Cumings, 'The Origins and Development of the Northeast Asian Political Economy', 44.

growth in the discussion above. For, both Korea and Taiwan self-consciously followed the model of Japan's export-propelled growth after the effectiveness of that model was demonstrably evident. Robert Wade points out that Japan was the 'textbook' for both Korea and Taiwan, and that 'MITI was the model for its counterparts both in Taiwan and Korea to accept the same responsibility for promoting new industries and advanced technologies.'[40]

However, the adoption of the model did not occur spontaneously, but was done on American prodding, indeed under American pressure and direction. As Wade puts it, 'the United States "invited" Taiwan, Korea, and Japan to become economically strong,' with the underlying reason being their 'location and geopolitical importance'. They were invited 'because of their location on the West's defence perimeter (which made them more strategic than, say, the Philippines, Indonesia, or Brazil)'.[41] 'Invitation' is too mild a term for the process at work. To begin with, Japan was critically important in the titanic struggle between the US and the Soviet bloc because of its industrial capacity and potential. Then, in turn, Korea and Taiwan became important because their geographical location made them into daggers, as it were, pointed at the heart of Japan. The American role in the development of Korea and Taiwan was of immense and critical consequence. The US guaranteed their security through a direct military presence in their territories, and by building their military capabilities. It provided huge infusions of economic aid that, on a per capita basis, was matched in few other places at the time. And, significantly, it provided access to its markets for their goods resulting from the strategy of export-propelled growth. Not to be underestimated in all this, of course, is the role of the particular nature of the local polity, economy, and society.

The State and Development

Both Korea and Taiwan are classic examples of 'the developmental state'. In the period of their developmental breakthroughs, say from around the mid-1960s to the mid-1980s, both of them represented hard states, Taiwan perhaps more so with its Leninist-type ruling party KMT transplant from the mainland as against Korea with its military rule, periodically legitimated by electoral mandates under authoritarian

[40] Wade, *Governing the Market*, 326.
[41] Ibid., 346.

auspices. At the same time, both started their post-war economic history with considerable preparation for economic growth by virtue of their having been colonies of Japan for about the first half of the twentieth century. Joan Robinson had at one time stated that what was wrong with Western imperialism was not that it had exploited its colonies but that it had not exploited them enough, in the sense that it did not create an exploited and exploitable proletariat through sponsoring their industrialization. That accusation of neglect of not exploiting enough would be difficult to sustain against Japan. Japanese imperialism was altogether unusual in that, as a hard state, it created in its colonies the social, administrative, and financial infrastructure for economic growth and built heavy industry after the model that it knew best, that of its own 'catch-up' industrialization. Perhaps, it did so for reasons that its colonies were close geographically, and that it intended them to be permanent possessions.[42]

In his analysis of the economic impact of Japanese colonialism in Korea, Atul Kohli argues that 'Japanese colonialism, as brutal as it was, left an imprint on a political economy that later evolved into the high-growth, South Korean path to development…. As late colonizers, the Japanese made ruthless use of state power to pry open and transform Korea in a relatively short period.'[43] Japan's impact was both by way of creating a centralized state with a disciplined impersonal bureaucracy whose authority penetrated deep into society, and by using the state power so created to push the socio-economic transformation of its colonies. According to Cumings, 'colonial manufacturing growth in Korea, 1910–40, averaged 10 per cent per annum, and overall GNP growth was also in the 4 per cent range, as was Taiwan's…. both Korea and Taiwan experienced higher GDP growth rates than Japan between 1911 and 1938 (Japan, 3.36 per cent; Korea, 3.57 per cent; Taiwan, 3.80 per cent).' Significantly, 'Japan had begun to export iron and steel, chemical, and electric-generating *industries*, although much more to Korea than to Taiwan.'[44] To extract an agricultural

[42] Atul Kohli, 'Where Do High-Growth Political Economies Come From? The Japanese Lineage of Korea's "Developmental State"', in Woo-Cumings (ed.), *The Developmental State*, 100.

[43] Ibid., 95.

[44] Cumings, 'The Origins and Development of the Northeast Asian Political Economy', 45–6, [emphasis added].

surplus, Japan also transformed the countryside by creating property rights in land.[45] Kohli's conclusion on the implications of past experience is instructive:

> The key elements of the eventual path it adopted, however,—a Japanese-style, state-driven export economy—were deeply etched into the social fabric. More specifically, the Korean economy, especially the southern Korean economy, had already been export oriented, its entrepreneurs had considerable experience in selling abroad, and the state within this economy had learned from its own history that strong support for business and exports, along with tight control over labour, was a route to high economic growth.[46]

However, the path to this pattern of export-led growth in the post-war period was not straight and narrow. Initially, both Taiwan and Korea adopted import-substitution industrialization (ISI) as the strategy for economic growth.

Import Substitution and Aid Dependence

Korea and Taiwan were pulled into the ISI strategy for economic growth as a result of the external compulsions arising out of the geopolitical reorganization of the region following World War II. The collapse of the Japanese empire in the wake of the defeat of Japan resulted in the loss by these states of their traditional markets for their goods. Social and political turmoil as a consequence of war and partition in Korea and of the occupation and repression by the KMT forces in Taiwan, and the potential for war in its conflict with the mainland, made economic reconstruction extremely urgent as a task for the governments, while pervasive export pessimism worked in favour of ISI policies. From the outset, both states were heavily dependent on military and economic aid from the US. However, the US remained indulgent toward their inward-oriented economic policies in view of the geopolitical importance of these states in the global conflict, the immensity of their economic needs, and the intransigence of their political elites, who favoured ISI.

[45] Stephan Haggard, *Pathways from the Periphery: The Politics of Growth in the Newly Industrializing Countries* (Ithaca, NY: Cornell University Press, 1990), 52.
[46] Kohli, 'Where Do High-Growth Political Economies Come From?', 131.

During the period from 1953 to 1958, Korea received an average annual inflow of economic aid amounting to $270 million, that is, about $12.00 per capita annually, which formed some 15 per cent of the per capita income. According to Evans, Korea 'received more aid per capita during the 1950s than any other developing country'.[47] Similarly, in the period from 1951 to 1965, American economic aid to Taiwan amounted to about $1.5 billion, that is, an annual inflow of about $100 million or some $6 per capita. American military aid was twice as much as the economic aid to the two states.[48] The economic aid by the US played a critical role in the economic development of the two states. During the 1950s, American economic aid to Korea covered five-sixths of its imports; according to one estimate, it constituted some 80 per cent of the country's gross domestic capital formation between 1953 and 1962.[49] Such aid to Taiwan amounted to 6 per cent of its GNP and constituted nearly 40 per cent of its gross investment; the US supplied about 35 to 45 per cent of Taiwan's imports. As Wade underlined: '"With that much aid who couldn't industrialize?" it is sometimes said. Certainly US aid was very important.'[50] Most probably, as a consequence, both states demonstrated superior economic progress during the decade of the 1950s, with Taiwan doing much better than Korea, the latter

[47] Peter Evans, 'Class, State, and Dependence in East Asia: Lessons for Latin Americanists', in Deyo (ed.), *The Political Economy of the New Asian Industrialism*, 203–26.

[48] Hagen Koo, 'The Interplay of State, Social Class, and World System in East Asian Development: The Cases of South Korea and Taiwan', in Deyo (ed.), *The Political Economy of the New East Asian Industrialism*, 165–81.

[49] Evans, 'Class, State, and Dependence in East Asia: Lessons for Latin Amerianists', 210. Haggard's account is similar: 'American aid was the key to the political economy of import-substitution in the 1950s. The significance of US support for the regime can hardly be overstated. Aid financed nearly 70 per cent of total imports between 1953 and 1962 and equalled 75 per cent of total fixed capital formation.' Haggard, *Pathways from the Periphery*, 55.

[50] Wade, *Governing the Market*, 82. Haggard notes: 'The dependence of the new regime on aid was roughly equal to Korea's. Of a total current-account deficit of $1.3 billion between 1951 and 1962, aid financed $1.1 billion. Total economic commitments, including PL 480 shipments allocated between 1951 and 1965, were almost $1.5 billion.' He adds: 'An additional $2.5 billion came in the form of military equipment grants.' Haggard, *Pathways from the Periphery*, 84.

having been through a war with North Korea in 1950 and 1951. Between 1950 and 1960, Taiwan's GDP grew at an average annual rate of 7.6 per cent while that of Korea's at 5.1 per cent.[51]

American Pressure and Export Orientation

Notwithstanding their commendable economic performance, both states started to encounter serious problems usually associated with the ISI strategy, such as the saturation of the domestic markets, rent-seeking and corruption, underutilization of industrial capacity, overvalued currency, and current account deficits.[52] As a consequence, economic growth began to decline. In Taiwan, the growth rate fell year after year between 1952 and 1956. The year 1957 witnessed a worsening of the balance of payments problem. Meanwhile, the military crisis in the Taiwan Straits in 1958 led to some changes in the economic and political leadership. These changes, in turn, made for the formulation of 'a new political strategy that focused explicitly on building up the island's economy as the foundation from which other political objectives might be realized'.[53] In this manner, the first requisite of economic growth as a hegemonic project of the developmental state was met in Taiwan, which was already a hard state.

External pressures were crucial in the change to an outward-oriented strategy. To begin with, Taiwan faced a worsening foreign exchange situation in late 1957. The first instalment of reforms toward an export-led strategy began in April 1958 with the devaluation of the currency by over 40 per cent, and the simplification of the multiple exchange rate system. The US then weighed in, urging further reform. More important, it employed the leverage of Taiwan's dependence on American aid both as carrot and stick and made strategic use of its role in joint decision-making to push for reform. Haggard explains:

> In the same year the Americans began to play a more active role in the reform process.... Aid was used in the short run, through both threats and

[51] Richard E. Barrett and Soomi Chin, 'Export-Oriented Industrialization States in the Capitalist World System: Similarities and Differences', in Deyo (ed.), *The Political Economy of the New East Asian Industrialism*, 23–43, Table 1.

[52] Haggard, *Pathways from the Periphery*, 90–1.

[53] Ibid., 91.

promises, for the purpose of extracting, but also supporting, reforms. The process of influence is described by Jacoby: 'In Taiwan, the US AID Mission often played the role of "whipping boy" for the development-minded officials of the Joint Commission and the Council. These officials could argue for economic reforms within the Chinese government on the grounds that they were under pressure by the US government.'

Following a visit by Under Secretary of State C. Douglas Dillon in 1959, AID proposed an eight-point programme including liberalized exchange controls, the sale of more government enterprises and more effective management of those retained, and noninflationary monetary and fiscal policies.[54]

Some have seen American pressure for reform in Taiwan as one of the 'clearest cases in economic history of cause and effect'.[55]

The similar push to an export-propelled growth strategy in Korea had to wait for a few years because of political instability. An opposition movement marked by severe rioting led to the resignation of the unpopular Syngman Rhee government in 1960, but the successor democratic regime proved to be short-lived. A military coup under Park Chung-Hee in 1961 laid the foundations of the developmental state in Korea. Initially, the military regime continued with the ISI strategy. But, when it encountered serious economic problems, both internally and externally, the US exerted pressure for reform, in particular toward an export-oriented growth strategy. Here, as in Taiwan, the US skillfully wielded the instrument of aid and the American role in Korea's decision-making to press Korea for reform:

more important, the director of AID had independently suspended aid disbursements in 1962 in an effort to force the government to bring spending and income into line.... the United States used the aid weapon to force policy changes, both through the short-run manipulation of aid to achieve limited goals and through an announced intention to reduce aid commitments over the longer run....

Finally, in April 1963, the government negotiated a major stabilization programme with the United States, including ceilings on growth of the money supply, the budget deficit, commercial bank credit expansion, and foreign-exchange reserves. The next American target was the exchange rate. Drawing on a study commissioned by AID, the United States pressed

[54] Ibid., 92–3.
[55] Cumings, 'The Origins and Development of the Northeast Asian Political Economy', 70.

devaluation despite strenuous objections from Korean business and
government officials....

Inflation, balance-of-payments problems, and forced stabilization taught
the Park regime important lessons. Economic difficulties forced a reassessment
of the inward-looking growth strategy the military had initially favoured;
they also provided an object lesson in the political costs of aid dependence.
Reliance on the Americans made the Korean government extremely
vulnerable to changes in aid levels. Political pressure from the Americans
pushed Park to adopt policies that would increase his economic independence
by creating alternative sources of foreign exchange. As Anne Krueger puts
it succinctly, 'the export-promotion policies of the government were
adopted as a means, not as an end.'

The final moves toward an outward-looking strategy evolved during the
two years following Park's assumption of the presidency in January 1964.
These had their origins in a group of American advisers working closely with
mid-level planners in the Economic Planning Board and the Ministry of
Commerce and Industry. A Joint US-Korean Economic Cooperation
Committee, formed in July 1963, became a locus for the discussion of the
development strategy, including the promotion of exports, the coordination
of commercial and investment relations, and fiscal and financial reform.[56]

The reforms proceeded at both the macro and the micro level. In
May 1964, Korea devalued its currency and later moved to a single
floating exchange rate. At the micro level, it set up the Joint Export
Development Committee, with representatives from AID, government
ministries and the private sector, which was instrumental in promoting
policies to push exports. The committee's export programme centred
on using incentives to spur new exports.[57]

Exports and Economic Growth

With the export-propelled growth strategy adopted under the
auspices of the developmental state, both Korea and Taiwan went on
to enact their economic miracles over the next two decades, despite
their having had to adjust to the oil price shocks. Behind their annual
rates of growth of over 8 per cent lay the fantastic growth in exports,
testifying to the powerful impact of exports on growth of national
income. The average annual growth rates of merchandise exports for
Taiwan during 1960–70 and 1970–82 were 23.7 per cent and 9.3 per
cent respectively; the corresponding figures for Korea were 34.7 per

[56] Haggard, *Pathways from the Periphery*, 68–70.
[57] Ibid., 70.

cent and 20.2 per cent. Equally remarkable is the shift to manufactured goods in their merchandise exports. At the end of the second period, manufactured goods had come to form about 90 per cent of the merchandise exports of both countries; note that their share for Korea in 1960 was only 14 per cent.[58] Both states also benefited from the Vietnam war, as did Japan again, in their export drive because of American procurement policy.

A noteworthy aspect of the economic growth of the two countries is that their geopolitical importance (with the US having some 40,000 troops in Korea) is reflected, as in the case of Japan, in the American willingness to absorb their exports of manufactured goods. Korea has sent a third to one-half of its annual exports and Taiwan a quarter to two-fifths of its annual exports to the US.[59] In 1962, Taiwan ranked number 21 in the US import market of manufactured goods; in 1986 its rank had escalated to four. Similarly, Korea's rank jumped from 40 in 1962 to five in 1986.[60] One estimate for the period from 1981 to 1986 testified to the critical role of the exports, especially those to the US, in the economic growth of the two countries. It showed that exports to the American market over this period were responsible for 42 per cent of Korea's growth and 74 per cent of Taiwan's growth.[61]

Although both states achieved their economic miracles under authoritarian and labour-repressive regimes, it is impressive that once they had achieved developed-country living standards, confirmed by their having achieved high income country status, their political regimes transited to more open and democratic systems by the late 1980s.[62] In the process, they demonstrated the robustness of modernization theory's basic proposition that the accomplishment of

[58] Barrett and Chin, 'Export-Oriented Industrialization States in the Capitalist World System', 26, 32.

[59] Ibid., 33; and Pempel, 'The Developmental Regime in a Changing World Economy', 177.

[60] Wade, *Governing the Market*, 37.

[61] Lester Thurow, *Head to Head: The Coming Economic Battle Among Japan, Europe and America* (New York: William Morrow, 1992), 62.

[62] See Robert A. Scalapino, 'Democracy in Taiwan and Asia—Advances and Challenges', in Peter C.Y. Chow (ed.), *Taiwan's Modernization in Global Perspective* (Westport, CT: Praeger, 2002), 29–43.

economic development (as distinguished from the process of development) makes for stable democracy.[63]

Summary and Conclusions

Any model in the social sciences simplifies reality in order to sharpen our understanding of the world around us. It reduces complexity so as to limit or eliminate 'noise' or clutter, enabling us to focus on the relationships among the selected variables. However, if in the process the model misses out on the essential variables that bear on the explanation of outcomes, then its utility is plainly diminished.

There can be no doubt that the model of 'the developmental state' enhances our understanding of Japan's economic miracle as well as that of other countries that chose to follow Japan's example. But it is equally apparent that it is inadequate in facilitating a full comprehension of that phenomenon, insofar as it fails to specify the outward-oriented nature of Japan's economic strategy and, more importantly, the geopolitical context that led to the strategy's establishment and contributed as well to its success. By extension, the same comment applies to the cases of the economic miracles of Korea and Taiwan, which self-consciously sought to replicate Japan's experience.

A review of the economic miracles of Japan, Taiwan, and Korea reveals four common features among them that need to be specified beyond what the model of the developmental state incorporates. First, the economic breakthrough by way of fast-speed growth that led to their economic miracle status followed, and did not precede, the turn of these states to export-oriented strategies for economic growth. On the basis of the evidence presented above, it would be difficult to argue that this is merely a case of correlation. Rather, the evidence makes for a convincing case of cause (export orientation) and effect (high growth rates). In all the three instances, difficult economic circumstances made for a conscious decision to change economic strategy to export promotion in order to advance growth.

---

[63] Seymour Martin Lipset, 'Social Requisites of Democracy: Economic Development and Political Legitimacy', *American Political Science Review*, 53, 1 (May 1959), 69–105; Karl W. Deutsch, 'Social Mobilization and Political Development', ibid., 55, 3 (September 1961).

Second, the switch to an export-oriented strategy took place either under American dictation (Japan) or American pressure (Korea and Taiwan). In Japan, the US as the Occupation power directly enforced the export-oriented strategy; in Korea and Taiwan, the US deliberately used the dependence of these states on American aid as leverage to force the change in strategy.

Third, the US played a key role in the success of the export-oriented strategies of the three states by its willingness to open its market for their exports. The success of any export-oriented strategy is, no doubt, partly a function of the national effort to make the necessary structural adjustment in the local economy, society, and polity. However, it is also significantly dependent on the international economy's openness to receive the exports. In the circumstance of the time, American readiness to let in exports, military and non-military, from Japan, Korea, and Taiwan was crucial to the success of the change by these states to the export-oriented strategy.

Fourth, the willingness on the part of the US to receive such exports was not inspired by charity or altruism, but was part of the considered American geopolitical strategy for the containment of the Soviet Union.[64] In this effort, preventing Japan, with its great industrial strength, from slipping into the Soviet orbit was a foremost concern. The concern for Korea and Taiwan was derivative in that the security of these two states was seen as linked to that of Japan. Such derivative concern was, of course, not limited to them but applied also to quite a few other countries in Southeast Asia.

---

[64] In a sharp turn subsequently to a more radical orientation, Johnson has highlighted the importance of the readiness of the US, for geopolitical reasons, to receive the industrial exports from East Asia. Indeed, he holds the singleminded American obsession with animosity toward, and containment of, the Soviet Union as responsible, in a 'blowback' effect, for hollowing out the American industrial economy through welcoming East Asian exports. See Chalmers Johnson, *Blowback*, 32, 176–7, 195, 217–18, 223. However, this change in his views is less well known, and it is the original notion of the developmental state that succeeded in acquiring iconic status in development studies.

Chapter 9

THE SOUTHEAST ASIAN EMULATORS

The accomplishment of an economic miracle by Japan through an export-propelled strategy was understandably regarded as an anomaly initially. That may have been so either because the Japanese were considered culturally unique, or because Japan was before the war already a developed country and the miracle merely represented the post-war recovery of a major industrial power. But when Korea and Taiwan plus Hong Kong and Singapore—as the Four Dragons, or the Gang of Four (G-4), or the East Asian Tigers—joined Japan with their own economic miracles, the export-propelled growth strategy could no longer be dismissed as an anomaly. Instead, it was now elevated to the status of a new model of economic growth that was believed to be a necessary recipe for countries seeking rapid development.

Dissent on Export-Propelled Growth

Even as the Asian Tigers were demonstrating the effectiveness of the export-propelled growth model, however, there emerged warnings early on from many experts that the model, by virtue of having been successfully implemented by a small group of countries, was no longer feasible for other LDCs. For such experts, it was not simply that other LDCs lacked the comparable initial conditions that had existed in Japan, Korea, and Taiwan, such as greater economic equality through effective land reform, or widespread education, especially at the primary level, or a hard state, or even Confucian cultural values. These were, no doubt, important considerations, but the key obstacle for them was that there were strict limits to the absorptive capacity of the developed countries for the labour-intensive, low-technology exports from an ever-expanding circle of LDCs.

Systematically employing the method of comparative *statics*, William Cline did a rigorous quantitative analysis of export data, with 1976 as the base. He demonstrated that 'a generalized move to the G-4 export strategy' was just not feasible because 'the bulk of the market would be vulnerable to closure of access because of high import penetration.' The markets of the developed countries would simply be 'oversaturated with LDC supplies under the East Asian export model'. In Cline's view, 'even if only a limited number of NICs were to follow the G-4 model, there could be substantial risk of protectionist response.' Accordingly, he held that 'it would be inadvisable for authorities in developing countries to rely in their long-term plans upon the same kind of export results that have been obtained by the four East Asian countries.' The G-4 were just lucky in that they 'took advantage of the open-economy strategy before the export field became crowded by competition from other developing countries, and did so when the world economy was in a phase of prolonged buoyancy'.[1] Cline thus gave effective expression to a new 'export pessimism' in the face of a rising protectionism in the West. Similarly, Andre Gunder Frank argued that, in Hagen Koo's words, 'the very success of these [G-4] countries in the zero-sum world of international trade eliminated the possibility of similar successes elsewhere.'[2] Some highly respected specialists on East Asia also joined in this scepticism about the utility of the export-propelled growth strategy, though for different reasons.

Robert Wade emphasized the contingent external aspects of strategic location and geopolitical importance in the success of Japan, Korea, and Taiwan. He averred that 'to the extent these factors are different at other times and places, this throws doubt on the possibilities for other countries at other times to emulate East Asian success.'[3] On the other hand, for Chalmers Johnson, the originator

[1] William R. Cline, 'Can the East Asian Model of Development be Generalized?', *World Development*, 10, 2 (1982), reprinted in Charles K. Wilber (ed.), *The Political Economy of Development and Underdevelopment* (New York: Random House, 1988), 282–97.

[2] Hagen Koo, 'The Interplay of State, Social Class, and World System in East Asian Development: The Cases of South Korea and Taiwan', in Frederic C. Deyo (ed.), *The Political Economy of the New Asian Industrialism*, 169.

[3] Robert Wade, *Governing the Market*, 346.

of the concept of the 'developmental state', it was the particular internal set-up within these states that held the key to their success. 'Superficially,' he thought, 'it would be possible to argue that to the extent that the model implies export-oriented growth, its future prospects are poor because changes in the international environment have lowered the chances for dramatic expansions of exports.' But he rejected the notion that 'the environment is the main determining factor in the model'. Rather, it was his case that the developmental states have been, by their internal constitution, adept at adaptation to any environment, and therefore 'the capitalist developmental states will still outperform the others'. At the heart of the issue was the fact that 'they have discovered ways to surmount the rigidities of zero-sum domestic competition without falling into the trap of authoritarian displacement of the market and private enterprise.'[4]

Southeast Asia's Derivative Geopolitical Importance

Many of the LDCs may have been persuaded by this new generalized export pessimism, but some were not. Some of the states for which the model of the Asian Tigers had a considerable 'demonstration effect' were their neighbours in Southeast Asia, several of whom were organized in the regional bloc of ASEAN (Association of Southeast Asian Nations). As James, Naya, and Meier state: 'Other Asian developing countries began to follow the lead of the NICs.' They add, referring to the four major members of ASEAN, that is, Indonesia, Malaysia, Philippines, and Thailand: 'Surprisingly, a second group of Asian developing countries—the ASEAN-4—deliberately chose to become more export oriented in the 1970s.'[5] Focusing on Indonesia, Malaysia, and Thailand alone, Putzel confirms: 'All three Southeast Asian countries attempted to follow the tigers in promoting and encouraging the development of export-oriented production.'[6]

[4] Chalmers Johnson, 'Political Institutions and Economic Performance: The Government-Business Relationship in Japan, South Korea, and Taiwan', in Deyo (ed.), The Political Economy of the New Asian Industrialism, 164.

[5] William E. James, Seiji Naya, and Gerald M. Meier, Asian Development, 23, 207.

[6] James Putzel, 'Developmental States and Crony Capitalists', in Pietro P. Masina (ed.), Rethinking Development in East Asia: From Illusory Miracle to Economic Crisis (Richmond, Surrey, UK: Curzon Press, 2002), 161–88.

The connection between Southeast Asian countries and the model of the Asian Tigers is deeper than the latter's demonstration effect. Southeast Asia had been seen as geopolitically important in the security perceptions of the US because of the perceived intrinsic linkage of the region with the military and economic security of Japan. As Bowie and Unger maintain: 'The United States, as the regionally dominant power, nurtured Japan's post-war take-off and linked it to Southeast Asia's markets and raw materials, thereby shaping many aspects of Southeast Asia's development.... Thus, the economic choices of Southeast Asian decision-makers ought to be seen, in the first instance, as responses to the security concerns and geopolitical considerations of the United States and their regional consequences.'[7]

The recognition of the linkage of Southeast Asia to Japan's economic and political future had occurred quite early in the post-war period after the US had decided to adopt the course of containment against the Soviet Union. The intellectual father of containment policy and director of the State Department's Policy Planning Staff (PPS), George Kennan, had in an October 1947 document (PPS/10) underlined the consequences that may be expected for Japan in the case of the loss of its markets and the sources of its raw materials in Asia. He had noted that 'Japan faces, even in the best of circumstances, an economic problem of extremely serious dimensions,' and had gone on to highlight the importance of Southeast Asia for Japan. Meanwhile, one of his staff members, James Paton Davies, informed a conference of American diplomats in June 1948 that the US was 'tying Southeast Asia in as a regional block against Communism, just as we are trying to build up in Europe a regional organization against Communism and would like to do so in the Middle and Near East.'[8]

Kennan himself focused particularly on Indonesia, holding it to be 'the most critical issue of the moment in our struggle with the Kremlin'. He was concerned that if it fell to communism, it may 'lead

---

[7] Alasdair Bowie and Danny Unger, *The Politics of Open Economies: Indonesia, Malaysia, the Philippines, and Thailand* (Cambridge: Cambridge University Press, 1997), 26.

[8] Wilson D. Miscamble, *George F. Kennan and the Making of American Foreign Policy, 1947–1950*, 273–5.

to communist denial of our east-west global communications'. In what would later come to be described as the domino theory, he maintained that 'it would only be a matter of time before the infection would sweep westward through the continent to Burma, India, and Pakistan.' After the communist revolution in China, Southeast Asia's strategic importance to the future of Japan emerged even stronger for Kennan and Davies.[9] Together they developed a study on 'United States Policy Toward Southeast Asia' (PPS/51), the document which is said to have 'formed the basis of Asian containment doctrine for the next two decades'.[10]

Subsequently, in 1954, the US created the military alliance of the Southeast Asia Treaty Organization (SEATO) to safeguard the region against the threat of communism in the larger interest of Japan's security. For the same reason, it also became involved in the Vietnam War during the 1960s and early 1970s. In addition, the US developed bilateral security agreements with the Philippines and Thailand, and set up military bases there.

Japan's Role in the Development of Southeast Asia

Despite American endeavours to court Indonesia's President Sukarno, the country had veered in the 1960s toward a de facto alliance with China. What is more, the Communist Party of Indonesia began exercising increasing, perhaps decisive, influence in Sukarno's government. Fearing a life-or-death struggle with the communists, Indonesia's military carried out in 1965, much to the relief of the US, a successful putsch and seized power. In the aftermath of the seizure of power, Indonesia's Communist Party was crushed and hundreds of thousands of rural inhabitants suspected of being the party's cadres and supporters were slaughtered. These events marked a dramatic rupture in the post-Independence political history of the country. Following the immense political upheaval, General Suharto installed the New Order regime in Indonesia. Not long after, ASEAN was formed as a multilateral regional organization with the enthusiastic support of the US.

---

[9] Ibid., 273–5.
[10] Michael Schaller, *The American Occupation of Japan*, 159.

To recover from the economic disaster that had been left behind by the previous government, the new regime in Indonesia adopted, on the advice of the team of economic technocrats known as the 'Berkeley mafia', a liberal economic policy, marked by greater openness to the world economy. In effect, the new government enacted a virtual structural adjustment programme, before that term came into vogue in the 1980s to describe IMF-imposed economic restructuring in the LDCs. The turn to economic openness in Indonesia, as part of a political rupture, is not matched for its high drama among the other ASEAN countries. Fighting a war against the communists in Vietnam, the US was, however, gratified by the developments in Indonesia, and it encouraged Japan to extend substantial economic aid and cooperation to the new regime.

Subsequently, as the US proclaimed the Nixon doctrine in 1971 in an effort to bring its overseas commitments into balance with its capabilities, it seemingly devolved upon Japan a bigger role more generally in the region. It now favoured Japan assuming a larger burden in providing foreign aid to the countries of the region. Japan may have been inclined in that direction in any case in order to advance its own economic and geopolitical interests. Over the period 1964–73, Japan extended official development assistance (ODA) in the amount of $1,055 million to Indonesia (in the main, after the military coup). Besides, it provided $619 million to the other members of the ASEAN Four. Subsequently, Japanese ODA expanded vastly, with Japan pouring billions of dollars of foreign aid into the region. During 1987-91 alone, Japan provided $18,885 million in ODA to the four major ASEAN countries. Close to half went to Indonesia ($8,212 million), with Malaysia, the Philippines, and Thailand receiving $2,001 million, $4,599 million and $4,073 million, respectively. Japan's contribution was more than half of all aid received by each of them—Indonesia (51 per cent), Malaysia (78 per cent), the Philippines (51 per cent), and Thailand (51 per cent). The US had only a minor role in foreign aid to these countries in this period.[11]

Not surprisingly, the flag of Japanese foreign aid was accompanied by massive amounts of Japanese foreign investment. The regional networks of Japanese firms, in what had been at one time regarded as part of the Greater East Asian Co-Prosperity Sphere, facilitated the

[11] Bowie and Unger, *The Politics of Open Economies*, 41.

relocation of 'sunset' industries from Japan to Southeast Asia. Soon, Korea and Taiwan joined Japan in similarly investing in the region. As K. S. Jomo pointed out: 'Industrial relocation within the East Asian region contributed tremendously to the export-oriented manufacturing boom in the Southeast Asian HPAEs [High-Performing Asian Economies] for almost a decade beginning in the mid-1980s.'[12] Indeed, foreign investment driving the exports of manufactured goods can be considered to be a distinctive characteristic of the development model in Southeast Asia, differentiating it from the Northeast Asian model, in which there had been only limited reliance on foreign investment. Foreign direct investment was instrumental in making the ASEAN Four into powerful exporting states, but the dominant fact remains that they were, in the first instance, increasingly open to integration into the international economy, and to facilitating such investment and encouraging the export of goods produced by it.

Following the Miracle Economies

Indonesia, Malaysia, the Philippines, and Thailand as the most populous members of the original ASEAN have often been referred to as the ASEAN Four. The demonstration effect of the model of the East Asian miracle economies on all of them was profound, though it is difficult to make a straightforward cause-and-effect case to that effect. However, the long-term trend among all the ASEAN Four toward greater openness is clear, notwithstanding the zigzags and detours for a variety of reasons that differed from one country to the next. Thailand and Malaysia, of course, had already traditionally been more outward-oriented economies. In their case, the impact of the East Asian model was to fortify the orientation in favour of openness and to emphasize the export of manufactured goods rather than to simply continue to focus on commodity exports. While all four were attracted and eager to implement the East Asian model, they were not strictly examples of 'the developmental state' as conceptualized after the experience of Northeast Asia. For them, economic growth, though crucially important, could not be an

[12] K.S. Jomo, 'Rethinking the Role of Government Policy in Southeast Asia', in Joseph E. Stiglitz and Shahid Yusuf (eds), *Rethinking the Asian Miracle*, 463.

all-determining 'hegemonic project'; there were other competing social and economic priorities as well. Lacking the ethnic and cultural homogeneity and the greater social and economic equality of the Northeast Asian states, the decision-makers in the ASEAN Four faced serious social and political problems. As a consequence, industrial policy 'was much less coherently developed and applied in the Southeast Asian countries than in Northeast Asia'.[13] However, the role of the state varied; it was decisive in Indonesia and Malaysia, substantial in Thailand, particularly in assuring macroeconomic stability, and the weakest in the Philippines.

The decision-makers in Southeast Asia functioned under some severe handicaps. They had to make economic policy in the context of being beset by serious problems of ethnic diversity (Malaysia and Indonesia), political instability because of frequent disruptions either by popular movements or military interventions (Thailand), and dominance by powerful interest groups in society with their own vested economic interests (the Philippines). As a result, the strategy of export-propelled growth was not always vigorously or consistently followed, or it got undermined at times in the course of implementation. There were often strong nationalist temptations that led to episodes of misdirected import-substitution industrialization, especially in the context of windfall gains from the OPEC oil price hikes (Indonesia and Malaysia). There were equally strong compulsions of distributive justice on behalf of large indigenous populations, which undermined the cause of economic efficiency (Malaysia and Indonesia). At times, infirmities of the polity also led to 'crony capitalism' and the plunder of the state (the Philippines, and later, Indonesia).

Still, the ASEAN Four are recognized as having had a higher degree of openness to the international economy than most other LDCs. Significantly, 'the ASEAN Four in the 1960s and 1970s were, to greater or lesser degrees, practising the orthodoxy of the 1980s and 1990s.'[14] They became progressively more open with greater experience and did not always have to wait for an economic crisis in order to liberalize. Interestingly, they maintained their high degree of openness from the early 1970s onwards, despite the interruptions from time to time by episodes of import-substitution industrialization and the considerable turmoil in the international economy (given the

---

[13] Putzel, 'Developmental States and Crony Capitalists', 176.

[14] Bowie and Unger, *The Politics of Open Economies*, 1.

oil price hikes, fluctuations in commodity prices, high inflation rates, and the debt crisis). The ASEAN Four have been open not just in terms of exports, but more generally in regard to foreign trade and also, rather distinctively from the Northeast Asian states, in respect of foreign investment. Their high degree of integration into the international economy is evident in the large expansion of their exports, the transformation in the nature of the goods exported, and the vast amounts of foreign investment they have received.

Though not matching the performance of the Northeast Asian tigers, exports by the ASEAN Four saw considerable expansion, as a result of emulating the model of the tigers. As a proportion of GDP, exports were nearly three to four times higher in 2000, compared to 1970 (Table 9.1). The export structure in 2000 stood greatly

Table 9.1: Exports as Per cent of GDP

	1970	1980	1990	2000
Indonesia	13.45	34.18	25.33	38.55
Malaysia	41.41	56.69	74.54	125.49
Philippines	21.58	23.57	27.52	56.30
Thailand	14.99	24.11	34.13	67.04

Source: World Development Indicators.

changed in comparison with the situation in 1970, with manufactured exports constituting 57 per cent, 80 per cent, 92 per cent, and 76 per cent of merchandise exports for Indonesia, Malaysia, the Philippines, and Thailand (Table 9.2). In 1970, manufactured exports had been relatively of little importance, amounting to less than 10 per cent of merchandise exports. Especially abysmal was the figure of 1.1 per cent in the case of Indonesia. Particularly noteworthy is the significant place occupied in 2000 by high technology exports, with their proportion in merchandise exports being nearly 60 per cent in the case of Malaysia and the Philippines, and 16 per cent and 32 per cent for Indonesia and Thailand, respectively (Table 9.2). There is merit, then, in the observation that 'the ASEAN Four have demonstrated considerable success at rapidly increasing their production and changing the structure of their economies.'[15] The process was aided greatly, of course, by the massive foreign investments in their

[15] Ibid., 3.

Table 9.2: Manufactured Exports as Per cent of Merchandise Exports

	1970	1980	1990	2000*
Indonesia	1.1	2	46	57 (16)
Malaysia	8.2	19	49	80 (59)
Philippines	6.3	37	69	92 (59)
Thailand	5.2	29	80	76 (32)

*Figures in parentheses are for High Technology Exports as Per Cent of Manufactured Exports.
Source: The figures for 1970 are from William E. James, Seiji Naya, and Gerald M. Meier, *Asian Development: Economic Success and Policy Lessons* (Madison, WI: University of Wisconsin Press, 1989), 40. The figures for 1980, 1990, and 2000 are from the World Bank, *World Development Report 1983*, 166–7, *World Development Report 1992*, 248–9, and *World Development Report 2003*, 240–1, respectively.

economies. The ASEAN Four together received over $130 billion in FDI net inflows in the three decades from 1971 to 2000. Malaysia received the largest amount ($53 billion), followed by Thailand ($41 billion), Indonesia ($21 billion), and the Philippines ($16 billion) (see Table 9.3).

Table 9.3: Cumulative FDI Net Inflows (Current US$ Million)

	1971–1980	1981–1990	1991–2000	Total
Indonesia	2,053	4,176	14,938	21,167
Malaysia	4,103	11,048	38,298	53,449
Philippines	489	2,777	12,707	15,973
Thailand	882	7,336	32,490	40,708

Source: Based on World Development Indicators.

What is impressive is that the ASEAN Four, barring the Philippines—considered the laggard or outlier among them—have demonstrated a strong economic performance.[16] In the quarter-century from 1971 to 1995, the economies of Indonesia, Malaysia, and Thailand grew at rates of over 7 per cent, their average rates of GDP growth being 7.29 per cent, 7.45 per cent, and 7.64 per cent, respectively (see Table 7.2). The growth rate for the Philippines at 3.53 per cent was half that of the other three members of the

[16] Ibid., 1.

ASEAN Four. The financial contagion that struck East and Southeast Asia in 1997 affected the growth rates adversely for all of them during the last half-decade of the twentieth century.

The strong economic performance of the ASEAN Four is reflected in the increase in their per capita incomes. GDP per capita at constant prices increased from 1970 to 2000 by 3.34 times for Indonesia, 3.50 times for Malaysia, and 3.73 times for Thailand. Compare these figures with those for India and Pakistan, where per capita GDP increased by 2.11 times and 1.88 times, respectively. Again, the Philippines lagged behind the others among the ASEAN Four, with per capita GDP having increased by only 1.31 times. The ASEAN Four have, amazingly, exited from or remained out of the low-income-category country, with Malaysia having made it into the upper middle income category. (The experience of Vietnam in terms of better growth, after its opening to the world economy, is not taken into account here since it is recent.) The strong economic performance is manifest in the considerable change in their structure of production and employment, as is evident in Tables 9.4A and 9.4B.

Table 9.4A: Share of Agriculture and Manufacturing in GDP (Per cent)

	Indonesia			Malaysia			Thailand		
	1965	*1980*	*1996*	*1965*	*1980*	*1996*	*1965*	*1980*	*1996*
Agri.	51.0	24.8	16.3	16.0	22.9	12.7	27.0	23.2	10.4
Mfg.	8.0	11.6	25.2	14.0	19.6	34.5	19.0	21.5	29.3

Table 9.4B: Share of Agriculture and Manufacturing in Employment (Per cent)

	Indonesia			Malaysia			Thailand		
	1965	*1980*	*1996*	*1965*	*1980*	*1996*	*1965*	*1980*	*1996*
Agri.	75.0	55.9	44.0	63.0	37.2	16.8	84.0	70.8	40.4
Mfg.	8.0	9.1	12.6	12.0	15.5	27.0	4.0	7.9	16.5

Source: James Putzel, 'Developmental States and Crony Capitalists', in Masina (ed.), *Rethinking Development in East Asia*, 161–88.

Some have referred to the Southeast Asian countries as quasi-NICs in the light of their superior economic performance.[17] In its opus on the East Asian miracle, the World Bank characterized Indonesia, Malaysia, and Thailand (pointedly leaving out the Philippines) as

[17] James, Naya and Meier, *Asian Development*, 217.

High-Performing Asian Economies [HPAEs], alongside Japan and the Gang of Four, and included them under the category of *Newly Industrializing Economies* [NIEs].[18] Indeed, the World Bank has regarded the Southeast Asian states as better exemplars, rather than the Northeast Asian states, for the other LDCs. This is so in view of the fact that most LDCs share many of the social and political features that characterize Southeast Asian states. Among these features are: the lack of state autonomy and the weak state capacity compared to the Northeast Asian Tigers; the existence of ethnic and cultural diversity; the lower level of state interventionism; the relative absence of Confucianism; and the dependence on foreign investment for economic growth in Southeast Asia.[19] Others have concurred with this view of the World Bank.[20]

Even if lacking the dramatic proportions of the record displayed by Korea and Taiwan, the more open economies of Southeast Asia testify to the superior economic performance that is possible under an export-propelled growth strategy as compared to, say, the more inward-oriented economies of South Asia. Not to be ignored, however, in this better performance is the fact that the region had the geopolitical benefit of having been provided the security umbrella, political patronage, and economic largesse by the US, directly or indirectly. This is an aspect that the World Bank has tended to overlook through its excessively narrow preoccupation with economic indicators alone. Compared to the economies of South Asia, the economies of Southeast Asia performed far better, thanks to their decision-makers choosing to ignore the advice of academics who were convinced of the case for export pessimism. However, openness is no panacea as the case of the Philippines well illustrates; it cannot entirely compensate for the corrosive effects of predation by political and state elites, the weakness of the state, and the mismanagement of macroeconomic policy.

Notwithstanding the outstanding contribution that the export-oriented strategy made to economic growth, and the lifting of millions of people out of poverty, the strategy was somewhat tarnished by the contagion of the financial crisis that struck the region in 1997 and 1998. However, while it caused an awful lot of economic and social pain to the populace, the crisis proved to be short-lived; by 1999,

---

[18] World Bank, *The East Asian Miracle: Economic Growth and Public Policy* (New York: Oxford University Press, 1993).

[19] Ibid., 7.

[20] Bowie and Unger, *The Politics of Open Economies*, 9.

it had abated.[21] The region recovered quickly from it and has escaped, except for Indonesia, from falling into the low income category, which continues to be the lot of most of the countries of South Asia.

Conclusions

The Southeast Asia region has been geopolitically important to the US because of the latter's security interests in Japan and the region's own proximity to China. To counter the threat of communism, the US threw a security umbrella over the region, thus providing an environment of international security within which economic growth could take place. In that sense, geopolitics is not to be underestimated in the economic development of the region. Moreover, the US encouraged Japan to provide foreign aid, and to assume a more active role in the region's economic development.

By their spectacular performance, the miracle economies of Northeast Asia had a decided demonstration effect on the Southeast Asian countries, giving rise to emulation by the latter, with a focus on exports of manufactured goods. The emulation did not, however, follow a straight and narrow path. Rather, there were many twists and turns in policy. However, the ultimate result of greater openness of the economies of the ASEAN Four, as evidenced by the role of exports and foreign investment in their economic profiles, is clear. Beyond the demonstration effect, the Northeast Asian economies played a direct economic role in the economic advance of Southeast Asia through foreign investment. Compared to the economies of South Asia, the economies of Southeast Asia (barring the Philippines) performed much better, thanks to their decision-makers ignoring the advice of academics who were persuaded by export pessimism.

Since the ASEAN Four followed chronologically as imitators of the model of the miracle economies of Northeast Asia, though not in a straight line, it would seem legitimate to see their emulation as having a causal relationship to their subsequent strong economic performance in Indonesia, Malaysia, and Thailand. However, there is no more decisive illustration of this proposition than the experience of China, where the shift to an export-oriented strategy and the extension of a welcoming open door to foreign investment preceded the explosive growth in its foreign trade and GDP during the 1980s and 1990s.

[21] World Bank, *Rethinking the East Asian Miracle*, Joseph E. Stiglitz and Shahid Yusuf (eds), 3–4, 82.

Chapter 10

CHINA'S ECONOMIC MIRACLE

The rise of the miracle economies of Japan, Taiwan, and South Korea was of momentous significance not only for these states themselves but for others as well, for they became a model for the latter. The rise of these miracle economies demonstrated the importance of the shift to the strategy of outward orientation, which in these particular cases had clearly preceded their rise to the status of great trading nations and their transformation into developed countries. Their economic success testified to the strong element of a causal relationship, and not merely a correlation, between an export-oriented strategy and economic growth. Their experience, however, also suggests that the relationship between strategy and growth is not simply an economic one. Rather, it is one in which geopolitics is strongly and intimately implicated. For, the success of the strategy in Japan, Taiwan, and South Korea ultimately rested on the geopolitical posture of the US. Not only did the US press, even coerce, for the switch to the export-oriented strategy, but it was also willing, for larger geopolitical reasons, to receive the increased exports from these economies after the change in their economic strategy. Geopolitics was thus an essential and effective midwife in the economic transformation of these Northeast Asian states.

In the last two decades of the twentieth century, China enacted another economic miracle by its self-transformation from a slow-growth economy, not much different from those of South Asia, to a great trading nation and a major economic power. How do the two propositions drawn from the experience of the Northeast Asian states—(1) the export-propelled strategy of economic growth as the cause of the economic miracle; and (2) the key role of geopolitics in the strategy's success—stand up against the Chinese experience? The argument of this chapter is precisely about the robustness of these two propositions. Accordingly, this chapter first looks at China's economic transformation as a result of policy change, and then at the role of geopolitics in it.

China's Fast-Track Economic Transformation

China was a late imitator of the East Asian model, beginning its economic reforms toward that end not until as late as 1978. In shifting to the export-oriented growth strategy, China rejected the new 'export pessimism' that had arisen, in the wake of the rapid economic rise of Japan and the Gang of Four, to discourage other states from following their path in view of the growth of protectionism in the West. China's rejection of the new export pessimism is of extreme importance. For, China is no ordinary LDC. Its population of about one-and-a-quarter billion today is about a quarter of the combined population of the LDCs; around the time of the policy shift in 1978, its population of nearly one billion was about 30 per cent of the total for the developing countries.[1] The resort by China to the export-propelled growth strategy is, then, equivalent to dozens of LDCs simultaneously adopting that strategy. By the same token, countries that chose to forgo shifting to an outward-oriented strategy at that time missed out on an enormously beneficial opportunity that China so eagerly seized. Such countries also made a subsequent similar change harder for themselves since China had already pre-empted markets that could otherwise have been theirs.

Successive Reforms and Economic Transformation

China, however, did not implement the change to an export-oriented strategy wholesale as part of some grand strategic plan. Rather, it began by opening in 1978 a small wedge in the inherited monolithic structure of centralized planning of a long-standing communist state through making legitimate some limited participation in the market.[2] China did so by two small and tentative but, in retrospect, momentous

[1] European Commission, *European Social Statistics: Demography* (Luxembourg: 2000), 39.

[2] John McMillan and Barry Naughton, 'How to Reform a Planned Economy: Lessons from China', in Ross Garnaut and Yiping Huang (eds), *Growth Without Miracles: Readings on the Chinese Economy in the Era of Reform* (Oxford: Oxford University Press, 2001), 459–73.

steps. One, while gradually freeing up the market for agricultural commodities, China introduced some elements of personal property rights in agriculture. It did this through partial de-collectivization, whereby responsibility for production was invested in the household or close to the household, rather than in the commune as before, along with part of the output now allowed to be sold in the open market. Two, it endorsed, though not unambiguously, engagement with the world economy by 'expanding economic cooperation on terms of equality and mutual benefit with other countries on the basis of self-reliance, striving to adopt the world's advanced technologies and equipment'.[3]

In 1979, China additionally introduced reforms to support the export of manufactures; and, in a major shift from past policy, it allowed the entry of foreign investment.[4] This was a significant departure from its traditional ideological orthodoxy. For, until then, China had held its policy of economic self-reliance as the ideal model for the developing world. At that time, China and its radical supporters abroad had attacked other countries for their export and capital dependency on an exploitative capitalist world system, as it would allegedly only deepen their underdevelopment through intensifying social and economic pauperization, marginalization, and polarization. Now, however, breaking free from earlier ideological requirements, China made rapid economic growth the *hegemonic project* as is characteristic of the 'developmental state'. It has been correctly observed that 'rapid economic growth does not proceed unless the view is widely held in society that it is a prime objective. Growth attained this status in 1978, and has retained it since.'[5]

The market incentives introduced by China proved to be a potent stimulus to agricultural production and exports. The injection of the small wedge of the market generated increasingly intense pressures for incrementally widening the wedge more and more until the system came to be greatly transformed. The reforms triggered 'first,

[3] Geoff Raby, 'The "Neither This Nor That", Economy', and Dwight Perkins, 'Completing China's Move to the Market', in Garnaut and Huang (eds), *Growth Without Miracles*, 19–35 and 36–53.

[4] Perkins, 'Completing China's Move to the Market', 42.

[5] Ross Garnaut, 'Twenty Years of Economic Reform and Structural Change in the Chinese Economy', in Garnaut and Huang (eds), *Growth Without Miracles*, 16.

massive entry of non-state firms; second, a dramatic increase in competition, both among state firms and between state and non-state firms; and, third, improvements in the performance of state-owned firms resulting from state-imposed market-like incentives'.[6] In 1982, the party gave ideological support for limited markets.[7] Export subsidies were provided and special economic zones for export processing were established so that exporters, both foreign and local, would not have to face bureaucratic hassles. In 1985, China devalued its currency drastically from 1.7 yuan to the US dollar, fixed in 1981, to 2.9 to the dollar, and then again in 1990 to 4.8 to the dollar. The resulting total increase in the value of the dollar of over 182 per cent relative to the yuan was more than twice the 87 per cent rise in retail prices in China. The impact was immense. As Perkins noted, 'foreign trade responded to these incentives in dramatic fashion.... A Soviet-style economy geared to producing low quality goods for a captive domestic market was suddenly competing head-to-head with its East Asian neighbours, the most dynamic exporters of manufactured goods in the world.'[8]

In 1988, China launched the coastal development strategy in its drive to 'join the world division of labour according to its comparative advantage in labour-intensive manufactures, permitting international markets to determine the pattern of production and exports',[9] rather than having the planning authorities shape that pattern through a national plan. The opening up of the economy expanded progressively, and further reforms in foreign trade followed in 1990. The successive waves of reforms to open up the economy in terms of both foreign trade and foreign capital resulted in a stunning growth in capital inflows and, substantially as a consequence of that, in exports. That, in turn, has made China a major player in the international economy and a major economic power.

The Rise of China as a Great Exporting Power

The shift to an export-oriented growth strategy detonated an explosive growth in China's exports of goods and services. Between

---

[6] McMillan and Naughton, 'How to Reform a Planned Economy', 460.

[7] Raby, 'The "Neither This Nor That" Economy', 25.

[8] Perkins, 'Completing China's Move to the Market', 42.

[9] Raby, 'The "Neither This Nor That" Economy', 31.

1978 and 2000, such exports at constant 1995 US dollars grew by 25 times from $9,631 million to $239,006 million (see Table 10.1). The amazing impact of the strategy was immediately visible in the first two years of the reforms between 1978 and 1980, when exports tripled; the growth rates in 1979 and 1980 were extraordinarily high at 73.84 per cent and 65.78 per cent respectively. Over the two decades between 1981 and 2000, China's exports expanded at an average annual rate of 16.66 per cent (in particular years the decline in the growth rate, worked out on the basis of US dollars, is often the temporary result of devaluation). The share of exports in GDP increased more than five and one-half times from 4.60 per cent in 1978 to over 25 per cent in 2000, even as the GDP underwent a vast expansion. China's exports grew at a rate much higher than the growth rate for GDP, almost three-quarters higher. China's merchandise exports to the US alone amounted to $54,359 million (out of total exports of $266,140 million) in 2001 compared to a mere $325 million (out of total exports of $8,687 million) in 1978.[10]

As a consequence of the fantastic growth in its exports, China has established itself as a major economic power on the international scene, increasing its share of world exports from 0.72 per cent in 1978 to 3.91 per cent in 2000 (see Table 10.2). By way of contrast to China's experience after the adoption of the export-propelled growth strategy, India's exports increased only a little over five times from $10,614 million in 1978 (a level higher than China's in that year) to $56,484 million in 2000. The change in the share of exports in India's GDP was from 6.15 per cent to about 13.95 per cent—a level that was about half that of China's. Again, India's annual growth rate in exports over the period 1981–2000 was also, at 8.58 per cent, about half that of China's.

Particularly noteworthy is the change in the composition of exports. When China first started its export-oriented strategy in 1978, its leadership had counted on the expansion of exports of oil, minerals, and agricultural commodities. In fact, over the years, China has seen a drastic shift from the export of such primary commodities to manufactured goods, which in 2000 constituted 87.1 per cent of its exports (Table 10.3). Indeed, China has increasingly become an industrial workshop to the world, importing raw materials and components and processing them into manufactured goods. In this

---

[10] IMF, *Direction of Trade Statistics Yearbook* (1982 and 2002).

Table 10.1: Exports of Goods and Services, FDI Inflows and GDP: China

Year	Exports (1995 US$) Million	Exports Growth Rate %	Exports % of GDP	FDI Net (Current US$) Million	FDI Net % of GDP	GDP (1995 US$) Billion	GDP Growth Rate %
1978	9,631	–	4.60	–	–	145	10.21
1979	16,742	73.84	6.35	–	–	155	7.29
1980	27,755	65.78	7.61	–	–	164	5.96
1981	31,935	15.06	8.56	0	0.00	174	5.75
1982	32,872	2.93	8.90	430	0.21	191	9.57
1983	33,644	2.35	8.26	636	0.28	211	10.85
1984	41,422	23.12	9.42	1,258	0.49	243	15.23
1985	41,004	-1.01	9.99	1,659	0.54	274	12.59
1986	46,259	12.82	11.83	1,875	0.63	298	8.55
1987	53,278	15.17	13.65	2,314	0.86	331	11.18
1988	61,013	14.52	13.06	3,194	1.04	366	10.67
1989	68,184	11.75	12.73	3,393	0.99	381	4.12
1990	84,877	24.48	17.53	3,487	0.98	396	3.99
1991	99,039	16.69	19.43	4,366	1.16	433	9.19
1992	113,954	15.06	19.50	11,156	2.67	495	14.27
1993	123,504	8.38	17.08	27,515	6.37	561	13.54
1994	154,072	24.75	25.32	33,787	6.23	634	12.83
1995	167,960	9.01	23.99	35,849	5.12	700	10.53
1996	120,662	-28.16	21.03	40,180	4.92	767	9.58
1997	148,326	22.93	23.07	44,237	4.92	835	8.84
1998	158,950	7.16	21.92	43,751	4.62	900	7.80
1999	181,009	13.88	22.04	38,753	3.91	964	7.05
2000	239,006	32.04	25.89	38,399	3.56	1,040	7.94

Source: World Development Indicators.

Table 10.2: China's Share of World Exports (Million US$)

Year	World Exports	China's Exports	China's Share %
1975	805,600	5,798	0.72
1978	1,203,500	8,687	0.72
1980	1,869,300	17,087	0.91
1985	1,812,700	27,329	1.51
1990	3,330,300	64,500	1.94
1995	5,071,000	148,955	2.94
2000	6,368,700	249,195	3.91

Source: IMF, *Direction of Trade Statistics Yearbook* (various years).

Table 10.3: China's Exports: Market Share and Structure

Product	1985	1990	1995	2000
I. Market Share	1.6	2.8	4.8	6.1
1. Primary Products	2.4	2.6	2.5	2.3
2. Manufactures based on Natural Resources	1.1	1.3	2.1	2.7
3. Manufactures not based on Natural Resources	1.5	3.4	6.1	7.8
a. Low Technology	4.5	9.1	15.5	18.7
b. Medium Technology	0.4	1.4	2.6	3.6
c. High Technology	0.4	1.4	3.6	6.0
4. Others	0.7	0.7	1.4	1.8
II. Export Structure				
1. Primary Products	35.0	14.6	7.0	4.7
2. Manufactures based on Natural Resources	13.6	8.2	7.4	6.9
3. Manufactures not based on Natural Resources	50.0	76.2	84.6	87.1
a. Low Technology	39.7	53.6	53.5	47.6
b. Medium Technology	7.7	15.4	16.9	17.3
c. High Technology	2.6	7.3	14.2	22.4
4. Others	1.4	0.8	1.0	1.1

Source: *World Investment Report 2002*, 162.

development, it was fortunate to have been aided by the enormous relocation of industries first from Hong Kong, and then additionally from Taiwan, Korea, and Japan and even Southeast Asian countries, as firms there sought to take advantage of the relatively lower wages in China. As one observer has stated:

By the early 1990s, four-fifths of Hong Kong manufacturing firms had relocated to China. Such investments have reoriented Hong Kong–China trade patterns: Most trade activities are directly related to the subcontracting investment activities undertaken by Hong Kong firms in China. In 1993, 74 per cent of Hong Kong's domestic export to China was related to outward processing; of the import from China, it was 74 per cent in 1993. In effect, Hong Kong operates as a trading corporation that contracts out production in China—through the provision of production designs and materials—and purchases and distributes the finished goods worldwide.... Briefly stated, labour-intensive goods that previously came from Korea, Taiwan, Hong Kong, and a number of Southeast Asian countries are now increasingly coming from China.[11]

Despite becoming a major powerhouse in the export of labour-intensive low-technology goods around the world, China's exports have, in fact, included a high proportion of high-technology products, amounting to 22.4 per cent (see Table 10.3). India's exports, by contrast, have only a nominal share of high-technology goods.

Consistent with the massive increase in China's exports, there has occurred a sharp expansion in China's share in the world market, growing almost four times from 1.6 per cent in 1985 to 6.1 per cent in 2000 (see Table 10.3). Note, particularly, the change in low-technology manufactures, where China now has almost one-fifth of the world market (more precisely, 18.7 per cent) as against only 4.5 per cent in 1985. At the same time, its market share in high-technology products increased from 0.4 per cent in 1985 to 6.0 in 2000, while that in medium-technology products from 0.4 per cent to 3.6 per cent.

The Extraordinary Role of Foreign Investment

Foreign investment has played a huge role in the acceleration of China's exports. There was little to none of FDI in China in 1981. In 1982 and 1983, *net* FDI amounted to $430 million and $636 million, respectively (see Table 10.1). Between 1984 and 1990, it grew substantially, ranging between $1.3 billion and $3.5 billion; even the Tiananmen crackdown of 1989 failed to make any dent in capital

[11] Yasheng Huang, 'The Role of Foreign-Invested, Enterprises in the Chinese Economy: An Institutional Foundation Approach', in Shuxun Chen and Charles Wolf, Jr (eds), *China, the United States, and the Global Economy* (Santa Monica, CA: RAND, 2001), 147–92.

inflows. One authoritative account asserts that 'then an isolated, autarchic economy, China, through the mid- and late-1980s, absorbed about half of the direct foreign investment flows to developing economies'.[12] More importantly, soon after, in the early 1990s, the floodgates literally burst open in terms of FDI. In 1991, FDI had stood at $4.36 billion, but in 1992 a big jump occurred, when it increased to $11.16 billion; the next year, 1993, it more than doubled, constituting 6.37 per cent of China's much-expanded GDP. The following three years, it was around $35 billion annually. In 1996, net FDI crossed the $40 billion mark, and in 1997, it reached the figure of $44 billion.

In 2001, China received the unprecedented amount of $46.9 billion (current) by way of FDI inflows, a figure unmatched by any LDC.[13] If the figure of $22.8 billion in FDI for Hong Kong is added to the amount that China received directly in 2001, the inflow of foreign capital to the larger mainland China emerges as entirely stupendous. Even by itself, China has in recent years come to stand as the largest recipient of FDI among the developing countries (Table 10.4). Even if a quarter of the FDI inflows represents 'round tripping', that is, local capital recycled back into the country in order to avail

Table 10.4: Share of the Largest Recipients of FDI Flows among LDCs (Per cent)

Economy	1985	Economy	2000
Saudi Arabia	20.4	China	19.2
Mexico	11.3	Hong Kong, China	16.0
Brazil	9.2	Brazil	14.4
China	7.0	Argentina	6.5
Singapore	6.9	Mexico	5.6
Malaysia	5.5	Korea	4.0
Egypt	4.7	Singapore	3.1
Bermuda	4.6	Bermuda	2.8
Hong Kong, China	4.3	Chile	2.7
Argentina	2.7	Cayman Islands	2.4
Top 10 Total	76.6	Top 10 Total	76.7

Source: World Investment Report 2001, 52. The figures for 1985 and 2000 are the average for 1983–1985 and 1998–2000, respectively.

[12] Ross Garnaut, 'Twenty Years of Economic Reform', 1–18.
[13] *World Investment Report 2002*, 305.

of the privileges extended to foreign capital,[14] the figures for the FDI that has come to China are gigantic when compared to most countries. Although a large proportion of foreign capital may have come from ethnic Chinese sources in East and Southeast Asia, most of the Fortune 500 firms are present in China's economy. By September 1999, American firms had 28,249 direct investment projects in China, estimated to cost $50.9 billion.[15] At the same time, there were other enormous capital inflows to China. As one economist observed the scene:

> By the mid 1990s China had become one of the world's largest trading nations, the recipient of more foreign direct investment than any other country in the world, the largest borrower from the World Bank, the largest recipient of official development assistance in the form of low-interest, long-term concessionary loans from industrialized countries, and except for the Czech Republic, the only transition economy with ready access to international capital and equity markets.[16]

The impact of foreign capital on China's economy has been enormous. Consider first the sustained strong impact of FDI inflows on gross capital formation in China, which emerges sharply when compared to India's record. The average for FDI as a share of capital formation during the periods 1990–5 and 1996–2000 was 9.8 per cent and 12.7 per cent for China, as compared to India's 0.9 per cent and 2.9 per cent (see Table 10.5). More important, corresponding to the frenetic pace of capital inflows from the early 1990s onwards,

Table 10.5: FDI Inflows as a Percentage of Gross Fixed Capital Formation

	1990–1995 Average	1996	1997	1998	1999	2000
China	9.8	14.3	14.6	12.9	11.3	10.5
India	0.9	2.9	4.0	2.9	2.2	2.3

Source: World Investment Report 2002, 325.

[14] Henry S. Rowen, 'China and the World Economy: The Short March from Isolation to Major Player', in Chen and Wolf, Jr (eds), *China, the United States, and the Global Economy*, 211–26.

[15] Xianquan Xu, 'Sino-US Economic and Trade Relations', in Chen and Wolf, Jr (eds), *China, the United States, and the Global Economy*, 237–52.

[16] Nicholas R. Lardy, 'The Role of Foreign Trade and Investment in China's Economic Transformation', in Garnaut and Huang (eds), *Growth Without Miracles*, 385–98.

the share of exports by foreign affiliates in China's total exports exploded to 48 per cent in 2001 from less than 5 per cent in 1986. Their share had been less than 9 per cent even as late as 1989. Over 90 per cent of the exports by foreign affiliates consisted of manufactured goods, with machinery and equipment occupying a prominent place. Especially noteworthy is the fact that in the area of technology-intensive industries, the share of foreign affiliates jumped from 59 per cent in 1996 to 81 per cent in 2000. As against that, China's domestic enterprises tend to dominate in the low-technology sector, where they specialize in the export of toys, luggage, and fabrics.[17] Besides the area of exports, foreign affiliates have a substantial share, amounting to about a quarter, of the domestic sales in manufactures.[18] One considered judgement is that 'China has had rapid export growth, but this has depended to an unprecedented degree on foreign invested firms . . . rapid export growth from foreign invested firms, a large share of which is export processing, has limited backward linkages and the domestic content of exports is very low. To some extent, export industries appear to be enclaves.'[19] Perhaps, over time, this particular weakness will get rectified.

Meanwhile, apart from contributing capital, technology, and modern management practices, FDI, even when it is meant only for the purpose of assembly and processing, has provided considerable employment for Chinese labour, and has thus contributed to national income, especially when FDI inflows are on the scale that China has experienced. That is an economic benefit that other LDCs have been deprived of in not being able to get similar levels of FDI.[20] Moreover,

[17] *World Investment Report 2002*, 162–3. At another place, the report shows that the shares of foreign affiliates in China's total exports and manufacturing exports in 2001 were 50 per cent and 44 per cent, respectively, as against 17 per cent and 16 per cent 10 years earlier in 1991. In the case of India, the share was 3 per cent in both categories in 1991, just as it was in 1985. Ibid., 154.

[18] Huang, 'The Role of Foreign-Invested Enterprises in the Chinese Economy', 147.

[19] Lardy, 'The Role of Foreign Trade and Investment in China's Economic Transformation', 395.

[20] However, for a sceptical look at the role of FDI in China, see the seminal work by Yasheng Huang, *Selling China: Foreign Direct Investment during the Reform Era* (Cambridge: Cambridge University Press, 2003). Huang holds FDI in China to be abnormally high, in part substituting for the role that local

with the surge in Chinese exports of manufactured goods, there has occurred a change in the structure of employment. Employment in the primary sector has declined from 62.4 per cent in 1985 to 49.8 per cent in 1998; on the other hand, it increased from 20.9 per cent to 23.5 per cent in the secondary sector and from 16.7 per cent to 26.7 per cent in the tertiary sector.[21] However, despite the obvious benefits that China has derived from inflows of foreign capital, not everyone views the massive foreign presence in China's economy positively. As one perceptive observer has noted:

> In China, no less than in other countries, foreigners' growing presence in industries steeped in national and political symbolism can be an emotionally wrenching experience. It is no longer considered normal business competition, proclaimed one worried Chinese official from the auto industry; it is nothing short of geopolitical war. Of the four so-called pillar industries designated by the Chinese government, FIEs [foreign-invested enterprises] have a significant presence in two of them. In electronics and telecommunications, FIE's equity stake has already exceeded that of domestic firms, at 53 per cent in 1997. FIEs accounted for 47 per cent of the assets and 63 per cent of pretax profits.[22]

China's Rise as an Economic Power

The export-oriented strategy adopted by China has resulted in a tremendous boost to its national economy, for 'foreign trade has become the major driving force behind industry and even the entire economy.'[23] The growth in national income has been phenomenal and, as a consequence, 'China has emerged as the most dynamic large player in the world economy.'[24] Between 1978 and 2000, China's GDP in constant 1995 US dollars expanded more than seven times

---

capital was quite capable of performing, and had indeed been doing so. He takes the reason for its massive entry to be, until 1997, ideology-based discrimination by the state against the *domestic* private sector.

[21] Yuanzheng Cao, 'World Economic Restructuring and China's Economic Transformation', in Chen and Wolf, Jr (eds), *China, the United States, and the Global Economy*, 25–44.

[22] Huang, 'The Role of Foreign-Invested Enterprises in the Chinese Economy', 155.

[23] Cao, 'World Economic Restructuring and China's Economic Transformation', 39.

[24] Garnaut, 'Twenty Years of Economic Reform', 6.

from $145 billion to $1,040 billion (see Table 10.1). It grew at an annual rate of 9.7 per cent over the two decades between 1981 and 2000 (compared to India's growth rate of 5.45 per cent, only a little more than half that of China's) (see Table 7.2). In the process, China has elevated itself to the status of a lower middle income country; it is no longer a low income country. With a gross national income of $1,131 billion (current) in 2001, it has emerged as the sixth largest economy in the world in US dollar terms (after the US, Japan, Germany, the UK, and France). Perhaps, that assessment understates China's economic power, for in PPP international dollars, with a gross national income of 5,415 billion, it is the second largest economy (after the US).[25] Besides, China increased its net international reserves, according to the *World Development Indicators*, from a mere $1.6 billion in 1978 to a massive $168.3 billion in 2000.

Economic Transformation and World Politics

The achievement of phenomenal economic growth by China through the instrumentality of an export-propelled economic strategy has, no doubt, had some impact on its national autonomy. Of course, to begin with, China is an unusually powerful developing country because of the gigantic size of its territory, population, and economy, and its status as a great power by virtue of being a permanent member of the UN Security Council. However, in the course of implementing its high-growth economic strategy and as a consequence of achieving success in it, China has displayed a high degree of pragmatism, moderation, and restraint, even on important issues, which on the basis of its official ideology, would have been unthinkable in the past.

No longer does China encourage, sponsor, and support revolutionary groups and rebellions in the developing world. Gone, too, is the old clarion call for the immediate encirclement of the cities of the world (the developed capitalist world) by revolutionary bases in the rural areas (the developing world). While determined, even intransigent, in protecting its core interests, China has at the same time been flexible enough to compromise in order to assure access to foreign markets, especially the American market. The general Chinese passivity at the UN Security Council discussions in early 2003 on the issue of American pressure for war against Iraq was truly remarkable. While

[25] World Bank, *World Development Report 2003*, 234–5.

opposed to the American plans to attack Iraq, the Chinese were averse to threatening the use of their veto to bar the US. When asked by the BBC as to the reasons for the unwillingness to use the veto, Premier Zhu Rongji responded, 'It is not in China's immediate interest.'[26] It is noteworthy that, in the aftermath of the war, the US made no mention of China even as it chose to forgive Russia but to punish France and Germany for their opposition. Interestingly, Deng Xiaoping had specifically directed the Chinese leadership in the early 1990s that in its relations with the US it should: increase trust, reduce tension, develop cooperation, and avoid confrontation.[27] Some, indeed, see China as having finally become enmeshed in the capitalist world system. In a sweeping summary view of the shifting landscape across the entire Northeast Asia region during the last century, Bruce Cumings points to the recent change in respect of China from a world-system perspective:

> Still, the central experience of Northeast Asia in this century has not been a realm of independence where autonomy and equality reigned, but with enmeshment in another web: the hegemonic web. This web had a spider: first England/America, then America/England, then war and defeat, then unilateral America, then and down to the present, hegemonic America. Japan, South Korea, and Taiwan industrialized mostly within this web. North Korea and China defined themselves as outside the web, thereby endowing the web with overriding significance—and so they structured their states to resist enmeshment. Japan, South Korea, and Taiwan have thus had states 'strong' for the struggle to industrialize but 'weak' because of the web of enmeshment: they are semi-sovereign states. North Korea and China had states 'strong' for industrialization and 'total' for hegemonic resistance. But as the century ends, both are being drawn into the web. This suggests that the nearest thing to a new truth about the state since Hegel, Hintze, and Marx is that state machineries are embedded in the world system, that their autonomy within it is quite limited, and that the specific institutional forms states may take around the world cannot be understood apart from the workings of the whole. That whole is the one Marx called 'the grandest terrain', the world market.[28]

[26] G. Anandalingam, 'China Expands Its Influence', *Economic Times* Online, 25 April 2003.

[27] Hui Wang, 'US-China: Bonds and Tensions', in Chen and Wolf, Jr (eds), *China, the United States, and the Global Economy*, 257–88.

[28] Bruce Cumings, 'Webs with No Spiders, Spiders with No Webs: The Genealogy of the Developmental State', in Meredith Woo-Cumings (ed.), *The Developmental State*, 61–92.

That, however, is but one perspective. A different view would emphasize another element. The greater economic prowess that has accrued to China as a result of the export-propelled growth strategy has made possible the acquisition by it of greater economic and, therefore, military capabilities, thus adding to its comprehensive national strength and its ability to play a more significant geopolitical role. Indeed, many see China destined as a result to rise as the challenger to the present hegemon, the US.[29]

Such a prospect may still be some decades away, but even China's present accomplishment is extraordinary and genuinely constitutes an economic miracle; if anything, it would seem to surpass the achievement of the Northeast Asian states, which, for geopolitical reasons, had the massive strategically derived support of the US. However, an important question that arises here is whether the Chinese economic miracle was innocent of such support. The accounts by economists on the performance of the Chinese economy, focusing on economic strategy and indicators alone, would tend to have us believe so, as if it was all simply a matter of opening up the economy to foreign trade and capital, and introducing markets in agriculture and industry.

Quite the contrary, as the account that follows below convincingly demonstrates, the US was as much strategically implicated in the success of the Chinese economy, as it was in that of the other Northeast Asian states and, remarkably, with the very same adversary as the intended target of its policies. China's adoption of the export-oriented strategy was facilitated historically by a particular geopolitical context, even though its unintended consequences may be very different from what had been originally envisioned. The inflows of foreign investment, at least initially, were facilitated by that particular geopolitical context. Again, all the output produced for export by China would have availed little, nor would it have found the necessary foreign markets, had it not been for that same geopolitical context. During the first decade of the strategy's implementation, the role of the US in its success was absolutely critical, though China's own steely determination to succeed in this endeavour is not to be underestimated.

---

[29] See Ronald L. Tammen *et al.*, *Power Transitions: Strategies for the 21st Century* (New York: Chatham House, 2000).

The De Facto Sino-American Alliance

American involvement in China had been of long standing. However, the success of the communist revolution in China in 1949, the fraternal treaty between the resulting new regime and the Soviet Union, and the intervention by the US and China on opposite sides in the Korean War in 1950, had turned the latter two countries into deadly enemies. Subsequently, within a decade, the Sino-Soviet alliance broke down under the pressures of conflicting national interests and, consequently, disputes over ideology. The relations between the two Communist giants eventually deteriorated to such an extent that they massed several dozen divisions of their armies against each other on their common frontiers at the end of the 1960s. Though no war broke out, some bloody clashes did take place.

To counter what it perceived as a mortal threat to its national security from a more powerful adversary, China was ready to abandon its policy of self-imposed isolation and simultaneous encouragement to revolutionary wars around the world during the Cultural Revolution of the 1960s. It was willing to embrace even a former enemy in order to counterbalance the Soviet Union. Meanwhile, mired in a hopeless war in Vietnam and facing mounting anti-war protests at home, the US saw, in the Soviet Union, an increasingly ascendant power that was quickly developing into a threat to its global position of hegemony. Under President Richard Nixon, the US then masterminded a breathtakingly daring geopolitical stratagem in 1971 to restructure the global balance of power through aligning China with itself in order to jointly counter the Soviet Union. Fervent opposition to the Soviet Union as a common enemy was at the heart of the new relationship between China and the US; as Nixon was to express it later: 'During the Cold War, the United States and China were brought together and held together by our fears.'[30]

The relations between the US and China quickly blossomed, even if largely in secret, so much so that Kissinger could soon write to Nixon in March 1973 that 'we have progressed faster and further than anyone would have predicted, or the rest of the world realizes. *For*

---

[30] Richard Nixon, *Beyond Peace* (New York: Random House, 1994), 131, cited in Hui Wang, 'US–China: Bonds and Tensions', 258.

in plain terms, we have now become tacit allies.[31] From that point on for the next two decades, 'Washington proceeded to support, arm, share intelligence with, and nurture the economy of, a Chinese government it had previously attempted to overthrow.... Two countries with fundamentally different political and economic systems worked together to defeat a third nation, the Soviet Union, perceived as a more immediate threat to themselves.'[32] For the US, in its rivalry with the Soviet Union, the alliance with China was of tremendous value; it was the equivalent of NATO in Asia.

Building Up China Militarily

Interestingly, early during the development of their relationship, it became apparent to the US that among many officials in China's military there was little belief in the much-emphasized doctrine of 'people's war',[33] and that they were eager to acquire American technology. Indeed, the Americans were soon to discover that the Chinese appetite for modern military technology and for developing military relations with the US was insatiable.

Among the first ventures to strengthen China's military capabilities was the secret American authorization in 1975 to have Great Britain sell to China, without obtaining COCOM scrutiny and sanction, $200 million worth of Rolls-Royce engines to upgrade Chinese jet fighters. This deal was followed, soon after Mao's death in 1976, to sell Cyber 72 computers which, while having civilian applications, were intended for military purposes. At this time, technology was 'the biggest favour the United States could bestow', and gradually it was 'putting itself into position to provide China with the sort of technology that could be put to military use'. Military cooperation between the two states accelerated after President Jimmy Carter came to office. While the US was not yet ready to be seen as directly providing military equipment to China, apparently in order to avoid appearing provocative toward the Soviet Union, it asked its European allies to undertake supplying such equipment. Carter's national

---

[31] Cited in James Mann's award-winning book, *About Face: A History of America's Curious Relationship with China, from Nixon to Clinton* (New York: Alfred A. Knopf, 1999), 63; [emphasis in Kissinger's original note].

[32] Mann, *About Face*, 8.

[33] Ibid., 58.

security advisor Zbigniew Brzezinski, with his pronounced anti-Soviet inclinations, was especially active in this regard. As Secretary of State Alexander Haig described it later: 'Zbig told the Chinese, the US would see that they got weapons, and asked them for a list of what they want[ed]. The Chinese, in response to the US initiative, ... provided a list of 47 items. Zbig then went through Western Europe with the list, saying "We can't sell right now, but you do it".' Additionally, Brzezinski provided briefings to Chinese officials on Soviet troop deployments on their border, backed up with reconnaissance pictures of Soviet installations.[34]

The Carter administration pushed forward to normalize relations with China. By mid-December 1978, it had decided to officially recognize China as of 1 January 1979, and to invite Deng Xiaoping to the US for an official visit soon after. The relations between the two countries now increasingly took on a military cast, and 'the special view of China—that it was not so much a country as a military strategy—reached its apogee under Carter and Brzezinski.' The two countries developed cooperation in intelligence matters, with their intelligence bureaucracies working closely together. The US went on to establish signals-intelligence stations in western China aimed at the Soviet Union. In this intensive cooperation, the Carter administration chose to set aside other concerns, such as human rights violations, which Carter had made central to his foreign policy elsewhere in the world. The grand anti-Soviet strategy easily trumped such moral concerns. Interestingly, when Deng informed Carter, during his visit to Washington, that China intended to invade Vietnam, Carter did not oppose the move or attempt to dissuade him from the use of force. Instead, he merely asked for restraint, thus giving what 'amounted to a green light for the Chinese invasion'. Deng then went ahead with the Chinese invasion of Vietnam in February 1979. Mann comments:

> What remained secret was the extent of America's day-to-day involvement in the Chinese invasion. At the White House, Brzezinski met with Chinese Ambassador Chai Zemin virtually every night throughout the military conflict to turn over American intelligence on Soviet deployments. This was vital information, the product of American satellite reconnaissance, which gathered far beyond anything Chinese intelligence could have collected.[35]

[34] Ibid., 74, 76, 86, 87.
[35] Ibid., 97–100.

It is well worth remembering that all this military cooperation or collusion between the US and China long pre-dated the Soviet intervention in Afghanistan in December 1979.

With the Soviet intervention in Afghanistan, the military cooperation intensified. The US now agreed to sell 'non-lethal' military equipment to China directly. This was a major breakthrough, for: 'The die was now cast. America was selling China what it had long sought—hardware and advanced Western technology with military applications.'[36] After the Reagan administration entered office, military cooperation with China intensified, with the spigot opened wide for sale not only of advanced technology but also of 'lethal' weaponry, and that, too, with American financing under the Foreign Military Sales programme. China immediately expressed interest in Hawk missiles, anti-submarine torpedoes, and armoured personnel carriers. The Reagan years in office constituted the 'golden years' of Sino-US military cooperation. During the second half of the decade of the 1980s, with arms sales to China having become the centrepiece of the Sino-US military relationship, China bought a series of weapons systems. One senior Pentagon official noted that prior to the Tiananmen incident, '60 to 70 per cent of the military relationship was arms sales'. Indeed, arms deals became 'in many ways, a symbol of the entire relationship between the United States and China in the 1980s'.[37] Not entirely, however!

Building Up China Economically

There was another extremely important element in the relationship, which was not newsworthy during the Reagan years, because, by then, it had simply become routine—that of economics. Here, the key development was the extension to China during the Carter administration of the Most Favoured Nation (MFN) status. Kissinger had broached the subject of MFN with China in 1973, but China had then evinced little interest, perhaps because Mao Zedong was still around, and enmeshment in the capitalist world-system would have stood out as a glaring contradiction to his ideology. When Kissinger brought up the issue again in 1975, China was more anxious that MFN not be offered to the Soviets than in obtaining it for itself.

[36] Ibid., 111.
[37] Ibid., 141–2.

China's interest in MFN had to wait for the passing away of Mao Zedong and Zhou Enlai, for the discrediting of the old policy regime, and for economic reforms to start at home first. So, when Deng came to Washington in late January 1979, a sea change in China's attitude was manifest: 'Chinese officials now eagerly wanted MFN, and Deng eagerly pressed for the trade benefits during his meetings in Washington. If China got MFN status, he forecast, its trade with the United States would be ten times larger than American trade with Taiwan.... Moreover, the Chinese leader said, once trade was established, America would be able to sell its technology to China. As usual, Deng was not modest in his requests. He said to Carter's Cabinet, "We want your most up-to-date technology, not even that of the early 1970s, do you understand?"' Action soon followed, and the Carter administration gave China the MFN status that it had sought, which was endorsed by Congress with little discussion. With this approval, 'MFN then disappeared as a political issue in Sino-American relations for a decade'.[38]

The approval of MFN for China was a momentous event. Without it, China's export-oriented strategy would have been smothered at birth, for then the prohibitively high tariffs of the Smoot-Hawley Act would have applied, which would have made the penetration of the American market awesomely difficult. The extension by the US to China of MFN and other economic privileges coincided precisely with the turn to the export-propelled strategy reliant on the export of manufactured goods, and is the explanation for the sudden burst in China's exports and their sustained growth rate. Military intimacy and trade expansion proceeded hand in hand. Interestingly, underlining the strategic thrust of the MFN decision, and more generally of international economic processes, is the fact that the MFN status was not extended to the Soviet Union. Along with MFN, the Carter administration also made available to China, while again denying them to the Soviet Union, other economic privileges such as access to Export–Import Bank credit and the relaxation of export controls.[39]

All these measures, both economic and military, were part of the American grand strategy to consolidate the Sino-US de facto alliance against the Soviet Union. They were undertaken with great zest, though often without public knowledge. But there were some

[38] Ibid., 106–10.
[39] Ibid., 108.

dissident voices. Edward Luttwak asked in *Commentary*: 'Is it our true purpose to promote the rise of the People's Republic to superpower status? Should we become the artificers of a great power which our grandchildren may have to contend with?' Similar was the comment of former US ambassador to the Soviet Union Malcolm Toon before Congress. He said, 'It does seem to me that far down the road, a China armed to the teeth, as she intends to be, with a fairly strong economy, probably is not going to be very benign in her attitude toward the United States, because they are against the sort of things we stand for.'[40] In the larger cause of defeating the Soviet Union through the Sino-US alliance, however, such criticisms were brushed aside.

The Tiananmen Rupture and the Recovery in Relations

Then, suddenly in 1989, when Chinese security forces ruthlessly crushed the student movement for the promotion of democracy at the Tiananmen Square, there developed a serious rupture in the relationship between the US and China. The military crackdown caused extreme bitterness in the US, especially in the Congress, for the advancing economic reforms and rapid economic growth in China had given rise to the illusion of the possibility of a gradual relaxation of political controls and a peaceful evolution to democracy. The Bush administration imposed sanctions on China in the areas of exports of munitions and lending by the Export–Import Bank and international financial institutions. It did so with some reluctance and sadness, and it was desperately eager to prevent damage to the overall relationship. At times, it was moved to act in order to prevent more radical measures by Congress.[41]

However, the relationship was too valuable to the two countries, and they both sought to restore normalcy to it in the midst of much public recrimination and exchanging of threats. Gradually, the sanctions were allowed to wither away, even though the sense of the earlier intimacy had been lost. The Bush administration endeavoured

[40] Ibid., 109–10.

[41] On the relationship under George Bush, see Robert S. Ross, 'The Bush Administration: The Origins of Engagement', in Ramon H. Myers, Michel C. Oksenberg, and David Shambaugh (eds), *Making China Policy: Lessons from the Bush and Clinton Administrations* (Lanham, MD: Rowman & Littlefield, 2001), 11–44.

to establish as close relations as possible against the background of the bitterness that had emerged with the Tiananmen incident. Indeed, it was in the closing years of the Bush administration that the policy of 'engagement' had its origins in an attempt to deal with China consistent with its special status and power:

> Engagement as a bilateral policy toward China seeks to manage conflicts of interest and expand cooperation through negotiation and mutual accommodation reflecting the interests and relative capabilities of both sides. Thus engagement does not promote one-sided cooperation on the part of China or the United States through either the threat to use or the use of punitive sanctions or through appeasement. It essentially acknowledges the reality that China is not like countries that are subject to overwhelming US superiority in every measure of power and influence. Engagement is premised on the fact that China is a great power and that pursuit of US interests requires the United States to acknowledge Chinese interests and China's ability to significantly harm American interests.[42]

The entry into office by President Bill Clinton opened the possibility of a fresh beginning in bilateral relations, but China was not high on the new administration's priority list.[43] Equally, after its anger at the sanctions following Tiananmen, China was in a truculent mood and in no state of mind to be easily pacified. Besides, Clinton initially suffered from the handicap of having attacked George Bush during the election campaign for coddling the Chinese dictators, whom he had referred to as 'the butchers of Beijing'.[44] Moreover, the attempt to develop a workable relationship with China needed to overcome some serious problems that had arisen in their relationship. The list of these problems was long and included human rights violations in China, repression in Tibet, the fate of Chinese dissidents, the status of Taiwan, the American supply of F-16 fighter jets to Taiwan, the visit of President Lee Teng-hui from Taiwan to the US, alleged Chinese contributions to campaign financing, charges about Chinese spying in sensitive areas like nuclear weapons in the

---

[42] Ross, 'The Bush Administration', 39

[43] On the Clinton period, see Nancy Bernkopf Tucker, 'The Clinton Years: The Problem of Coherence', in Myers *et al.*, *Making China Policy*, 45–76.

[44] Robert G. Sutter, 'Domestic Politics and the US–China–Taiwan Triangle: The 1995–96 Taiwan Strait Conflict and Its Aftermath', in Robert S. Ross (ed.), *After the Cold War: Domestic Factors and US–China Relations* (New York: M.E. Sharpe, 1998), 48.

US, unauthorized supply of sensitive technology by American firms to China, and proliferation of missile and nuclear technology by China to Pakistan and the Middle East.

Despite the multiplicity of problems confronting it, the Clinton administration had early on decided to continue with the overall policy inherited from the Bush administration, though it added a new prefix and called it 'comprehensive engagement'. However, the administration was internally divided, and its policy suffered from drift and incoherence. Attempts by the Clinton administration in its early years to link relations with China to the issue of human rights were rebuffed by the Chinese, who, knowing of the divisions within the administration and the US, proved to be intransigent on the issue. Clinton finally determined that China was too important a power for relations, especially economic ones, to be held hostage to the single criterion of its performance on human rights. Not everyone was pleased with the new posture of the Clinton administration. During the election campaign for Clinton's second term, the well-known right-wing commentator Patrick Buchanan declared: 'I think the policy [of the Clinton administration] has degenerated into reflexive accommodation and appeasement of Communist China.' He went on to admonish: 'I think we have to stop babying this regime. It is not some lovable wayward child that merely needs indulgence and affection... [We have] to stop empowering a potential enemy of the United States of America ... and make China pay some price for her belligerence, hostility and arrogance.'[45]

Despite such admonishments, President Clinton pushed on to elevate the relationship to 'strategic partnership' in his second term, even though the term itself had originated with the Chinese.[46] In turn, the Chinese now spoke of a developing 'constructive strategic partnership' between the two countries, particularly after President Jiang Zemin's state visit to the US in 1997. In what appeared like reinvigorated cordiality, Clinton reciprocally visited China in 1998, but the policy labels seemed somewhat exaggerated: 'Strategic partnership, like engagement, did not endow Clinton's China policy with a broad-gauged rationale. If engagement seemed descriptive rather than substantive, strategic partnership suggested a degree of

[45] Cited in Sutter, 'Domestic Politics and the US–China–Taiwan Triangle', 48.

[46] Tucker, 'The Clinton Years', 59.

intimacy in US–China relations that objective reality did not support.'[47] Still, Clinton's legacy was highly significant. Earlier, in 1996, as an omen of things to come in his second term, President Clinton had already delinked MFN for China from human rights considerations and put it on a permanent basis. Subsequently, in 1999, under his stewardship, the two countries also came to an agreement on China's entry into WTO.

The Countervailing Power of Economics

Regardless of the state of the strategic relations between the US and China, the impressive fact remains that the economic arena has become, at least for now, immune to the vagaries of their political relations. In a strange reversal, their economic relationship has come to influence their political and strategic relationship unlike the situation before Tiananmen. This consequence is, ironically, in part, the side-effect of economic globalization in which the two states are deeply enmeshed.

Of course, their strategic relationship was affected by more than Tiananmen. The collapse of the Soviet bloc and of the Soviet Union brought about a change in the equation between China and the US in their mutual relationship. For one thing, China no longer perceived a security threat from a much-reduced and weakened Russia as a successor state to the Soviet Union. China therefore did not any more need the protection of the US against a threat from the north, nor did it require the power of the US to counterbalance a more powerful neighbour and adversary. Rather, Russia had become a source of supply of technologically sophisticated arms to build up the military capabilities of China. Interestingly, China increasingly treated the US as the primary source of threat to its strategic and economic interests. At the same time, China masterfully, almost coercively, persuaded the US to treat its strategic interests seriously by its own activities in the area of arms and technology proliferation. Thus, the American supply of F–16 fighter planes to Taiwan in the 1990s called forth a Chinese riposte by way of supply of M–11 missiles to Pakistan on top of the earlier proliferation of nuclear technology and equipment to that country. What is more, the US was paralysed from making a determination on China's violations of American laws and from

[47] Ibid., 69.

applying the sanctions mandated by them for fear of further adverse actions by China.

However, looming above all in restraining the US vis-à-vis China has been the unintended impact on the bargaining position of the US as a result of China's stunning economic progress, the large inflows of American capital into China, and the flowering of trade relations between the two countries. These developments have made the US, perhaps more accurately, powerful interests within the US, a stakeholder in the Chinese economy and, as a consequence, the US has acquired a vested interest in the success of the Sino-US economic relationship and, therefore, the flourishing of the Chinese economy. Paradoxically, China has made the American economy dependent on China for the supply of cheap mass-produced consumer goods; American consumers have become hooked on such goods, and any disruption of their supply for political reasons evokes protests on their behalf. At the same time, many of the Fortune 500 companies have made investments running into billions of dollars in China; indeed, a considerabie part of the Chinese exports are the products of American affiliates in China. As a consequence, there are powerful lobbies in the US to plead for their own interests and, therefore, of China's. These lobbies, in turn, have strong supporters in the executive and legislature to exert influence on policy. Their power is reinforced by the fact that there is periodic interchange of personnel between government and business in the US, so that former officials who have since joined business houses continue to have access to the corridors of power.[48] The Chinese have also skilfully used personal capital built with former diplomats in pursuing their national interests in the US.

Long before the Tiananmen incident, Secretary of State George Shultz had been struck by the fact that American business leaders repeatedly articulated 'the standard Chinese line'.[49] However, by the time of that incident, the American business community had become far more influential in relation to policy on China. In the aftermath of the Tiananmen incident, American businessmen were quite vocal about their concerns. Reebok's chief executive warned against revocation of MFN status because it would hurt his shoe-making

---

[48] On the different lobbies in regard to American policy-making on China, see Kerry Dumbaugh, 'Interest Groups: Growing Influence', in Myers *et al.*, *Making China Policy*, 113–76.

[49] Mann, *About Face*, 132.

business in China. Toy dealers complained that stopping Chinese imports would mean 'Christmas 1990 would definitely be lost; Christmas 1991 quite possibly would be lost as well'. Wheat growers protested that the cost would be 'simply too high for US wheat producers to bear'. At the same time, suppliers of military equipment and satellites, some of them big contributors to campaign finance, wanted their own interests protected. Let alone revoke MFN, the Bush administration, along with the other industrialized nations, soon rescinded the restrictions on international lending to China. As Barber Conable Jr, former World Bank president, put it: 'Procurement won out over idealism.' In summary, the advice proffered to opponents of China by one ardent supporter of sanctions against China, William C. Triplett II, the minority chief counsel to the Senate Foreign Relations Committee at the time, is extremely pertinent. He admonished, 'MFN was a losing issue, because the power of US corporations would always hold sway in Congress.'[50] Similarly, another observer noted that 'the business community has been essentially invincible on the issue of MFN status.'[51]

The same factors that precluded the revocation of MFN made untenable the linking of MFN by President Clinton to Chinese performance on human rights. As two authorities observe: 'Meanwhile, powerful American corporations were lobbying the administration to jettison its linkage policy. This new lobby persuaded Congress to back away from imposing sanctions on the PRC, and vote for improving Sino-American trade and investment relations.'[52] The linkage policy, therefore failed. Eventually, the US was led to put MFN on a permanent, rather than annual, basis and to support China's membership of WTO. Interestingly, at one time, some in the Clinton administration proceeded on the assumption that China would have to make concessions because of its dependence on the American market, access to which was regarded as important to the Chinese economy. On the other hand, Chinese decision-makers had come to the realization that they could afford to be intransigent, for the administration did not have the support of business to be able to coerce China to submit to its conditions:

---

[50] Ibid., 199, 217, 219, 232, 240, 244.

[51] Steven M. Teles, 'Public Opinion and Interest Groups in the Making of US–China Policy', in Ross (ed.), *After the Cold War*, 40–69.

[52] Ramon H. Myers and David Shambaugh, 'Introduction: The Legacy of US–China Policy, 1989–2000', in Myers *et al.*, *Making China Policy*, 1–17.

Beijing believed MFN would pass regardless of China's human rights record. Clinton's retreat simply confirmed the view among Chinese leaders that they had little to fear from Washington, that recalcitrance paid off, that business was more important to Americans than their principles, and that business leaders could be counted upon to fight China's battles. When Secretary of Commerce Ron Brown arrived in Beijing that August with a phalanx of CEOs in tow eager to sign huge contracts and uninterested in human rights, China's leaders knew their gamble had paid off.[53]

Engagement thus continued, but the terms of engagement had changed. Mann summarizes the transformation perceptively:

America's preoccupation in dealing with China switched from Cold War strategy to business, yet some of the underlying dynamics were the same. In the 1970s, the Chinese had tried to exert their will over America by suggesting that Beijing might restore its ties to Moscow. In the 1990s, they instead threatened to award business contracts to other countries.

Indirectly, at least, this new 1990s basis of the US relationship with China also had its origins in the Cold War. The United States had opened its markets to Chinese goods, encouraged American firms to invest in China, and granted the country most-favoured-nation status, thus developing commercial ties broader than with any other Communist country. These efforts were carried out with the hope of strengthening China as a partner against the Soviet Union. The economic infrastructure developed in the last years of the Cold War, especially the opening of America's market to Chinese exports, helped China to become in the 1990s a much more prosperous and powerful nation, with which American firms were much more eager to do business.[54]

Strategic Partnership or Strategic Rivalry?

After the end of the Cold War, the strategic relationship between the US and China changed fundamentally, because no common goal existed to sustain the earlier de facto alliance. The collapse of the Soviet Union made the US the sole superpower in a unipolar system. Given the asymmetry in power between the US and China, the former could not but impinge on Chinese interests, directly or indirectly, in East Asia. On the other hand, China's explosive economic growth transformed it into a potential challenger to the hegemony of the US. If China were to continue on its present course of economic performance, and the balance of capabilities were to

[53] Tucker, 'The Clinton Years', 53–4.
[54] Mann, *About Face*, 371–2.

change in China's favour, a crucial tipping moment would arrive in the strategic situation in East Asia. At that point, America's present allies, tacit or open, would defect and the American-led alliance structure in Asia would unravel. As China gets economically and militarily stronger, it is suspected that it will also become assertive and constitute a threat to peace and stability in the region. It is quite possible that as China undergoes economic transformation as a result of industrialization and modernization, its political regime will also undergo change, perhaps toward a more open, pluralistic, and democratic system. This would perhaps then make for harmony between the US and China because, if the democratic peace theory is correct, democracies do not go to war with each other. Strategic engagement, on the part of the US with China, is supposed to have been based on some such premise. Such an outcome will certainly be welcome to the votaries of peace and democracy. However, as between the hegemonic power and the challenger, peace or democracy is not really the issue, it never is; what is at issue is primacy.

Confronted by a rising challenger, the hegemonic power has several options.[55] At one extreme, the hegemonic power can act to defeat the possible threat of the rise of a challenger in the future through confrontation now. This is the strategy that the US had adopted toward the Soviet Union during the Cold War, and it included such measures as encirclement through alliances and economic warfare by cutting off outside markets and technology supplies in order to degrade the economic and technological capabilities of the challenger. Notwithstanding the immense power of the US, perhaps it is not within the capacity of the US to adopt such a strategy, for other advanced countries may not be willing to join it in isolating China. If the US had serious problems in 2003 in rallying Germany and France against Iraq, how much more difficult would it be to do so in regard to China!

Equally, for its part, China is no ordinary power, but as a major nuclear and missile power, besides its enormous economic strength, it has many assets that it can employ to make trouble for the US in retaliation. It can do so in Northeast Asia (through North Korea),

---

[55] The discussion on the typology of options follows Robert S. Ross, 'Engagement in US–China Policy', in Alastair Iain Johnston and Robert S. Ross (eds), *Engaging China: The Management of an Emergent Power* (London: Routledge, 1999), 181–4.

Southeast Asia (through territorial disputes), South Asia (through Pakistan), and more generally in the Middle East (through proliferation). In any case, 'there is little support for this policy [of thwarting China's rise] in the United States.'[56] Meanwhile, China is preparing in a race with time to pre-empt the possibility of the US frustrating its rise to hegemonic power in East Asia. It is doing so by foiling any possible attempt at encirclement through cultivating relationships with a wide variety of countries around it and with multilateral forums, such as ARF and ASEAN. It is also doing so by reducing the asymmetry with the US in economic vulnerabilities through diversifying economic relationships and joining rule-based organizations, such as WTO. More ambitiously, China aims to transform the world power structure in accord with a new strategic architecture, that of multipolarity, which is in essence a code word for the reverse containment, in effect, of the US. In this endeavour, China has the cooperation of some venerable allies of the US, such as France.

At the other end of the spectrum from defeating the emergence of a threat from China as a challenger is for the US to recognize the inevitability of the rise of China as a great power and to 'accommodate itself to a pax-Sinica premised on Chinese hegemony over East Asia'. This option assumes that China's inexorable rise to power 'will cause China's smaller neighbours to bandwagon with China, thus excluding the United States from East Asian affairs'. It is best, then, that 'the United States should also bandwagon with Chinese power so as to avoid counterproductive conflict and to maximize the potential for cooperation in order to benefit from PRC hegemony'.[57] The US, however, would find this bandwagoning strategy simply unacceptable as it runs so counter to its self-perception as a hegemonic power and to its notions of national destiny. Accordingly, the US will not be willing to just concede hegemony in East Asia to China. There is sufficient belief on the part of the US in its own power and in its capacity to rally support to resist Chinese hegemony from other countries in East Asia, who are seen as preferring cooperation with the US rather than with China.

In between the extremes represented by the options of preventively undermining China's ability to be a contender and of bandwagoning with it lies the option of balancing China, which 'is the approach

---

[56] Ibid., 181.
[57] Ibid., 181.

implicitly advocated by a broad cross-section of American foreign policy specialists'. It is assumed that China will continue to grow in power. But there is the realization under this option that the resulting strategic situation will be one where there will be competition between the US and China for influence in East Asia 'in which neither great power will have the ability to establish region-wide hegemony'. The broad consensus on balancing has, however, not led to agreement on the precise policy to be pursued toward China, and debate has centred on two policy packages under the rubric of balancing— 'engagement' and 'containment'. Both policy packages are premised on the notion that a powerful China will be a challenge to American supremacy in Asia, but they view Chinese intentions differently, with opposed consequences for policy. The proponents of 'containment' believe that the foreign policy of China as a revisionist power, is internally-driven, and that as China succeeds in its military modernization it will employ force in its various territorial and political conflicts. Since the US will prove to be the principal obstacle to China's foreign policy ambitions, they see conflict between the US and China as ultimately inescapable. Viewing Chinese intentions as not being reactive, they see 'little benefit in trying to reach compromise solutions to conflicts of interest'. The stance of the advocates of containment is to follow the model of the stern American posture toward the Soviet Union during the Cold War. Interestingly, meanwhile, 'they view US–China economic ties as providing Beijing with the technological know-how and financial resources to eventually challenge US economic and strategic interests.'[58]

The other policy package of 'engagement' also opposes the emergence of China as the hegemon in East Asia. However, it takes it to be within the capacity of the US to influence the degree of tension and conflict between the two powers within the balance of power system in East Asia. Engagement assumes that China's policy toward the US is not already predetermined. Instead, Chinese behaviour is likely to be influenced by American behaviour, with friendly policies evoking a friendly response and hostile measures meeting with animosity. Although as ideal types, the two policy packages are counterposed against each other as exclusive, in reality each package represents a mix of overlapping elements. What leads to the characterization of the package as one rather than the other

[58] Ibid., 182–3.

is the balance among the elements within it. As Kissinger once famously observed, 'détente presupposes containment. So, similarly, does engagement.'

Engagement was the overall label for the policy that President Bill Clinton pursued toward China during his second term, when he chose to characterize the relationship with China as one of strategic partnership. Symbolic of the growing strategic partnership between the two powers was the state visit of President Jiang Zemin to the US in 1997, and the return trip of Clinton to China in 1998. Interestingly, Clinton went directly to Beijing without visiting Japan en route. But it is noteworthy that these moves at the engagement of China and the elevation of the bilateral relationship to a strategic partnership had been preceded by the containment-like consolidation of the American alliance ties with Japan in 1997 through the agreement on 'Guidelines of US–Japan Defence Cooperation'.

In the realist lexicon, however, as between great powers there can really be no engagement. Such powers are inexorably led to hegemonic conflict. Engagement is only an exercise in illusion; it can only be ephemeral and cannot be a stable arrangement. Consequently, near the end of the Clinton presidency, the realist scholar John Mearsheimer concluded his authoritative opus on the great powers with a dire warning that 'a rising China is the most dangerous potential threat to the United States in the twenty-first century.' Depending on China continuing its fast-speed modernization, he believed, 'the most dangerous scenario the United States might face in the early twenty-first century is one in which China becomes a potential hegemon in Northeast Asia.' He took it for granted that rapid modernization would lead to China becoming the greatest economic power, which would, in turn, enable the building of a mighty military machine. A thrust to regional hegemony would then automatically follow. He thought that China 'might be far more powerful and dangerous than any of the potential hegemons that the United States confronted in the twentieth century,' because no other challenger packed as much latent power as does China. In view of this analysis, Mearsheimer was led to the conclusion that 'the United States has a profound interest in seeing Chinese economic growth slow considerably in the years ahead.' Quite the contrary, he was struck by the fact that 'for much of the past decade, however, the United States has pursued a strategy intended to have the opposite effect. The United States has been committed to "engaging" China, not "containing" it.' In his view, the US was entirely mistaken in its approach:

> This US policy on China is misguided. A wealthy China would not be a status quo power but an aggressive state determined to achieve regional hegemony. This is not because a rich China would have wicked motives, but because the best way for any state to maximize its prospects for survival is to be the hegemon in its region of the world. Although it is certainly in China's interest to be the hegemon in Northeast Asia, it is clearly not in America's interest to have that happen.... it is not too late for the United States to reverse course and do what it can to slow the rise of China.[59]

It would seem that the new administration that came to power in 2001 under President George W. Bush (junior), with its more assertive and muscular approach to foreign policy, because of the leadership's consciousness of the very unprecedented nature of contemporary American power, was of this same persuasion. During the election campaign, Bush left no one in doubt that he thought of China not as a strategic partner but as a strategic competitor. This, then, was the mindset that the Bush administration had brought with it to office. If this, indeed, was the case, the Bush administration would soon have come face to face with a major dilemma, because the US would then have had a dual but contradictory relationship with China on its hands. Under the circumstance, at the strategic level, the US would be regarding China as a competitor, while at the economic level, its domestic structure had evolved to compulsively propel China's economic power to higher and higher peaks. How the Bush administration would resolve this contradiction, however, remained to be seen.

Before the Bush administration had figured out what implications its strategic assessment had for its economic policy in relation to China, there occurred the shocking terrorist attacks on the American homeland on 11 September 2001 (9/11). These attacks came as a stunning blow to the prestige, collective psyche, and hitherto permanent sense of mainland security of the US. The 9/11 attacks served to radically alter the administration's strategic priorities in order to focus on the terrorist threat from groups and states that it considered to be part of 'the axis of evil'. China astutely extended support to the US in its war on terrorism, and earned considerable American

---

[59] John J. Mearsheimer, *The Tragedy of Great Power Politics*, 362, 401–2.

goodwill. No doubt, the President's authoritative national security strategy document of 2002 insisted that the US fully intended to remain the sole superpower, hegemonic in a largely unipolar system. It warned: 'Our forces will be strong enough to dissuade potential adversaries from pursuing a military build-up in hopes of surpassing, or equalling, the power of the United States.'

The US, however, now saw terrorism as the primary threat to its security. Indeed, the national security strategy document welcomed 'the emergence of a strong, peaceful, and prosperous China'. To be sure, the US found disconcerting the lack of democratic development in China as also China's military build-up. The document admonished: 'In pursuing advanced military capabilities that can threaten its neighbours in the Asia–Pacific region, China is following an outdated path that, in the end, will hamper its own pursuit of national greatness.' Still, with cooperation already existing in various areas where their interests overlapped, such as the war on terrorism and promotion of stability in the Korean peninsula, it also promised to seek 'a constructive relationship with a changing China'.[60] Significantly, Bush visited China twice and also entertained President Jiang Zemin at his ranch in Texas. There thus emerged a different pattern in the relationship than had been envisaged during the Bush election campaign. As an authoritative Chinese academician observed:

> Bush has called China a 'friend', leaving behind his campaign rhetoric about China being a 'strategic competitor'. Despite enhanced US military cooperation with Taiwan, he has publicly assured Beijing that he does not support Taiwanese independence. As commerce between the two nations continues to thrive, the Chinese believe their relationship with the United States is the best it's been since the Cold War ended.
>
> Paradoxically, therefore, a more aggressive United States does not represent a greater threat to China than before, as long as the Bush administration continues to identify the 'crossroads of radicalism and technology' (to quote its national security strategy) as the gravest threat to the United States. Terrorism and nuclear proliferation (especially on the Korean peninsula) are problems for China as well. For these reasons, Beijing has reacted positively to Bush's new discourse of 'great power cooperation'.[61]

---

[60] President of the United States, *The National Security Strategy of the United States of America*, 27, 30.

[61] Wang Jisi, 'A View From China', *Foreign Policy*, (July/August 2003), 31.

The perception among American observers was similar: 'In short order, Beijing has gone from Washington's strategic competitor to being its security collaborator and a major trade and investment partner.... The change has been abrupt ... the Bush administration virtually reversed its China policy.'[62] Increasingly, the Bush administration viewed China, conditional on its continued cooperative behaviour, as a potential member of a concert of powers that would help maintain a regional and global order, no doubt of American design.[63]

Since the Bush administration sees the terrorist threat as lasting for a generation or more, over which period regime change across the Middle East is envisaged as becoming pervasive, does that mean confrontation between the two great powers—the hegemon and the challenger—stands postponed for that length of time? That remains to be seen. What the relative economic strength, and therefore military power, of the two powers will be at that time cannot be foreseen at this juncture.

Summary and Conclusions

The evidence is compelling on the point that the acceleration of economic growth in China and the rise of China as a major economic power in the world economy was a consequence of the change in its economic strategy from inward orientation to export promotion. The change in economic strategy preceded, and did not follow, the explosion in China's economic growth. It is as close to a cause-and-effect relationship as one can get in the social sciences. Equally, it is manifest that the success of the export-oriented strategy was greatly aided by the geopolitical circumstance of the tacit Sino-American alliance against the Soviet Union. That alliance led the US to grant most favoured nation status to China, and to allow the entry of China's

[62] Morton Abramowitz and Stephen Bosworth, 'Adjusting to the New Asia', *Foreign Affairs*, 84, 4 (July/August 2003), 119–31. Note also the more critical, observation by Joshua Kurlantzick, 'China: Economic Power, Political Enigma', *Washington Quarterly*, 25, 3 (Summer 2002), 50–67: 'The administration has reverted to the toadyish, Clintonesque strategy of ignoring China's flaws and atrocities.'

[63] Rosemary Foot, 'Bush, China and Human Rights', *Survival*, 45, 2 (Summer 2003), 167–85.

massive exports into its market, besides facilitating vast FDI inflows into China.

At the same time, the Chinese endeavour in combining realpolitik and economic strategy for a stunningly successful economic performance provides a superb and instructive lesson in statecraft. It evokes awe for China's dogged determination and brilliance in managing the outside world. It also shows how a weaker party can at times triumph in its relations with a stronger one. A weaker party can, as China did, do so through clever bargaining, often feigning injury and playing on the sentiment of having been harmed and humiliated. It can also do so through occasional bluffing, astute defiance, and the single-minded but flexible pursuit of national interests, and as well through creatively developing stakeholders in the protection of those interests. China seized its opportunities as and when they became available, and it also created the opportunities that it could seize. Its behaviour provides a model in its own right for other countries just as much as that provided by the Northeast and Southeast Asian states.

The international system is a dynamic arena, where change is constant. China and the US entered into a fruitful relationship aimed at the containment of the Soviet Union. At the time, the US found it in its interest to strengthen China economically and militarily. However, the collapse of the Soviet Union transformed the international system into a unipolar one with the US as the sole hegemon. The change did not leave the Sino-American relationship unaffected, with both parties treating each other with a high degree of wariness. There is a considerable body of opinion that holds China's emergence as a challenger to the US a matter of certainty in the not-too-distant future, if China keeps up its current scorching pace of economic growth.

Meanwhile, in line with the theory of 'path dependence',[64] the US is constrained by the consequences of its past policies whereby some highly influential domestic actors have become stakeholders in making China stronger and stronger. Ordinarily, the US would have

[64] On the theory, see Douglass C. North, *Institutions, Institutional Change and Economic Performance* (Cambridge: Cambridge University Press, 1990), 92–104, 112–17. See also, Geoffrey M. Hodgson, 'Economic Evolution: Intervention Contra Pangloss', *Journal of Economic Issues*, 25, 2 (June 1991), 519–33.

confronted a serious dilemma, torn as it would have been, between a rising China constituting a threat to its hegemony and a powerful part of its business community committed in its own interest to fuelling, precisely the power of that rising China. However, the emergence of the new threat of terrorism in 2001 and after, has sidetracked the US from having to contend with this dilemma, at least for now.

It is, no doubt, difficult to make predictions about what adjustments the US will find necessary in its future posture toward China in order to preserve unipolarity and its hegemonic position within it. The US may well feel that the successful completion of modernization will eventually lead China to have a stake in the present international system, presided over by the US. Moreover, the distance between American and Chinese power is so vast that it cannot be quickly traversed, and thus may not cause immediate concern to the US, especially in view of the latter's structure of alliances and military bases in Asia. Besides, China's own dependence on the American market also has its constraining effects for it as well, not just for the US.

Chapter 11

INDIA

Subaltern Geopolitics and Economic Policy

With its weakening as a result of World War II, Great Britain found it increasingly difficult to hold on to its empire in the Indian subcontinent and decided to quit. The consequence of the dismantling of the British Empire was the emergence in 1947 of two states in the shape of India and Pakistan, rather than one, marking the triumph of both the ethnic heterogeneity of the subcontinent and of the imperial policy of divide-and-rule. Religion had formed the basis of the partition of the empire into two states, with Pakistan founded as a homeland for the Muslims. The fact that religion led to partition implies that a single united successor state would hardly have been propitious for the organization of 'the developmental state' in the subcontinent on the pattern of the mono-ethnic Northeast Asian states.

Despite the partition, however, rampant ethnic heterogeneity (religious, linguistic, caste) remains the dominant characteristic of both successor states, and it constitutes a formidable barrier to the construction of the developmental state. Both states have nonetheless engineered episodes of considerable length during which economic development was apparently a 'hegemonic project', but with indifferent, and at times tragic, results. One scholar exclaims in the opening sentence of an article that 'India must be the most dramatic case of a failed developmental state,' and attributes the failure to India's 'embedded particularism'.[1] In Pakistan, the single-minded pursuit of

---

[1] Ronald J. Herring, 'Embedded Particularism: India's Failed Developmental State', in Meredith Woo-Cumings (ed.), *The Developmental State*, 306–34.

economic growth in the 1960s by an authoritarian regime, to the neglect of the task of nation-building, made for the alienation of the country's major ethnic component that constituted more than half the population, and led to its secession in the form of Bangladesh.

Ethnic heterogeneity, however, is not the sole determinant of a country's political and economic destiny. Public policy, including its effective implementation, also matters. Of course, behind public policy lies a whole set of factors—the nature of political leadership and the vision it holds, the type of polity and party system, the kind of support base that the leadership and party have in society, and the political and cultural values of the populace. Despite the shared characteristic of widespread ethnic heterogeneity and the common experience of having been under British colonial rule, India and Pakistan have differed radically in these aforementioned aspects and, accordingly, their political and economic paths have been quite different from early on after their emergence as separate states.

For more than half of its history, Pakistan has been under military rule. In contrast, despite suffering from some serious infirmities, the political system in India has been from its very inception under civilian control within a representative parliamentary system, with the military strictly subordinate to the elected political leadership. Some have, indeed, regarded the continued operation since independence of a democratic parliamentary system in India's far-flung federation as 'a political miracle', a mark of 'Indian exceptionalism' among the less developed countries.[2] As in the political sphere, so in several other areas, India and Pakistan have manifested divergent patterns of policy and behaviour. In examining the different patterns of economic policy and outcomes, this chapter deals with India while the next chapter looks at Pakistan.

Economic Performance and Policy Change

In regard to economic performance, India's post-Independence history can perhaps be roughly divided into two long periods, with the divide being placed flexibly at either 1975 or 1980. In the first period, the average rate of economic growth is about 3.5 per cent,

---

[2] Myron Weiner, *The Indian Paradox: Essays in Indian Politics* (New Delhi: Sage Publications, 1989).

which has been derisively labelled as 'the Hindu rate of growth'. The impact of such a slow growth rate, sustained over a long period of time, was devastating. It included not just largely stagnant per capita incomes, but also deepening poverty, social and political conflict, and ultimately the decay of political institutions. In the second period, the average rate has been significantly higher at around 5 per cent or more.

Table 7.2 provides summary data on GDP growth rates in five-year averages since 1961. The average growth rate for 1961–75 works out to 3.56 per cent; that for the slightly more extended period 1961–80 is not much different at 3.48 per cent. The figure for 1976–2000 is 5.00 per cent, while that for the shorter period of 1981–2000 is 5.45 per cent. The argument here is that the difference in the average growth rate between the two periods is a function of policy change, disputing, in the process, the notion of cultural predestination implicit in the earlier description of the first period as symbolizing the Hindu rate of growth. Given the slow pace of policy change within India's democratic framework and federal structure in a continent-sized civilization-polity, however, it can be a matter of dispute as to exactly when, and to what degree, can policy change be regarded as having actually taken place.

Policy change has been largely a very gradual and incremental process. The Indian state is unlike the developmental states in terms of authority and decisiveness in the area of economic policy. After all, the very term 'the soft state' was coined to describe economic and political development in India. Many terms have been used to characterize the Indian state: the 'soft state', the 'imprisoned or structurally trapped' state, the 'overextended state', the 'iron-frame' state, or the 'contested federal' state. However, it is interesting that 'consistently lacking from dominant characterizations of the Indian literature is the "strong state" presumed to be crucial for successful developmental statism.' In contrast with the 'embedded autonomy' of the Northeast Asian states, the bureaucracy in India 'does suffer structurally from vertical and horizontal incoherence, much introduced by constitutional federalism, much by inadequate self-awareness in an extraordinarily complex organism operating over a continental political economy'.[3] However, notwithstanding the gradual and incremental nature of policy change, resulting from the very character

[3] Herring, 'Embedded Particularism', 313–16, 322.

of the Indian state, the direction of change has, nonetheless, been quite clear.

Geopolitics of the Subaltern Kind

In an interesting study on post-revolution China's economic record, three Chinese scholars attribute the slow growth during the period before the economic reform initiated by Deng Xiaoping in 1978 to the particular economic strategy of import-substitution industrialization employed by China, which had focused excessively on heavy industry. They remark: 'The evidence clearly suggests that the fundamental reason for China's high-cost and low-efficiency pattern of economic growth before the reform was the choice of an inappropriate development strategy.' Significantly, in support of their argument about the impact of economic strategy, they specifically discuss the Indian case, where the implementation of a like strategy had also led to a slow growth rate. Maintaining that 'both countries adopted the heavy industry-oriented development strategy', they reiterate that the strategy—which they also refer to as 'the leap forward strategy'—led to results that were similar in the two countries in terms of growth rate and employment structure. They conclude: 'The leap forward strategy failed not only in China and other socialist countries, but also in India and other developing capitalist countries. This suggests that the fundamental reason for the failure in China's economic development before the reform was the adoption of the leap forward strategy.'[4]

The question that arises is, as to why both China and India had gone in for the heavy industry strategy in the first place. In relation to China, the aforementioned three scholars offer what seems to be an anodyne technical rationale, expressed in strictly economic terms. They remark: 'The intended goal of giving priority to the development of heavy industries was to circumvent the constraints of capital shortage so that the economy could quickly overcome the adverse effect of a weak heavy industry base on the nation's growth and development. It was hoped that in this way the national economy

---

[4] Justin Yifu Lin, Fang Cai, and Zhou Li, 'Pre-Reform Economic Development in China', in Ross Garnaut and Yiping Huang (eds), *Growth Without Miracles*, 59–76.

could grow quickly, and could achieve the goal of surpassing advanced economies in the shortest possible amount of time'.[5] This rationale sounds uncannily similar to that provided by India's then planning czar, P.C. Mahalanobis, in the mid-1950s for the heavy industry strategy inaugurated under the Second Five Year Plan (1956/7–1960/1). In 1953, his thinking, which eventually led to the heavy industry strategy in the Second Plan, focused on removing the constraint of locally available capital goods in economic development in a closed economy:

> In the initial stage of development, the larger the percentage [of] investment on consumer goods industries, the larger will be the income generated. But there is a critical range of time and as soon as this is passed, the larger the investment in investment goods industries [read: heavy industries] the larger will be the income generated. Hence, it would be desirable to invest relatively more on the consumer goods industries: provided we are interested in the immediate future. If, on the other hand, we are interested in the more distant future, relatively larger investment on investment goods industries would give distinctly better results.[6]

At the preparatory stage of the Second Plan in 1955, Mahalanobis averred:

> In the long run, the rate of industrialization and the growth of national economy would depend on the increasing production of coal, electricity, iron and steel, heavy machinery, heavy chemicals, and the heavy industries generally which would increase the capacity for capital formation.... The heavy industries must, therefore, be expanded with all possible speed.[7]

Of course, the economic planning model of the Soviet Union—which, too, from the very beginning under Stalin, had favoured heavy industry—had been tremendously influential with both China and India. Soviet planners had offered a similar rationale as well. However, rationale is not the same thing as motive.

In following the Soviet model, both China and India were not necessarily persuaded by the economic rationale as such, but more

[5] Lin, Cai, and Li, 'Pre-Reform Economic Development in China', 62.

[6] P.C. Mahalanobis, 'Some Observations on the Process of Growth of National Income', *Sankhya*, 12, 4 (1953), 309.

[7] P.C. Mahalanobis, 'Draft Recommendations for the Formulation of the Second Five Year Plan 1956–61', in Government of India, Planning Commission, *Papers Relating to the Formulation of the Second Five Year Plan, 1955* (Delhi: Manager of Publications, 1962), 31.

by the larger encompassing architecture of nationalism and national power that underlay the strategy. The leaders of all three countries saw a direct link between heavy industry and military power that was regarded as necessary for national security. As the socialist economist Oscar Lange pointed out in 1943, 'The Soviet economy was planned not for the harmony of the different branches, but for one single purpose, namely the most rapid industrialization and preparation of effective national defence.' He further underlined the fact that 'Soviet economic planning did not serve the objectives of a harmonious socialist welfare economy, but served political and military objectives to which all other aspects of economic planning were sacrificed.'[8] The classic statement on this linkage was made by Stalin, in his 'We Do Not Want to be Beaten' speech in 1931, in the course of justifying not letting up the pressure to fulfil the First Soviet Plan.[9]

---

[8] Oscar Lange, cited in Oleg Hoeffding, 'State Planning and Forced Industrialization', *Problems of Communism*, 8, 6 (November–December 1959), 39.

[9] At the time, Stalin had declared:

It is sometimes asked whether it is not possible to slow down a bit in tempo, to retard the movement. No. This is impossible. It is impossible to reduce the tempo! On the contrary, it is necessary as far as possible, to accelerate it. To slacken the tempo means to fall behind. And the backward are always beaten. But we do not want to be beaten. No, we do not want this! The history of old Russia is the history of defeats due to backwardness. She was beaten by the Mongol Khans. She was beaten by the Turkish beys. She was beaten by the Swedish feudal barons. She was beaten by the Polish–Lithuanian squires. She was beaten by the Anglo-French capitalists. She was beaten by the Japanese barons. All beat her for her backwardness—for military backwardness, for cultural backwardness, for governmental backwardness, for industrial backwardness, for agricultural backwardness. She was beaten because to beat her was profitable and could be done with impunity.... That is why we must no longer be backward.... We are fifty to a hundred years behind the advanced countries. We must cover this in *ten* years. Either we do this or they will crush us.

Joseph Stalin, 'We Do Not Want to be Beaten', cited in Irving Louis Horowitz, *Three Worlds of Development: The Theory and Practice of International Stratification* (New York: Oxford University Press, 1966), 13–14.

Note also Stalin's comment: 'The industrialization of the country would ensure its economic independence, strengthen its power of defence and create the conditions for the victory of Socialism in the USSR.' *History of the Communist Party of the Soviet Union (Bolsheviks): Short Course*, cited in

Given the history of the experience of China and India with Western imperialism and their intense nationalist struggles to overthrow it, it should not occasion surprise that the two countries would want to safeguard their hard-won independence by undergirding it with the sinews of power. Nothing different can be expected in the case of modern China, given the famous words of its founding father Mao Zedong that 'power flows out of the barrel of a gun'. China's First Five Year Plan cites Mao in justification of the heavy industry strategy: 'Without industry, there can be no solid national defence, no people's welfare, and no national prosperity and power.' The same Plan immediately followed it with a statement in elaboration: 'The purpose of adopting a positive policy of industrialization, that is, a policy which gives priority to the growth of heavy industry, is to provide a material basis on which to strengthen our national defence, meet the needs of the people and bring about the socialist transformation of our national economy.'[10] Subsequently, the proposals of the Communist Party of China for the Second Five Year Plan declared: 'The central task of our Second Five Year Plan is still to give priority to the development of heavy industry. This is the chief index of our country's socialist industrialization, because heavy industry provides the basis for a strong economy and national defence, as well as the basis for the technical reconstruction of our national economy.'[11] Note the priority accorded to defence in all these statements in justification of the heavy industry strategy.

In recognizing the centrality of heavy industry to national defence, India was not any different from China. Elsewhere, I have argued with sufficient and compelling evidence that motives of national and military power underlay India's adoption of the heavy industry strategy, to the neglect of agriculture and consumer goods (just as in the case of China), with the inauguration of the Second Five Year

---

John H. Kautsky, 'An Essay in the Politics of Development', in Kautsky (ed.), *Political Change in Underdeveloped Countries: Nationalism and Communism* (New York: John Wiley, 1962), 61.

[10] People's Republic of China, *First Five Year Plan for Development of the National Economy of the People's Republic of China in 1953–57* (Peking: Foreign Language Press, 1956), 16.

[11] Communist Party of China, *Report on the Proposals for the Second Five Year Plan for Development of the National Economy* (Peking: Foreign Language Press, 1956), 13.

Plan in 1956.[12] These motives stemmed from the leadership's experience with imperialism and its understanding of the international system as an arena of incessant conflict where national self-reliance in military capabilities was an essential requirement for survival and national autonomy. The record abounds in declarations on the latter point by India's first Prime Minister, Jawaharlal Nehru (1947–64), whose personal vision lay behind the Second Five Year Plan at a time when he was at the peak of his power. To provide a flavour of his position, it should suffice to call attention to one particular lengthy discourse by him on the issue before parliament in 1956. During that discourse, he reminded the legislators that for purposes of defence, apart from the armed forces, 'you have to have an industrial and technological background in the country.' In the absence of the latter, he felt, there can be no military strength, for in that case 'the army depends on outside factors, foreign machines, foreign economy, foreign help. Such a country is essentially a dependent country, though called independent.' He elaborated:

> The real strength of a country develops by industrial growth, which implies the capacity to make weapons of war for the army, the navy, or the air force. You cannot develop an isolated industry without a general background of industrial development. You cannot have a factory producing tanks in the absence of other industrial development in the country. A factory producing aircraft can be erected only if there is a large supply of technically trained people. Therefore, our immediate object should be, both from the point of view of economic development and that of defence, to build up industry, heavy industry in particular.[13]

Countless other statements on Nehru's part can be advanced to reinforce the point.

Beyond the perception of the relationship between heavy industry and military power to assure national survival, there has additionally been the influence of the leadership's ardent vision of China and India as potential major powers on their economic strategy, with heavy

[12] Baldev Raj Nayar, *The Modernization Imperative and Indian Planning* (New Delhi: Vikas, 1972), chapter 3. See also Nayar, 'The Political Mainsprings of Economic Planning in the New Nations: The Modernization Imperative versus Social Mobilization', *Comparative Politics*, 6, 3 (April 1974), 341–66.

[13] Jawaharlal Nehru, *Jawaharlal Nehru's Speeches: Volume Three: March 1953–August 1957* (Delhi: Ministry of Information and Broadcasting, 1958), 41–2.

industry recognized as essential to actualizing the potential. Again, this may be self-evident in the case of China, but it is as well true of India as has been demonstrated in a different context.[14] The vision is thus addressed to the larger global structure of power in the international system, not simply to defence against local adversaries.

What is manifest here is the other side of geopolitics than what has been seen in the behaviour of the hegemon to render some states into foreign policy satellites or protectorates of the hegemon. In that context, the hegemon has often determined the economic strategies of those states, and made them dependent on itself by integrating their economies with its own. As against that behaviour of the hegemon, evidently some other states that perceive themselves to have the potential to become major powers endeavour, in the first instance, to build the necessary capabilities to safeguard their national autonomy, and to avoid coming under the domination of the hegemon. In this respect, their behaviour is *reactive* or *defensive* in relation to the more activist thrust of hegemonic behaviour. Beyond this element of Fear, as a motivation in pursuing mercantilist policies and undertaking the building of autarkic economies, there may also lie Ambition, in terms of changing the very structure of world power in order to contain the power of the hegemon. The situation, consequently, becomes pregnant with the possibility of conflict between the hegemon and those states that aspire to such ambition.

Two contrary impulses, then, seem to be at work here. One impulse, that on the part of the hegemon, is to contain or exercise dominion over other regional powers and possible challengers. The other impulse, that on the part of potential major powers, is precisely to resist such containment or domination through the building of economic and military capabilities on an autonomous basis. Whether they can succeed in this endeavour is another matter. In India's case, nonetheless, the quest for autonomy under Nehru's leadership was visible along a broad front, not simply in the gigantic import substitution industrialization effort with a concentration on heavy industry. It was evident in pioneering and persisting with a policy of non-alignment between the two power blocs, and in rallying the developing countries to follow a non-aligned policy. It was also

---

[14] Baldev Raj Nayar and T.V. Paul, *India in the World Order: Searching for Major-Power Status* (Cambridge: Cambridge University Press, 2003), chapter 4.

manifest in developing friendship with the Soviet Union, as a counter
to what was perceived to be the regional containment of India by
the US through its military aid programme to build up Pakistan,[15]
and in mobilizing Soviet aid for India's heavy industry to advance
India's capabilities. All this was done while India maintained a
parliamentary system at home, remained a member of the
Commonwealth of Nations, and availed of economic aid from the
US and other Western countries in the 1950s and the 1960s.

The Costs of Over-Ambition

The inward-oriented heavy industry strategy, which was inaugurated
with the Second Five Year Plan (1956/7–60/1), was intended to make
a break with the inherited colonial economic structure of a backward
agriculture and agriculture-based industry. It was repeated in the

---

[15] The then Vice-President Richard Nixon had forcefully argued before the
National Security Council that the US provide military aid to Pakistan 'as a
counterforce to the confirmed neutralism of Jawaharlal Nehru's India'. See
Ralph de Toledano, *Nixon* (New York: Henry Holt, 1956), 164; see also Selig
S. Harrison, 'America, India, and Pakistan: A Chance for a Fresh Start', *Harper's*,
No. 233 (July 1966), 67, and *New York Times*, December 9 and 10, 1953.

In a wider context, Huntington states: 'In terms of power, the United States
and the secondary regional powers have common interests in limiting the
dominance of the major states in their regions.... The United States ... has
worked with Pakistan to balance India in South Asia. In all these cases,
cooperation serves mutual interests in *containing* the influence of the major
regional power.' Samuel P. Huntington, 'The Lonely Superpower', *Foreign
Affairs*, 78 (March–April 1999), 35–49, [emphasis added]. The theoretical
treatment of the issue is in George Liska, 'The Third World: Regional Systems
and Global Order', in Robert E. Osgood *et al.*, (eds), *Retreat From Empire*,
326. He states: 'Great powers can treat and have reason to treat individual
middle powers as regional rivals, and be led to help still lesser states to contain
them under the pretence of restraining, unilaterally or cooperatively, all Third
World conflict.'

Nehru's own perception of the aims of military aid to Pakistan was in line
with these assessments. He believed that American decision-makers 'imagine
that an alliance between Pakistan and the US would bring such overwhelming
pressure on India as to compel her to change her policy of nonalignment'. See
Kuldip Nayar, *India After Nehru* (Delhi: Vikas, 1975), 52. For a more extensive
discussion of the issue, see Nayar and Paul, *India in the World Order*, 5–6, 66–
79, 146–9.

Third Five Year Plan (1961/2–1965/6) and was going to be repeated again in what proved to be the abortive Fourth Five Year Plan (1966/7–1970/1). The strategy so long as it lasted, no doubt, succeeded in establishing a large industrial base in the country, with the capacity to produce on a considerable scale the metals and capital goods necessary for further industrialization, albeit with not the most modern technology. At the same time, however, the strategy became the source of serious distortions, disequilibria and shocks in the economy.

To begin with, the ambitious scale on which the heavy industry strategy was planned, proved to be simply beyond the means of the economy.[16] The strategy ran into a foreign exchange crisis in 1957 soon after it was launched, and it was bailed out for the time being by foreign aid from the major economic powers. There was rivalry at the time between the American and Soviet blocs, which proved advantageous to India in extracting aid from both. The occasion, however, established a pattern of dependency on foreign assistance, which deepened over time in the 1960s. Between the years 1960/1 and 1966/7, foreign aid utilized by India amounted to an average of 3.11 per cent of its GNP.[17] In this manner, even though the strategy had, as its aim, the achievement of economic independence by India, ironically it made the country dependent on foreign aid for its execution. The consequence of this aid dependency was foreign intrusion in India's economic decision-making. As India's economic condition worsened and a crisis loomed by the mid-1960s, the World Bank and the US insisted that India implement an elaborate liberalization package as a condition for further foreign aid.[18] In its situation of serious food shortages, high inflation and resource scarcity, India had perforce to agree. As the first step toward economic liberalization, India devalued its currency sharply by almost 60 per cent in June 1966. However, the devaluation resulted in widespread public opposition on account of the perception that it represented surrender to American dictation.

[16] See Nayar, *The Modernization Imperative*, chapters 2–5.

[17] Jagdish N. Bhagwati and Padma Desai, *India: Planning for Industrialization* (London: Oxford University Press, 1970), 174.

[18] Baldev Raj Nayar, *Globalization and Nationalism: The Changing Balance in India's Economic Policy, 1950–2000* (New Delhi: Sage Publications, 2001), chapter 3; Francine R. Frankel, *India's Political Economy, 1947–1977: The Gradual Revolution* (Princeton: Princeton University Press, 1978), 269–71.

The devaluation also turned out to be a major economic failure, because the prevailing drought conditions prevented the expected expansion of exports. Additionally, the devaluation, together with inflation and food shortages, made for severe electoral losses for the ruling Congress Party, which eventually split. In the face of these developments, the government under Prime Minister Indira Gandhi rejected the remainder of the liberalization package, and, instead, swung to a more radical course, which included the nationalization of the country's banking system as well as large parts of the private sector.

It was not simply the over ambitious nature of the heavy industry strategy that proved to be economically counterproductive. There were problems inherent in pursuing that strategy in the Indian context. On the one hand, the strategy was incongruent with India's democratic framework, which set limits to sacrifices by the populace for a forced-march industrialization on the pattern of the Soviet Union and China. On the other hand, given the long-gestation period required for the heavy industries to come on stream, there was no immediate pay-off or economic gratification for the public from the vast investments that were being made. Moreover, the mechanism of centralized planning through which India chose to implement the heavy industry strategy compounded these problems. As a necessary corollary to socialist planning, the state imposed an extensive administrative regime of discretionary controls and licensing to operate the largely insulated mixed economy. This regime made for considerable rent-seeking in the system. Besides, because of the ideological commitment to socialism and the perception that the private sector was incapable of industrializing the country, the state decided to occupy the 'commanding heights' of the economy, with much of the new heavy industry under state ownership. In addition, it nationalized large parts of the private sector, turning the public sector into an economic leviathan. Instead of becoming an instrument of a vibrant socialism, however, state ownership failed to generate the expected surpluses to plough back into new investment for advancing economic growth.

Most critically, the focus on heavy industry had made for the neglect of agriculture in an already food-deficit country. The result was that the country became increasingly dependent on the US for food aid, which amounted close to 1 per cent of India's GNP during the period 1960/1 to 1966/7.[19] The food scarcity reached crisis proportions by the mid-1960s, when India's urban areas had to depend, for their food, on American charity. The food dependency on the US also brought, in its train, intense American pressure on India to change its foreign policy, especially in regard to the American war in Vietnam. In sum, during the period of the heavy industry strategy India witnessed not only a slow economic growth rate, but also enountered severe problems in terms of inflation and shortages of foreign exchange, food, and consumer goods, as well as in safeguarding national autonomy.

The Turn to Economic Liberalization

Although the adoption of the Green Revolution strategy by India in the mid-1960s had brought some relief on the food and agriculture front by the late 1960s, the early 1970s again saw serious economic deterioration. Severe economic problems emerged as a result of: the influx of ten million refugees from East Pakistan following the military crackdown there in 1971; the Bangladesh War of 1971, during which the US and China in collaboration backed the Pakistani military regime; the termination of American economic aid because of the war; the Indian renunciation of concessional food aid out of anger at American actions; and the first OPEC oil price shock in 1973. In addition, India faced prolonged agricultural stagnation because of failing monsoons. Together, these various factors created raging inflation and widespread shortages of food and essential goods. These latter developments were a source of great deprivation for the public. They generated numerous mass protests, while the trade unions threatened to shut down the economy with a countrywide railway strike.

Confronted with this grim crisis, Prime Minister Indira Gandhi finally responded with decisive action. She crushed the railway strike, and proceeded to impose in late 1974 a ruthless stabilization package. Joshi and Little point out: 'Mrs Gandhi decided that inflation had reached the limits of political tolerance and had to be dealt with. Breaking the strike was itself an anti-inflation measure.... After the strike was broken, an interministerial task force of senior bureaucrats was formed to devise an anti-inflationary policy. When it came, the

[19] Bhagwati and Desai, *India*, 174.

crackdown was savage.'[20] This turn to economic orthodoxy was indicative of severe disillusionment on the part of Mrs Gandhi with her economic radicalism of the recent past. The nationalization spree starting with bank nationalization in 1969 and the tightening of discretionary controls on the private sector had proven counterproductive. She now halted her earlier relentless drive for nationalization, and also introduced some measures of economic liberalization to give more freedom to the private sector.

Because of this course reversal, 1975 can therefore be regarded as marking the starting point in India's subsequent gradual and halting, but progressively increasing economic liberalization. The stabilization package had been primarily focused on the domestic economy. In the meantime, India had moved to open up the economy somewhat to the international economy, even if surreptitiously. The inward-oriented heavy industry strategy had contained a structural bias against exports even as high inflation had resulted in making the rupee overvalued. Explicit devaluation was not deemed feasible because of the perceived popular revulsion against it in view of the past experience with the 1966 devaluation. However, as fixed exchange rates were jettisoned on a wide scale in the wake of the collapse of the Bretton Woods regime in 1971, the government quietly linked the rupee to the weak British pound.[21] This linkage resulted in a more realistic exchange rate, which boosted exports subsequently. The de facto devaluation thus facilitated a closer integration of the Indian economy with the world economy. Elsewhere, in a quantitative analysis, it has been shown that India's participation in foreign trade was very low in 1970, being less than 8 per cent of GDP, while exports were less than 4 per cent.[22] However, there was some advance in India's trade during the 1970s after 1973. Between 1974 and 1987, the share of foreign trade in India's GDP expanded from 10.21 per cent to 14.05 per cent. Over the period from 1988 to 1991, there was a significant jump in the share, followed by a leap over the next four years, with the share crossing the level of 20 per cent in 1993, and reaching the unprecedented figure of almost 25 per cent in 1995.

[20] Vijay Joshi and I.M.D. Little, *India: Macroeconomics and Political Economy 1964–1991* (Washington, DC: World Bank, 1994), 55.

[21] Ibid., *India*, 56.

[22] Baldev Raj Nayar, 'Opening Up and Openness of Indian Economy', *Economic and Political Weekly*, 36, 37 (15–21 September 2001), 3529–37.

The next step in the gradual unfolding of economic liberalization took place subsequent to Mrs Gandhi's return to office in 1980, after the interregnum of 1977–9 when she was out of power, having been repudiated in the 1977 elections. Her new start in power took place in difficult economic circumstances because of an extremely severe drought the previous year, which had reduced India's food production by more than a sixth, and also because of the second OPEC oil price shock. Despite the immense crisis facing the country, Mrs Gandhi was determined to see that India continued on her path of higher economic growth. To that end, she was anxious to avoid the protectionist policies of the past, and to continue on the path of economic liberalization. She had no pretensions to socialism any longer; by this time she had already shed both her socialist ideology and her earlier socialist colleagues. She successfully approached the IMF for a massive loan, but before doing so she pre-empted any imposition of IMF conditionalities by implementing an economic reform programme of India's own design. India adopted a new liberal industrial policy in July 1981, facilitated technology, and capital goods imports, and removed subsidies on several basic goods. In addition, Mrs Gandhi adopted a tough attitude toward the public sector, demanding improved performance.[23] As an earnest of her seriousness in this regard, she set up a committee to recommend reforms for the public sector. However, her plans for economic reform were overwhelmed by the increased salience of the problem of national integration, in the course of handling which she was assassinated in October 1984.

Mrs Gandhi had taken the small but significant steps in economic reform in the context of economic crises. Her son and political successor, Prime Minister Rajiv Gandhi, then carried forward the process of economic reform, but remarkably his efforts in this direction took place in the absence of an economic crisis. They owed more to his personal fascination for modern technology, his deep concern at India's slow economic growth and its economic marginalization internationally, and his passion to see India enter the twenty-first century as an advanced industrial power. Interestingly, unlike his mother, who had continued, no doubt for shrewd reasons, to proclaim her commitment to socialism even as she pressed forward with reform, Rajiv Gandhi forthrightly made liberalization the

[23] Nayar, *Globalization and Nationalism*, 112–20.

centrepiece of his political programme without masking it behind socialist rhetoric. He hastened the pace of change and enacted reform along a considerable front.

The key feature of the changes under him was reliance on the private sector—instead of the public sector—as the mechanism for economic growth in the future, and the provision of the required resources and appropriate environment to facilitate its performance. Major reforms were undertaken in the areas of taxation, industrial licensing, and trade policy. Soon, however, he encountered resistance, not only within his own party but also among the public where liberalization came to be identified as a policy for the rich, which made the government politically vulnerable. As a result, in the final analysis, his liberalization effort did not cut very deep, and amounted to only tinkering within the existing system rather than making a break with it. Still, his tenure in office, from 1985 to 1989, changed the nature of the debate on the economy, where, as against the earlier ideological hegemony of socialism and mercantilism, it now became legitimate to regard liberalization as an appropriate alternative economic strategy.[24]

In spite of the various doses of reform from 1974 to 1990, India remained a comprehensively and stringently controlled economy, both internally and externally. Indeed, Joshi and Little maintained that 'In June 1991 India was the most autarkic non-communist country in the world,' while the IMF noted that India was 'one of the most heavily regulated economies in the world'.[25] Starting in that month, however, the most substantial instalment of economic policy reform so far in India took place over the next two years. The reform came in the wake of the economic crisis in 1991, which had been building up over the previous year. The crisis had reached the point where India would have had to take recourse to defaulting on its foreign obligations. The fundamental source of the crisis was the pattern of persistent annual fiscal deficits over the preceding decade, in turn a consequence of heavy subsidies to important political groups. Relatedly, the balance of payments situation had become critical. The final coup de grace was delivered by the Gulf crisis and war in 1990 and 1991,

---

[24] Ibid., 120–6.

[25] Vijay Joshi and I.M.D. Little, *India's Economic Reforms 1991–2000* (New Delhi: Oxford University Press, 1996), 63; and Ajai Chopra, *India: Economic Reform and Growth* (Washington, DC: IMF, 1995), 57.

which resulted in escalation of oil prices but, more importantly, in the drying up of inward remittances from Indian expatriate labour in the Middle East. India had to therefore, approach the IMF for support for a stabilization package. Devaluation and austerity through contractionary policies followed, as a matter of course.

But, significantly, India soon went beyond the conditionalities to undertake major economic restructuring, stemming from disenchantment with its earlier policies, and awe at the advance made by the economies of East and Southeast Asia. Reforms were energetically undertaken, both in the internal and the external spheres of the economy. Externally, besides devaluation, the rupee was made convertible on the current account, licensing was virtually abolished for imports, and tariff levels were drastically cut. Further, foreign direct investment was allowed to the extent of 51 per cent automatically, in a wide range of industries even as portfolio investment was welcomed. Internally, the entire edifice of industrial licensing was abolished except in the case of 15 industries of strategic or environmental importance, and anti-trust legislation was amended to facilitate expansion and diversification of capacity by large firms. Moreover, the number of industries reserved for the public sector was drastically reduced to only six. The taxation system was rationalized, while tax rates were slashed. Major reforms were also introduced to put the banking system on a sounder footing.[26]

With little evident embarrassment, the top leadership had made a 'paradigm shift'—what critics called a 'U-turn'—from the state to the market, openly and enthusiastically embracing integration of the Indian economy into the world economy. Although not all that was intended was achieved, a substantial movement took place in the direction of liberalization and openness of the economy. As one eminent economist noted: 'These reforms taken together constitute a comprehensive and thoroughgoing overhaul of the economic policy regime.' Similarly, the World Bank declared that 'India has fundamentally altered its development paradigm' and that the reforms 'have ended four decades of planning and have initiated a quiet economic revolution'.[27]

[26] Nayar, *Globalization and Nationalism*, chapter 4.
[27] Raja J. Chelliah, *Towards Sustainable Growth: Essays in Fiscal and Financial Sector Reforms in India* (New Delhi: Oxford University Press, 1996), 9; and World Bank, *India: Five Years of Stabilization and Reform and the Challenges Ahead* (Washington, DC: 1996), xvii, 31.

As already indicated, the period after 1975 has seen India attain a higher economic growth rate and an improved performance in terms of exports. There has also been an unprecedented accumulation of foreign exchange reserves after the early 1990s. Particularly noteworthy has been the rise of a world–class software industry, with substantial penetration by it of the world, especially the American market. It would be difficult to ascribe the outcome that has taken place in the wake of the reforms to anything other than the reforms themselves. Certainly, the flourishing of the software industry was a result of the dismantling of physical controls in the economy, and the providing of greater scope for private enterprise to flourish. Change in strategy from inward orientation to outward orientation thus preceded the improvement in the growth rate of the economy, and is causally related to it.[28]

[28] For a revisionist position that challenges the view that the shift to a higher growth rate began with the economic liberalization of the early 1990s, see Dani Rodrik and Arvind Subramanian, 'From "Hindu Growth" to Productivity Surge: The Mystery of the Indian Growth Transition' (available online; Cambridge, MA and Washington, DC: March 2004). The authors argue that, in fact, the shift began around 1980, and was generated by attitudinal change in the state toward a pro-business (in contrast to a pro-liberalization) approach. See also, for a somewhat similar position, Arvind Virmani, 'India's Economic Growth: From Socialist Rate of Growth to Bharatiya Rate of Growth' (Working Paper No. 122; New Delhi: Indian Council for Research on International Economic Relations, February 2004). A forceful critique of the Rodrik–Subramanian thesis appears in Swaminathan S. Anklesaria Aiyar, 'The 1980s Revisited', *Economic Times* Online, 17 March 2004. He maintains: 'Rodrik–Subramanian argue that the 1980s reform was internal rather than external. Yes, mainly. Caveats: The liberalization of foreign collaboration, a major factor, was external rather than internal. So was the aggressive exchange rate depreciation and income tax exemption given to exports in the second half of the 1980s, leading to an export boom.' Besides, he states: 'In 1981 India got the biggest loan in IMF history that made some modest opening up obligatory.'

Aiyar's position broadly coincides with the stand taken here and earlier in Nayar, *Globalization and Nationalization*, chapters 3–4. For an adequate comprehension of the issue, it is essential to take a broad 'big picture', rather than a hair-splitting, view of it. The successive instalments of economic reforms starting from 1974, though undertaken fitfully and incrementally, cumulatively meant the repudiation of, and the shifting of course from, the heavy industry strategy with the state in control of the economy's 'commanding heights'. That strategy was structurally biased against the consumer, agriculture, the market, and integration with the world economy.

It may be of some significance that the fuller turn to liberalization took place in the context of the collapse of the Soviet model in the 1980s, the subsequent disintegration of the Soviet Union, and the emergence of unipolarity in the international system under the hegemony of the US. However, it would perhaps be inappropriate to draw any causal connection between these events and economic reform in India. As has been seen above, long before Margaret Thatcher and Ronald Reagan came on the political scene, Mrs Gandhi had initiated the process of reform in late 1974, albeit tentatively and hesitantly. The fundamental reasons behind the change were initially internal, principally dissatisfaction with the adverse impact of the earlier strategy on economic growth and national autonomy, and the consequent search for new policies. Subsequently, the rise of 'the Asian Tigers' and the turn to reform and integration with the world economy on the part of China had a significant impact, chiefly the fear of becoming marginalized in the world economy. It is noteworthy that, during the 1990s, the relations between the US and India were not particularly friendly. Rather, India perceived the US as attempting to curb and constrain its defence capabilities and potential through a variety of international control regimes.

Economic Liberalization and National Security

Does the turn to liberalization betoken a divergence between economic strategy and geopolitics? At first blush, the break in economic policy in 1991 seems to mark a disjuncture in the government's earlier integration of the goals of national security and economic autonomy into the very design of Nehru's economic strategy of heavy industry.[29] However, the relationship between national security and economic policy is more complex, and is not limited to a single variant and certainly not for all time. In part, the break in economic policy itself was a consequence of the fact that Nehru's economic strategy, while no doubt laying a substantial base for a defence-oriented and self-reliant economy, also led to a considerable marginalization of India on the international scene.

[29] Joydeep Mukherji, 'Commentary: India Seeks an Economic "Tryst with Destiny"', *Standard & Poor's*, December 1999, 1–6.

India fell far behind many other developing countries that had started out from a similar economic base, but with a different economic policy. India's economic performance was starkly unimpressive in terms of per capita income, alleviation of poverty, and its share in the world output and exports.

The implications of such an economic performance were, as Paul Kennedy would have predicted, profoundly inimical to national security,[30] for it led to a gross imbalance between India and other major powers in national capabilities. In this state of affairs, no major power role could be obtained, and no national security could be assured. A flourishing economy was essential to national security, to economic autonomy, and to an adequate international role. In contrast, the country's economic performance in the 1960s and 1970s aggravated the nation's political and military vulnerabilities. Within less than a decade between 1962 and 1971, the country faced three wars, all of which were initiated by other powers. The economic performance crippled the nation from asserting itself on the international scene. Its vulnerabilities in terms of food and aid dependence, compounded by internal threats to political stability and national unity, made the country cautious in pursuing its foreign policy aspirations for fear of alienating the chief aid donors.

India's economic marginalization on the world scene was an important stimulus to economic policy reform. Though this was articulated primarily in economic terms, the disquiet over its implications for security and autonomy was not far from the surface. Significantly, it was in the context of the higher economic growth of the 1990s, which added to the resources and self-confidence of a new political elite in power, that India took the decision to defy the major powers to go in for the nuclear tests in 1998. It did so in the assurance that, with an improved economy, combined with its self-reliant base, it could take the resulting economic sanctions in its stride. However, the concern with national security is not a one-shot affair, it is of enduring relevance. As one of the more sober-minded ministers in the central government, Arun Shourie, has commented:

> As does the danger that lurks if we fail to achieve our potential: the growing economic distance between China and India will get translated into a

[30] Paul Kennedy, *The Rise and Fall of Great Powers.*

growing distance between our respective military capabilities, and that will constitute an irresistible temptation to many.[31]

It is evident that national security cannot be disassociated from economic performance and, therefore, from economic policy, though the form in which the relationship manifests itself may change over time.[32] To be sure, there are constraints that also accompany economic interdependence, but they pale in comparison to those that emerge from economic stagnation and marginalization.

Summary and Conclusions

India's experience reinforces the point that outward orientation has been associated with higher economic growth rates while inward orientation seems to have depressed growth rates. That a higher growth rate has followed the shift to outward orientation suggests the causal potential of such orientation. The outward orientation did not occur full-blown but developed gradually and haltingly from 1975 onwards, taking varyingly the form of tacit and explicit devaluation, facilitation of technology imports, and trade liberalization as part of a larger programme of economic policy reform.

India's experience as well suggests that geopolitics, albeit of a different kind than that relevant to the hegemon, has not been absent from questions of economic strategy in its case. The country's initial but long-drawn economic strategy of concentration on heavy industry, which resulted in a slow growth rate, was influenced by considerations of national autonomy—to which India has always attached high value—and by strategic aspirations for a major power role. As Selig Harrison has pointed out: 'The Indian development experience cannot be meaningfully judged in a narrowly economic context. For the implicit rationale underlying Indian policies has been a nationalist rationale, a readiness to bear inordinate costs, if necessary, to maximize the independent character of the industrialization

---

[31] Arun Shourie, 'Getting Our Act Together', *Indian Express* Online, 21 March 2003.

[32] For the argument that liberalization and globalization have been beneficial from the viewpoint of autonomy, see Baldev Raj Nayar, 'Globalization and India's National Autonomy', *Journal of Commonwealth and Comparative Politics*, 41, 2 (July 2003), 1–34.

achieved.'[33] Eventually, however, the Indian leadership, too, had to reckon with the high costs of its particular economic path. The inward-oriented heavy industry strategy resulted not only in a slow growth rate, but also made for dependency rather than autonomy. But, as it realized the costs of the strategy, the Indian leadership changed course even though the change has been stretched out over a long period of time.

Despite the better economic performance since the mid-1970s, more particularly after 1980, India's improved growth rate has been only modest. India has not yet succeeded in establishing on a sustained basis, the high growth rates that have been witnessed in the case of the Asian Tigers and China, even as there is widespread recognition that a high growth rate is absolutely essential to alleviating poverty. In part, the reason for the modest nature of the growth rate is that India has been slow in enacting economic policy reform because of the difficulties in building policy consensus in a far-flung federal structure situated in an ethnically heterogeneous continental polity.

[33] Selig S. Harrison, *The Widening Gulf: Asian Nationalism and American Policy* (New York: The Free Press, 1978), 326.

Chapter 12

PAKISTAN

Military Rule, Alliances, and Economic Performance

In political terms, Pakistan presents a dramatic contrast with India. It has seen three major military coups d'état (1958, 1977, 1999), and the military has ruled the country for more than half the years since the founding of the state (1958–71, 1977–88, 1999–). Even when civilian governments have formally been in power, they have not been civilian in substance. They have been, in effect, excluded from the arena of defence and foreign policy, which has become a prerogative of the military in terms of effective control. Besides, the military and its intelligence services have purposely penetrated the civilian bureaucracy and the key institutions of society.

Unlike the Indian case, where there is a major divide in the post-Independence years, distinguishing a period of low growth from that of medium growth, Pakistan manifests a pattern of *alternation* or *oscillation* between a low growth rate and a high growth rate. At least, that is the case over the first five of the six different periods (see Table 12.1). The record for the last period, however, is tentative since the political dispensation of that period has not yet come to an end, but it bids fair nonetheless to follow the earlier pattern. Is this pattern of alternation or oscillation unrelated to geopolitics and national security? While undoubtedly, many factors may have gone into the emergent pattern, geopolitics and national security have been a dominant influence in the outcome.

At one level, there seems to be a visible correlation between the better performance by way of a high growth rate and military rule in Pakistan. Indeed, the phenomenon of the better economic performance under military rule has had a major impact on the

Table 12.1: GDP Growth Rates in Pakistan over Different Periods

Period	GDP Growth Rate (%)		Nature of Rule
1. 1947–58	2.90	(1947–58)	civilian
2. 1958–71	6.63	(1960–71)	military
3. 1971–7	4.12	(1972–7)	civilian
4. 1977–88	6.86	(1978–88)	military
5. 1988–99	4.06	(1989–99)	civilian
6. 1999–	4.17	(2000–4)	military

Source: Except for the first and last periods, the figures are based on data in World Development Indicators; the periods in parentheses represent the actual years on which the figures are based. The figure for the first period is from Shahid Javed Burki, *Pakistan: The Continuing Search for Nationhood* (Boulder, CO: Westview Press, 1991), 118. The figure for the second period differs from that by Burki for the years 1958–1971 at 5.3 per cent. However, elsewhere Burki gives the figure of 6.8 per cent for GNP growth rate for those same years; see Shahid Javed Burki and Craig Baxter, *Pakistan Under the Military: Eleven Years of Zia ul-Haq* (Boulder, CO: Westview Press, 1991), 90. His figures in these two sources also differ for the third period; they are indicated as 5.4 per cent and 4.6 per cent, respectively. The figure for the last period is based on the editorial 'SBP Report', *The Nation* Online, 29 June 2003, with the growth rates being 2.4 per cent, 3.4 per cent and 5.1 per cent for the fiscal years 2000–1, 2001–2 and 2002–3, respectively, and on the story '5.5 to 5.8 pc GDP Growth Likely, says State Bank', *Dawn* Online, 31 March 2004, for the fiscal year 2003–4.

political thinking of some important authorities, such as the former senior World Bank official, Shahid Javed Burki. The correlation has led them to support the construction of a political regime that maintains a civilian façade but preserves the hegemony of the military, in the conviction that this is the best possible political arrangement in the given conditions of Pakistan.[1] However, taking the correlation at face value may be too simplistic. It also happens to be the case that, whether by human design on the part of the military rulers or by divine intervention or both, military rule has coincided with

[1] This assessment is based on the reading of Burki's weekly column in the newspaper *Dawn* Online during 2002 and 2003. The present military regime under General Pervez Musharraf intends to legally entrench the domination of the military over the polity through the establishment of a National Security Council, where it would have preponderant influence. See Ayaz Amir, 'Platos from the Drill Square', *Dawn* Online, 9 April 2004.

an explicit or implicit military alliance between the US and Pakistan.[2]

The military alliance with the US invariably results in a very substantial input of American largesse into the economy of Pakistan. But the economic consequences of the military alliance are much wider than direct American economic and military aid. The alliance with the US additionally brings in economic aid from other American allies in Europe, such as Great Britain and Germany, and in Asia, such as Japan. Moreover, the US and its allies then assure Pakistan a more sympathetic hearing for loans from the international financial institutions (IFIs), such as the IMF and the World Bank. Again, the alliance between the military rulers and the US endows legitimacy on the former, who having overthrown a civilian regime lack it, and are largely isolated internationally. By the same token, it also signals to local and foreign private investors that there is likely to be political stability and better economic prospects in Pakistan under the umbrella of the alliance and the accompanying input of increased foreign aid from the US and its allies. Therefore, as Omar Noman says, 'External resources have tended to ebb and flow in line with the state of US–Pakistan relations.'[3] That ebb and flow of aid is correlated, at the same time, with the variation in the outcome by way of Pakistan's growth rates because of the contribution it makes to Pakistan's economic fundamentals. As Noman puts it:

> In the economic arena, aid has played a significant role in physical capital formation, and in providing balance of payments support, particularly for industrial development. Donors have made an increasingly important contribution to policy reforms.... Pakistan has been a major recipient of aid which has helped relieve the investment constraint, particularly on physical infrastructure and the balance of payments constraint on growth.[4]

Despite the advantages of economic largesse from the US and its allies, and the higher growth rates that have resulted from it, the consequences of such an arrangement have, however, at times been disastrous for Pakistan when seen in their totality. There is merit,

[2] On the relations between the two countries, see Dennis Kux, *The United States and Pakistan, 1947–2000: Disenchanted Allies* (Washington, DC: Woodrow Wilson Centre Press, 2001).

[3] Omar Noman, *Economic and Social Progress in Asia: Why Pakistan Did Not Become a Tiger* (Karachi: Oxford University Press, 1997), 137.

[4] Ibid., 135, 176.

nonetheless, in the old saw that the three really important forces in Pakistan through its history have been 'Allah, Army, and America',[5] with the intensity of the influence of each varying over time. These three elements are, however, not unrelated.

Religion, Military Dominance, and the United States

Pakistan is by self-declaration, an ideological state. It was founded as a homeland for the Muslims of the subcontinent, and was the result of a spasmodic mass mobilization of the Muslim community in the 1940s by its political and religious elites on the basis of the slogan of 'Islam in Danger'. The spearhead of the mobilization was the Muslim League, an organization with which the British colonial bureaucracy was in tacit alliance. As the renowned authority Khalid Sayeed averred, 'the Muslim League during the pre-Partition period had sought the assistance of the *ulama* and other religious leaders in the election campaigns and had promised the voters that Pakistan would be an Islamic state.' The preambles to Pakistan's various constitutions since the founding of the state have declared that the 'sovereignty over the entire Universe belongs to Almighty Allah alone, and the authority exercisable by the people within the limits prescribed by Him is a sacred trust.'[6] Accordingly, the state has implemented by instalments the Islamic system of law, the Sharia, and has also officially characterized some groups that perceive themselves to be Muslim, such as the Ahmadiyyas, as heretical.

Islam is a comprehensive theological system that encompasses spiritual, social, and political aspects of life in this world and beyond. Of special interest here is its position on the role of the military in political life, and its posture toward other states. Writing in a major

---

[5] Anatol Lieven, 'The Pressures on Pakistan', *Foreign Affairs*, 81, 1 (January–February 2002), 106–18. The venerable political scientist, Anwar Syed, says: 'We have come to believe that nothing of consequence even in our internal governance and policy-making can happen without the consent of the United States. The road to power in Islamabad, it is said, goes through Washington. This belief pervades the thinking of both the power-elite and the counter-elite in our polity.' Anwar Syed, 'The Right Policy Recipe', *Dawn* Online, 25 May 2003.

[6] Khalid B. Sayeed, *The Political System of Pakistan* (Boston, MA: Houghton Mifflin, 1967), 68, 160.

professional journal, a Canadian political scientist of Pakistani origin, Saleem Qureshi, compellingly relates the dominance of the military in Muslim majority states directly to Islamic theology.[7] No doubt, military intervention in politics has been a wider phenomenon in the developing world and is not confined to Pakistan only, but the same general causes do not necessarily hold good for every state or category of states. To recognize only general causes as being true in every individual instance or part of a sample is to fall prey to the *ecological fallacy*, as it is to deny the specificity of causes in particular cases. At the same time, to maintain that a country's deep-rooted principal religion is like all other religions or that it has no impact on political phenomena is really to say, counter to the position of the believers themselves, that it is meaningless. Quite the contrary, religion can have a powerful impact on social and political behaviour in specific settings. Besides, not to take others seriously when they declare that they act out of their ideology and ideological convictions is to implicitly accuse them of hypocrisy.

In Islamic doctrine, the world is sharply divided in a Manichaean fashion into *Dar al-Islam* (the world of peace) and *Dar al-Harb* (the world of war), and it has been the historic mission of Islam to convert the world of war into the world of Islam. Qureshi says:

> To fight against unbelievers either to convert them to Islam or to subdue them or to destroy them—in case they choose to fight—in order to spread Islam, and to make it triumphant over all religions is considered a sacred duty of Muslims.
>
> The religious duty to universalize the rule of God, first by defending the Islamic state against external, non-Muslim threat, and second by expanding the realm of Islam and thus reducing the non-Muslim realm, is called *Jihad*. As the famous fourteenth-century Islamic historian Ibn Khaldun says, 'the holy war is a religious duty [and the Muslim's obligation is] to convert everybody to Islam either by persuasion or by force'.

There may be some controversy over the precise interpretation of the concept of the stark division of the world into the inherently warring zones of Islam and non-Islam, and also that of *Jihad* in resolving the conflict between them. However, no one of authority

---

[7] Saleem Qureshi, 'Military in the Polity of Islam: Religion as a Basis for Civil–Military Interactions', *International Political Science Review*, 2, 3 (1981), 271–82.

in Islam or Islamic polities has ever repudiated these concepts.[8] Besides, differences in interpretation should not bar analysts from inquiring as to what the dominant or principal interpretation is, and whether or not practice is in accord with it. In addition to the injunctions of the Islamic doctrine, there is the further fact to consider of the Prophet himself being a military commander, and of his immediate successors going on 'an unending conquest of the world'. As a result of these various elements, Qureshi concludes that 'the attraction of the military for the Muslims seems magnetic' and 'they tend to convert their states very readily to military rule'.[9]

---

[8] In addition, future generations are being continuously socialized into these concepts, which form part of the school curricula in Pakistan, not only in social studies but also in biology. Any attempt to remove or modify them in the direction of greater tolerance is met with strong resistance. See Zubeida Mustafa, 'A Curriculum of Hatred', *Dawn* Online, 31 March 2004, which underlines the findings of think tanks and scholars that: 'the curricula and textbooks in Pakistan were insensitive to the existing religious diversity of the nation, incited militancy, and violence, and encouraged prejudice, bigotry and discrimination toward fellow-citizens, especially women and minorities... our textbooks construct India and Hindus as enemies and ... incite permanent enmity, hatred and alienation with India... these books promote militarism and violence, and indirectly justify a heavy defence expenditure.'

[9] Qureshi, 'Military in the Polity of Islam', 275, 277, 280.

Another Muslim scholar says in a matter-of-fact manner, 'According to the majority view in the classical sunni school of thought, the world is divided into *dar-al Islam*, the domain of Islam, and *dar-al harb*, the non-Islamic territory. It is a collective responsibility of the *ummah* to expand the boundaries of *dar-al Islam*. The instrument to achieve this end is *jihad*, the holy war.' See Syed Aziz-al Ahsan, *Islamization of the State in a Dualistic Culture: The Case of Bangladesh* (Ph.D dissertation, Montreal, McGill University, 1990), 58.

Note that, in a Foreword, the then military ruler of Pakistan, signing himself as Chief of the Army Staff, General M. Zia-ul-Haq commended the book by Brigadier S.K. Malik, *The Quranic Concept of War* (Lahore: Wajidalis, 1979), for its exposition of 'the Quranic philosophy on the application of military force, within the context of the totality that is *Jehad*'. He added: 'The professional soldier in a Muslim army, pursuing the goals of a Muslim state, cannot become "professional" if in all his activities he does not take on "the colour of Allah".'

In the Preface to the book, the eminent lawyer A.K. Brohi declares: 'Islam views the world as though it were bipolarized in two opposing camps—Darus-Salam facing Darul-Harb—the first one is submissive to the Lord in cooperating with the God's purpose to establish peace, order, and such other pre-conditions

Thus understood, Muslim states are innately revisionist. It may well be that *all* states are inherently revisionist, given the anarchical nature of the international system.[10] However, realist theory also takes states to be rational actors, which act strategically on the basis of a calculation of costs and benefits. The distinctive function of ideology, however, is precisely to disrupt the cost–benefit calculus. Thus, revisionism under ideology stands on an altogether different footing than in realism. Perhaps, the force of circumstances may deter ideology-driven states from revisionism, and compel them to accept the status quo in relation to other states. Interestingly, however, an American scholar who was sympathetic to Pakistan, the late Wayne Wilcox, had concluded on the basis of his analysis of the relations between India and Pakistan that:

> Most India–Pakistan interstate conflict since 1947 has been generated by Pakistan. The weak party, in this situation, is also the revisionist power, and at times, it has pursued what Boulding could characterize as 'rational aggression', 'the deliberate, planned conflict or game of ruin' against India, in the calculated hope of relative benefit.[11]

It may be that the Islamic doctrine has special force in relation to India, because the members of the majority community of the Hindus as infidels are not even 'people of the book', a concept that may have, at times, moderated Muslim conflict with the Christians and Jews. Besides, the fact that India is a much larger and more

---

of human development, but the second one, on the other hand, is engaged in perpetuating defiance of the same Lord.' In justifying the unending conflict of the world of Islam against non-Muslims, he says: 'The defiance of God's authority by one who is His slave exposes that slave to the risk of being held guilty of treason and such a one, in the perspective of Islamic law, is indeed to be treated as a sort of that cancerous growth on that organism of humanity, which has been created, "Kanafsin Wahidatin", that is, like one, single, indivisible self. It thus becomes necessary to remove the cancerous malformation even if it be by surgical means (if it would not respond to other treatment), in order to save the rest of Humanity.' Ibid., vi–vii.

[10] John J. Mearsheimer, *The Tragedy of Great Power Politics*, chapters 1–2.

[11] Wayne A. Wilcox, 'India and Pakistan', in Steven L. Spiegel and Kenneth N. Waltz (eds), *Conflict in World Politics* (Cambridge, MA: Winthrop Publishers, 1971), 240–60. For a theoretical treatment, see T.V. Paul, *Asymmetric Conflicts: War Initiation by Weaker States* (Cambridge: Cambridge University Press, 1994).

powerful state not only causes insecurity for Pakistan but can, by its very existence, be perceived as an affront by the latter. For, after all, the Muslims were the rulers over the Hindus of India for over 600 years and their great monuments, such as the Taj Mahal and the Red Fort, are today located in India. In any case, Pakistan has eagerly undertaken to neutralize India's superiority by attempting to match its military capabilities, and to block its emergence as a major power. As Lieutenant General A.I. Ikram of Pakistan expresses:

> Pakistan, thus, became an obstacle in India's march to greatness. If Pakistan would not accept India as a great power, the rest of the world was not likely to do so either. Pakistan had to be removed from the path of the Indian march to glory, but Pakistan had no intention of being so removed. This led the two countries on a collision course, and they collided again and again.
>
> They are still on the same collision course, in spite of the reduction in size of Pakistan, which is partly compensated for by the internal weakening and disruption within India and the rise of divisive elements in that country. This state is likely to continue so long as India retains its designs of hegemony over South Asia, pre-eminence in Asia, and a great power role in the world.[12]

In short, Pakistan's overall national posture is Indo-centric; all Pakistani policies, or nearly all, are explained by its fundamental hostility, in the final analysis religion-based, toward India. India is the master key to understanding most Pakistani behaviour. The 'centrality of India in Pakistani thinking' that Lieven refers to[13] is not confined to any single issue, but is pervasive across issues. Making India the central focus of Pakistan's posture on the world has, however, been extremely costly. As Anwar Syed points out:

> Pakistan has fallen into the pits partly because it has adopted goals that are out of proportion to its means. Its security problem is focused on India whose resources are much larger. It wants to wrest Kashmir from Indian control, which it has not been able to do in spite of several resorts to military force. Further, Pakistan has been reluctant to accept the fact that it is a smaller power; it has all along wanted to be treated as India's equal. These goals have not only been unattainable, they have been very expensive to maintain.[14]

[12] Lt General A.I. Akram, 'Security and Stability in South Asia', in Stephen Philip Cohen (ed.), *The Security of South Asia: American and Asian Perspectives* (Urbana: University of Illinois Press, 1987), 163–80.

[13] Lieven, 'The Pressures on Pakistan', 107.

[14] Anwar Syed, 'The Right Policy Recipe', *Dawn* Online, 25 May 2003.

In order to achieve its aims in relation to India, alliance with external powers is absolutely essential for Pakistan, for, otherwise, it does not have the capacity to match Indian capabilities—and that is where America comes in. Early in Pakistan's post-independence years, while it was under civilian rule, the military in Pakistan under General Ayub Khan had directly approached and cultivated authorities in the US Defence Department with a view to establishing a special relationship. To that end, it and the larger regime staged a posture of sincere anti-communism in order to extract military support from the US against the communist bloc, even though the real object was to countervail against India. For its own purposes, regardless of whether they were a wider opposition to the Soviet Union or building a regional counterweight against India or both, the US was willing to oblige. The two countries then joined together in a military alliance in 1954, and soon Pakistan became known as 'the most allied ally', because of its membership in several regional military blocs sponsored by the US and its European allies.

The newly forged alliance started a massive flow of technologically advanced weaponry from the US to Pakistan, serving in effect to cancel India's superiority in numbers, which was the real intent of the alliance, at least of one of the parties. That Pakistan's anti-communism had been staged to mislead the US emerges as self-evident from the fact that Pakistan developed, when it became feasible, a de facto alliance with the communist regime in China even before a decade had elapsed after it had entered into the military alliance with the US. The target of the later alliance with China, too, was India. Meanwhile, large-scale economic aid from the US became a critical factor in the economic performance of Pakistan. Thus, American geopolitics in relation to economic development was in play in Pakistan, much as it was in the Northeast Asian states.

The military aid had two consequences for Pakistan, one internal and the other external. The abundant availability of resources from the US directly to the Pakistani military had the result of undermining the balance between the civilian and military wings of Pakistan's political system. It bloated the military establishment of Pakistan beyond that country's capacity, and also threw it out of balance with the rest of society and polity. It was no longer an organic part of the national system, but stood above and over it. It was an easy transition from that situation to direct military control of the entire society and polity. The domination of the military over the nation meant that policies that were presented as being justified by the national interest simply represented, most of the time, the interests of a single institutional interest group, the military. No doubt, 'the army is Pakistan's only effective modern institution and the backbone of the Pakistani state,' but:

> Over the years, Pakistan's military has been responsible for diverting a huge proportion of the country's resources to support itself. The military has always argued that such huge subsidies are essential for defence against India. But this massive spending has left disastrously little for infrastructure, education, and other fundamentals of economic development. Over the past ten years, military spending has averaged more than 30 per cent of the budget, and most of the rest has been spent on debt servicing.[15]

As a simple rule of thumb, Pakistan's defence expenditures as a proportion of GDP, although varying over time, have been twice or more than twice those of India's.

In terms of the external arena, the achievement of technological superiority by the Pakistan military as a recipient of American weaponry, no doubt, imparted greater self-assurance to the military. It reinforced the belief that one Pakistani soldier was the equal of five or more Indian soldiers. But it also made Pakistan intransigent toward resolving its disputes with its neighbours and, even more, emboldened it to undertake a military adventure against India in 1965 that proved extremely costly, as the consequences of the war reverberated throughout the political system.

Foreign Aid, Economic Strategy, and Political Consequences

Unlike India, Pakistan was—following the beliefs of its founder, Mohammed Ali Jinnah—not fascinated by socialism and the accompanying thrust for the state to occupy 'the commanding heights' of the economy. It was more committed to private enterprise, and at the same time to giving it all possible state support. Some regard the greater role given to private enterprise in Pakistan as 'a key explanatory factor' in the country's better economic performance.[16] Pakistan demonstrated amazing powers of resilience in the years immediately after partition, and its industry advanced substantially,

---

[15] Lieven, 'The Pressures on Pakistan', 108, 112.

[16] Noman, *Economic and Social Progress in Asia*, 19.

albeit from a narrow base, with the entrepreneurial effort of the business communities that had migrated from India.

However, Pakistan soon encountered serious political problems, stemming from its ethnic heterogeneity and lack of consensus over the structure of the state, including the role of religion. After the assassination in 1951 of its first Prime Minister, Liaquat Ali Khan, there ensued considerable political turmoil. The bureaucracy inherited from the colonial era, both civil and military, was contemptuous of the political leadership, and began to intervene wantonly in politics to manipulate the political parties and their leaders. In effect, it determined which politicians would come to and remain in power until 1958, when finally General Ayub Khan, in a military coup d'état, established a garrison state. Foreign economic aid had only a minimal role during the first period until 1954, when the entry into alliance with the US brought in larger amounts of aid. In the years from 1954 to 1958, the US committed itself to provide $700 million in aid; it financed more than half of the public sector development expenditure, and a third of the country's imports.[17]

In the second period under military rule, the role of foreign economic aid escalated and it had a decisive impact. Literally, the financial floodgates now opened for Pakistan. Massive aid flowed in not only from the US but also from its allies. Table 12.2 demonstrates the dramatic change that took place with the entry into alliance and especially after the military came into power. In 1952, economic aid was a mere five million Pakistani rupees; by 1956 it was nearly a half-billion Pakistani rupees; in 1960 it stood at a billion Pakistani rupees; by 1967, it had tripled to three billion Pakistani rupees, and

Table 12.2: Foreign Aid to Pakistan: Selected Fiscal Years

	1952	1956	1960	1967	1968	1970
Actual (Rs Million)	5.0	472	1068	3105	3334	3570
As a share of GNP	0.02	2.1	3.4	7.5	5.7	5.8
As a share of dev. expenditure	0.5	34.8	38.1	42.2	37.7	34.0
As a share of imports	0.1	18.6	31.1	55.8	47.0	49.8

Source: Omar Noman, *Economic and Social Progress in Asia*, 143, which is based on the information from the Pakistan Planning Commission.

[17] Ibid., 138–9.

by 1970 it had grown to three and a half billion Pakistani rupees.
As a proportion of GNP, aid jumped from an almost non-existent
0.02 per cent in 1952 to 7.5 per cent in 1967. In contrast to 1952,
when aid as a proportion of development expenditure stood at a
minuscule 0.5 per cent, it climbed dramatically to 42.2 per cent. Aid
as a proportion of imports was only 0.1 per cent in 1952, but its
average for the years 1967, 1968, and 1970 was more than half of
the country's imports. Foreign aid funded 40 per cent of the
development programme of Pakistan's Second Five Year Plan (1960/1–
1964/5), and its largest recipient was the industrial sector.[18] As Wade
had stated in relation to Taiwan, '"With that much aid who couldn't
industrialize," it is sometimes said. Certainly US aid was very
important.'[19] Little wonder that there was acceleration of the growth
rate in Pakistan's national income and its exports. Indeed, so
impressed was the world outside by Pakistan's success that, in the early
1960s, Korean planners visited Pakistan's Planning Commission in
order to find out what they could learn from its experience in pushing
development.[20] The US State Department at the time held Pakistan
to be a model for the developing countries that demonstrated how
a combination of political authoritativeness (read: authoritarianism)
and the right economic policies could generate rapid economic
growth.

Aid was not the only determinant in Pakistan's accelerated growth
rate. There was also economic policy, which had the endorsement of
American advisers; as Noman points out, 'aid resources and policy
input assisted in the acceleration of growth.'[21] Pakistan pursued
economic development with great determination, largely to the
neglect of social sectors. Relying on private enterprise, consistent
with the state's past approach, the military regime counted on 'the
social utility of greed' to catapult Pakistan into an industrialized
nation.[22] Believing in the doctrine of 'functional inequality', under

[18] Ibid., 142.

[19] Robert Wade, *Governing the Market*, 82.

[20] Noman, *Economic and Social Progress in Asia*, 6.

[21] Ibid., 161.

[22] For the concept, see the book by one of the American advisers, Gustav
F. Papanek, *Pakistan's Development: Social Goals and Private Incentives*
(Cambridge, MA: Harvard University Press, 1967), 242.

which the growth of inequalities was to be accepted in order to advance growth, it eagerly diverted resources to entrepreneurs by squeezing agriculture and suppressing the demands of industrial workers.[23] The resulting economic polarization led to 22 business families cornering much of Pakistan's wealth in industry, banking, and insurance. The public discontent with the increasing inequalities then boiled over into political turmoil after the war of 1965, which finally brought down the Ayub Khan regime.

Squeezing agriculture, however, had an ethnic dimension in that it meant the economic exploitation of East Pakistan, and the transfer of a vast economic surplus out of that region for the benefit of the industrialization of West Pakistan. In other words, the rapid industrialization of West Pakistan was achieved on the backs of the jute-growing peasantry in East Pakistan. The US and its allies were complicit in this process in that not only was the overall policy supported by them but also 'approximately 85% of aid resources went to West Pakistan, thus accentuating regional tensions'.[24] Eventually, the process led to the political alienation of East Pakistan and the disintegration of Pakistan, with the former region emerging as Bangladesh in 1971.[25] Thus, the single-minded pursuit of *state-building* by a military regime, insensitive to political realities on the ground, through an imbalanced growth strategy led directly to *nation-destroying*. Behind the urgent pursuit of industrialization itself, however, lay a crucial strategic element. Kalim Siddiqui, an author of Pakistani origin, shrewdly underlined:

> Economic development, which also became a 'national interest' as a result of Indian pressure, was pursued with a vigour unmatched in Asia or Africa outside China and Japan. As a direct result of alliances, Pakistan secured massive economic aid—more than twice as much per capita as India—which was needed to put Pakistan's industrial development on a par with India's in the shortest possible time. Makers of economic policy in Pakistan were singularly uninhibited by ideas of social justice or the equitable distribution of new wealth. The capitalist path—the accumulation of wealth

[23] Khalid B. Sayeed, *Politics in Pakistan: The Nature and Direction of Change* (New York: Praeger, 1980), 57; and Noman, *Economic and Social Progress in Asia*, 177–8.

[24] Noman, *Economic and Social Progress in Asia*, 143.

[25] Rounaq Jahan, *Pakistan: Failure in National Integration* (New York: Columbia University Press, 1972).

in the hands of those few who know how to multiply it in quick time—has been relentlessly pursued, because *growth of GNP is wanted primarily for its power content and only incidentally for its welfare value.*[26]

The third period in Pakistan's economic evolution saw the new civilian, but really Bonapartist, regime of Zulfikar Ali Bhutto, follow policies, in reaction to the earlier approach, that stood diametrically opposed to those pursued in the previous period. Bhutto's regime, with its claims to an Islamic socialism, marked a disjuncture in Pakistan's economic policy. It nationalized private sector firms on a wide scale and implemented projects, such as the steel mill with Soviet aid, that were long-gestating and low-yielding, and beyond the capacity of the Pakistani state. The regime had problems with the IFIs, with the World Bank unimpressed by the thrust for the public sector. This was also a period when the US was dismayed not only by Bhutto's radicalism but as well by Pakistan's drive for nuclear capabilities. Because of differences with the US, 'the USAID programme dwindled into virtual insignificance, reflected in the reduction of US personnel from over 1000 in the mid-sixties, to just 4 in 1977.'[27] It is not that Pakistan did not receive aid, but it came now more from the Soviet Union and the Islamic oil-producing countries. Combined with the change in economic policy, this aid was less productive for high growth rates. With the growing alienation of the middle classes, the business community, and the clerics, the military under General Zia ul-Haq intervened to overthrow Bhutto in 1977 and then in 1979 hanged him in what is considered to have actually been a judicial murder.

Zia then reversed the policies of the Bhutto regime through denationalization of businesses that had been taken over by the state, and he reverted to the policies of the Ayub regime in the 1960s that emphasized reliance on the private sector for growth. These actions may not have been sufficient for propelling Pakistan again to a high growth rate in national income and exports. However, a regime that was isolated initially, with President Jimmy Carter skipping Pakistan while on a visit to the subcontinent, was saved politically and economically by the intervention of fate. The Soviets came to the military rescue of the tottering regime in Afghanistan in 1979. With

[26] Kalim Siddiqui, 'Pakistan's External Environment', *South Asian Review*, 2, 2 (January 1969), 123, [emphasis added].
[27] Noman, *Economic and Social Progress in Asia*, 146–7.

that, Pakistan became a frontline state in the American effort to oust
the Soviet armed forces from that country, and the US and its allies
rallied to help Pakistan with generous aid. After Ronald Reagan
became President in 1981, the US decided to overlook Pakistan's
nuclear activities and, instead, provided it with a five-year aid
package worth $3.2 billion. After the utilization of that aid, the US
gave Pakistan another six-year aid package worth $4.02 billion.
Besides, Pakistan also benefited from its intelligence services being
the conduit for military and non-military aid to the Islamic rebels
in Afghanistan; these services husbanded the resources carefully for
their own future use. With all the new aid, Pakistan saw its average
economic growth rate for the period rise to match that of the 1960s.
Indeed, Burki argued that Pakistan had broken out of the mould of
South Asia and was on the verge of becoming a middle-income
country.[28] That hope, alas, has not yet turned out to be true; instead,
the Pakistan economy soon took to a course of regression.

Despite the high growth rates achieved by the economy under
General Zia, the financial mechanism employed for growth led to
serious problems. The high growth rates had been based on excessive
dependence on foreign aid and loans. The large-scale economic aid
and loans that Pakistan had been receiving earlier had a sting
attached to them in that they, or a considerable portion of them, had
to be paid back. Pakistan's debt was $9.9 billion in 1980, but by 1990
it had climbed to $20.7 billion (and then on to $32.8 billion in
2000).[29] In his budget speech in mid-1988, the acting finance
minister Mahbub ul Haq pronounced the economy to be 'bankrupt'.[30]
The government then negotiated a structural adjustment programme
with the IMF to cope with the situation.

Through its aid, the US was eminently successful in evicting the
Soviets out of Afghanistan. However, American aid to the *jihadi* rebels
was a major element in the subsequent rise of a Pakistan-sponsored
fundamentalist and terrorism-promoting regime in Afghanistan, and
in the 'blowback' resulting for the US in the form of the 9/11 attack
on its homeland. Equally, Pakistan's involvement in Afghanistan, while
beneficial in receiving an economic bonanza by way of foreign aid,

---

[28] Burki, *Pakistan: The Continuing Search for Nationhood*, chapter 3, which
bears the title 'Economic Development: An Emerging Middle-Income Country'.

[29] World Development Indicators. The figure for 1970 was $3.4 billion.

[30] Burki, *Pakistan*, 133.

proved detrimental to the country's larger interests. In a local version of 'blowback', it resulted in the development of a 'drug and Kalashnikov culture' with pervasive violence stalking the land. Also, Zia launched his own Islamicization of Pakistan for reasons both of conviction and regime legitimacy, and 'the Pakistani state was gripped by a menacing ideological puritanism'.[31] As a result, Pakistan faced increasing sectarian strife. Then, in 1988, Zia died in a suspicious air crash and, because of the rising public discontent, the military regime gave way to rule by political leaders.

The fifth period, which marks the return of the politicians to governance, found Pakistan to be in a difficult bind. Concerned over the Pakistani drive for the acquisition of nuclear capabilities, the US in 1990 imposed economic sanctions against Pakistan, and that put an end to the huge largesse the latter was getting from the US. Besides, Pakistan encountered severe problems of debt servicing. By June 1999, near the end of the period, Pakistan's foreign debt and liabilities amounted to 64 per cent of its GDP, while 60 per cent of its revenues went into debt servicing.[32] Pakistan had entered into an agreement in 1988 with the IMF for a structural adjustment programme, but it continued to remain intermittently under such programmes for more than fifteen years. Its economy was now on a course of deterioration. The average rate of economic growth, for the period as a whole, masks the progressively weakening situation. Between 1993 and 1999, the annual rate of GDP growth for individual years in percentage terms was 1.91, 3.90, 5.12, 3.86, 1.01, 2.55, and 3.66. Especially galling for Pakistani observers was the fact that, as a result, Pakistan's per capita income, which had been higher than that of India's by a very large margin, went on a path of relative decline until it was outstripped by India's (see Table 12.3). With the country's high population growth rate, the stagnation in per capita income growth vastly increased the percentage of people below the poverty line.

Benazir Bhutto and Nawaz Sharif alternated in office as Prime Minister during the period, having been duly elected, but the tenure of each was terminated prematurely by or at the behest of the military. Nawaz Sharif, the last one to hold that office, was eager to restore

[31] Noman, *Economic and Social Progress in Asia*, 37.

[32] Mehtab Haider, '$1 b Debt Write Off', *The Nation* Online, 6 April, 2003.

Table 12.3: Per Capita Income in Pakistan
and India (US$)

Year	Pakistan	India
1995	460	340
1997	490	390
1998	480	430
1999	470	450
2000	470	460
2001	420	460

Source: World Bank, *World Development Report* (various issues).

the power of the civilian wing, which policy orientation did not endear him to the military, even though at the beginning, he had been a political creation of the military. When India undertook the nuclear tests in May 1998, Pakistan under him responded with nuclear tests of its own, but the action elicited additional economic sanctions against it from the US. Meanwhile, though there is dispute over whether Nawaz Sharif acquiesced in the decision or not, the military under the direction of General Pervez Musharraf launched an attack in mid-1999 against India at Kargil in Kashmir. India responded with fury and Pakistan was rescued from this misadventure by the intervention of President Bill Clinton. There were increasing concerns at the time about Pakistan as a 'failed state' that had additionally made terrorism an active state policy in relation to its neighbours. Some in the US even wanted Pakistan to be declared a 'rogue state'. The conflict between Nawaz Sharif and the head of the Pakistan Army, General Musharraf, also sharpened, and in October 1999 the latter took over power in a military coup d'état.

The military coup resulted in still more American sanctions against Pakistan on account of the overthrow of democracy. The isolation of the regime was made vivid by its suspension from the Commonwealth, and by President Clinton spending a mere five hours in Pakistan as against five days in India during his trip to the subcontinent in 2000. Pakistan also came to acquire the image of being a key platform for terrorism, not only in Kashmir but also elsewhere. It was 'slipping into extremism and violence at a rapid rate, it had become a scourge to all of its neighbours, and it was a potential threat to friends and allies such as the United States and China'. However, fate again came to the rescue of the military regime. After the 9/11 attack on the US by terrorists trained in Afghanistan, Pakistan readily agreed to join the US once again as a frontline ally, this time ironically in the war against terrorism. It really had no choice: 'Pakistan absolutely had to receive international economic support to remain viable, and the West would doubtless "crash" Pakistan's economy if the government were not cooperative.'[33] Pakistan now made available its air space and air bases for the American invasion of Afghanistan. It was a bitter pill to swallow, for it was Pakistan that had installed the puppet fundamentalist and terrorist regime in Afghanistan in the first place in order to acquire 'strategic depth' against India and to play a major role in Central Asia.

The reward for Pakistan from the United States was legitimacy for the military regime, the withdrawal of economic sanctions, the cancellation of a substantial amount of debt, the rescheduling of a vast debt, and large amounts of foreign aid. One authority, Dr Moeed Pirzada, declared: 'It will be naïve to deny that it was also with the US help and goodwill that Pakistan managed a turnaround of its visibility, image, and economy since 9/11; the loan rescheduling of $12.5 billion by the Paris Club and an immediate cash injection of over one billion dollars are good examples in point.'[34] In an unusual gesture, President George Bush invited General Musharraf to Camp David and then provided him an additional five-year aid package worth $3 billion dollars, half in economic aid and the other half in military assistance.

Some assessments put the total of economic benefits for Pakistan much higher. In mid-July 2003, M.J. Akbar stated: 'In the last two years [actually a bit less] America's assistance to Pakistan has been upwards of $20 billion, give or take a few million. Not all of it has been in the form of the outright reward of three billion dollars given on 24 June. A year ago, Bush wrote off one billion dollars in debt at a New York press conference.... This was the appetizer. The big meal came quietly when America forced the IMF and other donors to give Pakistan two billion dollars in loans at marginal interest, and then helped Pakistan reschedule $12.5 billion of debt to the Paris

[33] Stephen Philip Cohen, 'The Nation and the State of Pakistan', *The Washington Quarterly*, 25, 3 (2002), 109–22.

[34] Moeed Pirzada, 'Camp David and Beyond', *Dawn* Online, 11 July 2003.

Club.'[35] Besides, the US and the EU extended preferential treatment toward certain imports from Pakistan, boosting its textile exports, even as India complained of trade diversion. In the eyes of a keen Pakistani observer, Pakistan has essentially been a rentier state, hooked on the rents of its strategic location.[36]

The new incoming aid and the more liberal trade policy of the donors toward Pakistan had a visible impact on the economy; its exports were on an upswing and its foreign exchange reserves rose to new highs. In the fiscal year 2002/3, exports reached 'the historic figure' of over $11 billion; government officials acknowledged, 'we were expecting an increase of $500 million in exports due to the concessions from the EU during 2002/3' but it actually reached $700–800 million.[37] In mid-2003, Pakistan's finance minister was proclaiming that his country, with a growth rate of 5.1 per cent in 2002/3, was the most dynamic economy in South Asia.[38] For the next fiscal year, he predicted an even higher growth rate at 6 per cent.[39] Membership in military alliances thus does seem to have its privileges.

Proceeding further, in order to rally Pakistani support in its pursuit of killing or capturing Osama bin Laden and his followers, the US, in early 2004, elevated Pakistan to the status of a 'Major non-NATO Ally'. In the process, the US ended the diplomatic isolation of the military regime and strengthened its hand against India.

Summary and Conclusions

Geopolitics has played a pre-eminent role in Pakistan's economic development. Its manifestation in respect of Pakistan is not that dissimilar from the pattern found in the Northeast Asian states, where the US provided a tremendous boost to economic growth through furnishing aid and markets in the larger interest of its global strategic goals. But the American role in Pakistan's economic development has, depending on the state of the relationship between the two countries,

[35] M.J. Akbar, 'Know Thine Friend', *Dawn* Online, 8 July 2003.

[36] Husain Haqqani, 'Causes for Concern', *The Nation* Online, 30 July 2003.

[37] Hamid Waleed, 'Exports Touch $11 Billion', *The Nation* Online, 11 July 2003.

[38] Sanjaya Baru, 'A Win-Win Race in South Asia', *Financial Express* Online, 13 June 2003.

[39] Sultan Ahmed, 'Growth without Relief', *Dawn* Online, 1 April 2004.

varied over the years from high intimacy to abandonment and even punishment, all with enormous impact. The periods of high intimacy between the two countries have coincided not only with high growth rates, but also, ironically, with military rule.

Pakistan's political development has been ruptured three times by military coups d' état. The close relations of the military regimes with the US have enabled the military to harness vast resources from the US and its allies for its own expansion and Pakistan's economic development. But the resultant policies have not always proven to be functional for Pakistan as such. This aspect is evident in the splitting of the country into two, the spread of the culture of drugs and guns throughout the land, and the turning of the country into a platform for terrorist activities, both at home and abroad.

Chapter 13

SUMMARY AND CONCLUSIONS

Globalization is a fact of life, and the world is more integrated economically today than it has ever been before in terms of trade and capital flows. It would be inaccurate to maintain, as the 'agnostics' or sceptics seem to, that the world economy was more integrated at the beginning of the twentieth century than it is now. The data on trade and capital flows do not any longer support that contention of the sceptics.

Moreover, the nature of international economic integration today is very different, in that it is of the 'deeper' kind than the 'shallow' one that was characteristic of the earlier era. This is evidenced by the composition of present-day trade, which consists largely of manufactures rather than raw materials, by the 'transnationalization' of the production process, and by the sharper financial integration in the world. In these respects, contemporary globalization is quite distinctive, compared to that of the nineteenth century.

The implication of globalization being an inescapable part today of the world economic reality, which is not within the power of most states to reverse or to shape, is that such states have to shoulder the costs of adjustment, essentially because being weak they are order-takers, not order-makers. However, insulation from the global economy is not a viable option for these states either, since that too, imposes costs. The question for them, then, really is how to carve out policies that would allow them to make the best of the situation as it exists, rather than quixotically tilt at windmills in attempting to counter the tide of globalization. Nor for that matter is the situation without substantial economic opportunities for those states that are eager to seize them.

The Geopolitical Limits to Globalization

Notwithstanding the deeper form in which it obtains today, globalization is not evenly distributed across the globe, and a high degree of concentration is a key characteristic of it. Globalization has a *truncated* character, given the concentration more or less of international economic interactions in the 'triad' of the US, Europe, and Japan. The data on trade and capital flows testify to its truncated nature. It seems justified therefore to conceptualize globalization as a process that is under way rather than a stage that has already been reached, despite what the 'enthusiasts' of globalization may say. Why is globalization truncated in this manner? Is it a random occurrence? Quite the contrary, the explanation for the truncated nature of globalization lies in geopolitics, which is often ignored as a factor, with analyses of globalization tending to focus on economic features alone. Power matters deeply in the international economy, and it is the powerful states that are the moulders of that economy. The world economy is therefore not an autonomous sphere of economics, rather it has been structured by geopolitics.

As the hegemonic power emergent at the end of World War II, the US purposively shaped the post-war world economy in order to serve its own interests and those of its allies. As a result, the benefits of globalization have largely flowed to the developed countries lodged in the triad. The members of the triad have, in accord with their 'embedded liberalism', employed a variety of mechanisms to shape globalization in the service of their interests and to pass on the costs of adjustment to the less developed countries (LDCs). Thus, capital flows, from which the triad benefits, are favoured but labour flows, from which the LDCs would benefit, are blocked or discouraged. Tariff barriers among the triad are reduced, but non-tariff barriers are raised against the LDCs. Besides, the comparative advantage of the LDCs in agriculture is undercut by the triad states through vast subsidies to their own agricultural sectors. Blocking labour flows, imposing non-tariff barriers, and massively subsidizing agriculture are all mercantilist policies. Ironically, they are pursued by the very states that are otherwise in the forefront of preaching the virtues of economic liberalism to the world. Globalization, as it is presently constituted, is, thus, designed principally for the developed countries, not for the world as a whole except as they may deign at their discretion to modify the structures of discrimination built against the LDCs.

Given the key role that geopolitics has played in shaping it, contemporary globalization cannot by the same token be regarded as an irreversible process. The assumption that globalization is on some unstoppable roll, an assumption so dear to the enthusiasts, that will sweep away long-standing institutional obstacles, such as the state, that stand in its way is decidedly an exaggerated one. For one thing, there is the highly instructive precedent of the fate of the first era of globalization in the nineteenth century, which quickly went up in flames in the geopolitical clash of arms among the major powers. Globalization then remained in abeyance for almost half a century. The enthusiasts of that earlier era's globalization were also convinced that the then prevailing international economic integration had conquered the geopolitical instincts of the major powers by enmeshing them in the new-found web of economic interdependence. The explanation for the collapse of globalization of that time lay precisely in geopolitics, not in economics. Even though they interact and influence each other, markets and states represent two different logics, both domestically and internationally. As an independent factor operative in the international system in its own right, geopolitics has not receded in the face of the march of contemporary globalization, contrary to what the enthusiasts of globalization imagine. In the context of a changing world economy, geopolitics necessarily assumes new incarnations. But a new incarnation does not equate to the erosion or end of geopolitics.

Evidence abounds on the continuing relevance of geopolitics. First, it is the hegemonic power of the US within a unipolar system that currently provides the overall framework within which globalization functions. Contemporary globalization arose in the context of a world economy that was structured by the hegemonic power of the US at the end of World War II, and it continues to be shaped by that power, which has now acquired imperial dimensions. Second, high defence expenditures by states, especially by the US, testify to the enduring importance of geopolitics. Third, the response to the 9/11 attacks on the American homeland on the part of the US and its allies in the areas of war and defence, international financial transactions, and immigration controls evidence the continued vitality of the state in the exercise of its powers.

Fourth, the increasing fragmentation of the world economy into regional economic blocs, a trend that really runs counter to globalization, is inspired by the promotion of the particular economic

262   The Geopolitics of Globalization

and political interests of the narrow groups of states constituting such blocs. In addition, these regional blocs serve as an insurance policy against possible disruptions of the world economy in the future, as a result of the eruption of either international economic crises or political conflicts among states. They are essentially a mercantilist device even though often promoted as advancing economic liberalism. States are Janus-faced; they aim to avail of the opportunities that the international economy provides, but they also want to protect themselves against the risks that participation in the world economy may bring. They therefore adopt a mix of liberal and mercantilist policies, with the proportions in the mix depending on circumstance. Because of these various factors, it would be remiss to neglect the independent, indeed prior, role of geopolitics and to assume that globalization is the sole operative process in the world economy.

Globalization and Development

Geopolitics has, as noted above, also been at the base of the truncated nature of globalization. Notwithstanding that truncated state, however, the world economy is a dynamic arena and not a frozen one. Its dynamism is illustrated, for example, by the changes in the country of origin of the world's 100 largest industrial corporations. In 1970, the US had 64, Europe 26, and Japan 8. By contrast, in 1988, the US had only 42, Europe 33, and Japan 15. Similarly, in 1970, North America had 19 of the world's 50 largest banks, Europe 16, and Japan 11. By 1988, North America had only 5, Europe 17, and Japan 24.[1] On a different plane, that of economic growth, it would seem that the pathway out of the periphery to the status of a developed country is not altogether closed. A couple of what were earlier LDCs (South Korea and Mexico) have, indeed, made it to the OECD, and quite a few LDCs have transited out of their peripheral status to at least the semi-periphery or, put another way, the semi-core.

The dynamic nature of the world economy is particularly evident in the economic advance made by a whole block of countries in East Asia and Southeast Asia, referred to as the newly industrializing economies (NIEs). The constituents of this block have broken out of the ranks of low income countries, and have joined either the

[1] Lester Thurow, *Head to Head*, 30.

middle-income or high-income categories through superior economic performance by way of high rates of economic growth. Japan may be viewed as a special case because of its economic accomplishments before World War II, but the set of NIEs includes Taiwan, Korea, China, Malaysia, Thailand, and Indonesia. Even though convergence in the world economy as between the developed countries and the large group of developing countries is nowhere near in sight, a strong tendency toward convergence is nonetheless evident in the progress made by these NIEs.

What stands out in respect of these economies is their greater integration into or openness to the world economy through their higher participation in international trade as a consequence of having purposively chosen outward-oriented growth strategies. To be sure, there is controversy over whether higher participation in foreign trade is the cause or the result of superior economic performance. However, the analysis of these economies in the post-war period through a series of case studies shows that the adoption of the export-oriented manufactures-reliant strategy preceded their economic advance. It can therefore be asserted with a reasonable degree of confidence, as against the position of the 'critics' of globalization, that openness is causally related to superior economic performance. The relationship finds a confirmation even in the case of the low income country of India, where the half-hearted economic liberalization preceded its better, though still modest, economic performance in the more recent period since 1975, compared to the period prior to that. It is evident, then, that by harnessing globalization to their development, the NIEs have been instrumental in modifying somewhat a salient feature of globalization, its truncated nature.

The implication of this finding, based on the East and Southeast Asian NIEs is clear—openness or integration is beneficial, contrary to what the critics of globalization, like the dependency theorists earlier, have maintained. That this empirical finding through the case study method is also in line with the more doctrinal position of the international financial institutions (IFIs) is only coincidental. Those countries that were influenced by dependency theorists, or by export pessimism that preceded it, paid a considerable price by forgoing higher economic growth through opting for inward-oriented strategies. Shortchanging themselves on higher economic growth on the part of such countries had the consequential result of preventing millions of their populace from being lifted out of poverty.

Geopolitics and Development

Valuable as international integration may have been for development in the NIEs in East and Southeast Asia, drawing on that experience as a lesson for other developing countries suffers from a serious limitation that emerges from the empirical analysis in this study. That limitation lies in the fact that geopolitics played a critical role in the success of the export–propelled growth strategies of these NIEs. Beginning with Japan, through Taiwan and Korea, and later the Southeast Asian countries, and then on to even the communist regime in China, the support of the United States, for extremely important geopolitical reasons, was a crucial factor in their success.

Spurred by its strategic conflict with the Soviet Union, the US felt compelled to aid these countries in their rapid economic march through export–propelled growth. It did so by mobilizing economic assistance for them, either from its own financial resources or those of its allies and the IFIs, by facilitating transfers of technology and capital to them and, critically, by providing access to its market for their exports. Interestingly, Pakistan, too, benefiting from a similar American geopolitical interest and the munificence that came with it, demonstrated early signs of emerging as a tiger contemporaneously with Taiwan and South Korea. One can, indeed, offer a counterfactual here that has considerable plausibility. If Pakistan had displayed constancy in its alliance with the US, rather than defecting from it, if it had shown some sensitivity in handling its ethnic heterogeneity, and if it had not squandered its opportunities in military misadventures, it would have been in the company of the NIEs today.

Sadly for other potential NIEs, it would seem that the propitious circumstance of the gigantic American geopolitical project of the containment of the Soviet Union is no longer available to them. Actually, however, geopolitical conflict never ceases, and it will continue to provide opportunities that some, though not all, developing countries may be able exploit for purposes of development. The more recent war on terrorism is an illustration of this proposition. Indeed, by joining the war on terrorism, a development that it had helped in part to create in the first place, Pakistan has again become a beneficiary of a massive largesse from the US and others prodded by the US. As one influential authority declared, 'What has provided the country with some clout is the role the administration of General Pervez Musharraf is playing in the US–led war against international terrorism.'[2] Pakistan has benefited from financial packages comprising direct economic and military aid, the cancellation and rescheduling of foreign debt, and special trade preferences by the US and the EU for its exports. Its economic recovery in the post-9/11 period after several years of economic stagnation, is directly a consequence of its having become an ally of the US in the war against terrorism. Some smaller states in eastern Europe that were earlier members of the Soviet bloc—'the new Europe'—have similarly benefited from their supporting the US on Iraq. Other states may also find opportunities as the US attempts to forestall the rise of challengers to its hegemony, or as the major powers construct regional economic blocs.

Of course, countries also create the opportunities that they then seize. During the 1950s, certain countries in Asia found it in their interest to facilitate having visiting American leaders come face to face with communist-led demonstrations, so as to extract more economic aid out of the US. Pakistan's staged anti-communism during that period was a manifestation of the same posture. Some American observers, such as Jim Hoagland and Selig Harrison among others, have suspected that Pakistan, after 9/11, has had a similar interest in seeing that the areas of Afghanistan near its borders continue to be embroiled in terrorist activity. International politics is not a morality play, and countries will exploit whatever opportunities come their way in order to advance their interests. Although any reference to the role of realpolitik and geopolitics in pushing development is likely to invite a moral sneer, it is apparent that quite a few countries have benefited from it in their drive to escape from underdevelopment and poverty.

The State and Developmental Breakthroughs

To highlight the importance of geopolitics in development is not to downplay that of other factors. It would be foolhardy to maintain that any single factor alone explains development. The consideration of the NIEs of East Asia and Southeast Asia makes it clear nonetheless that these economies achieved their breakthroughs in development while they were presided over by 'hard' states. The hard state rears its head too consistently in the saga of development of these economies

---

[2] Shahid Javed Burki, 'Trading with America', *Dawn* Online, 29 July 2003.

to be dismissed as simply incidental. Even Pakistan during its phases of rapid economic growth was under military dictatorship.

Of course, there is variation among the East and Southeast Asian NIEs in their degree of hardness, with the states in Southeast Asia not matching Taiwan and South Korea either in hardness or, perhaps not unrelatedly, in economic performance. India patently stands out as a soft state, and its economic performance even after its opening to economic liberalization, undoubtedly halting and fitful, has also been modest. From the limited number of case studies analysed here, there seems to be a correlation between the degree of hardness of the state and superior economic performance. Pakistan has alternated between the soft state and the hard state, and its economic performance has been roughly synchronous with political change, improving with the hard state.

No doubt, the relationship of the nature of regime to development is a controversial issue, with social scientists, largely of liberal inclination, apt to reject it out of hand.[3] But inclination alone cannot stamp out hard facts. Even the contemporary developed states transformed their agricultural economies into industrialized economies under non-democratic or pre-democratic auspices, just as the breakthroughs to industrialization in the post-war period have occurred, or are in the process of occurring, also under authoritarian auspices. The relevant sample of NIEs, besides those in East Asia and Southeast Asia, would include Brazil, Chile, and Mexico. In all these cases, authoritarianism and industrial transformation have gone together. It is hard to think of a democracy that would deserve inclusion in this list. It may well be that 'theoretically, democracies are not intrinsically less capable of generating these foundations of growth,'[4] but there is little empirical support so far for that

[3] Note, for example, that two eminent economists, Jagdish Bhagwati and Amartya Sen, who disagree fundamentally in their approaches to economics, are united on this aspect of the relationship between democracy and development, though their arguments are not very persuasive. See Jagdish Bhagwati, *The Wind of the Hundred Days*, chapter 41 on 'Globalization, Sovereignty and Democracy'. See also the address by Amartya Sen before the seminar on Development as Freedom, organized by the Federation of Indian Chambers of Commerce and Industry, on 31 July 2003; see *Times of India* Online and *Indian Express* Online, 1 August 2003.

[4] Larry Diamond and Marc F. Plattner, *Economic Reform and Democracy* (Baltimore, MD: Johns Hopkins University Press, 1995), xxii.

proposition. Even if correlation is not causation, the association between authoritarianism and industrial transformation is too powerful to ignore. To be sure, authoritarianism alone has not been sufficient for development. Other authoritarian regimes were not always successful. Still, on present evidence, while not sufficient, authoritarianism seems almost necessary.

The conclusion, of course, is not that LDCs that are democratic should shift to authoritarianism for the sake of rapid economic growth, but rather expectations in that regard would need to be moderated. The issue is linked to legitimacy, which can be of two kinds. One type is instrumental legitimacy, where governments must be effective in order to merit support, with effectiveness in economic performance commanding high priority in the modern era. The other can be called constitutive legitimacy, where certain political institutions are valued for their own sake, regardless—no doubt, within limits—of their implications for economic performance. A society may well prefer to opt for democracy for its particular mix of liberty and order, consent and coercion, even if it is at some cost to economic performance. Regardless, it would seem that contemporary globalization and geopolitics may enable some democracies to overcome the limitations that they would have earlier laboured under, because of the nature of their regime, in pushing decisively toward development.

The Receding Character of Requisites for Development

When Japan accomplished its fast-track economic growth as a result of its export-propelled growth strategy, its success was considered an anomaly, because of its past development history since the Meiji Restoration. It was, accordingly, not considered as having much relevance for the LDCs. In any case, it was objected, prematurely it would seem in retrospect, that the markets of the developed countries had already become saturated with Japan's labour-intensive low-technology goods, so as to preclude the addition of any more such exporters from among the LDCs. However, Taiwan and South Korea demonstrated that some additional LDCs could successfully replicate the Japanese experience of high-speed growth by following its model of export-propelled growth. The advocates of the new export pessimism then reiterated the case of market saturation with renewed vigour to warn against any further room being available for LDC exports. Yet, rather than choosing inaction or inward orientation, the ASEAN Four, and much more dramatically because its population is so huge and its economy so large, China, too, opted for the growth model of the Asian Tigers, and has successfully joined the group of NIEs. There have been, no doubt, continual cries for protection in the triad countries, but the impressive fact remains that the more recent group of NIEs accomplished their goals in good measure, and have changed the profile of East and Southeast Asia in the world economy.

It is not only market saturation that was held against the possibility of development in the LDCs, but other factors as well. At one time, it was maintained that the Northeast Asian Tigers, perhaps Taiwan not to the same extent, accomplished their development with little foreign investment. Consequently, it was asserted that the ASEAN Four were not likely to succeed because they were relying on foreign investment for growth. Foreign investment was considered inimical to their chances for development, since it would allegedly result in the transfer of economic surplus out of these countries. However, not only the ASEAN Four but, especially, China have successfully made use of foreign investment for their economic advance. Indeed, foreign investment served these countries well to overcome local limitations in terms of capital, technology, and management in pushing forward 'catch-up' industrialization. Since democratic regimes have difficulty in imposing sacrifices on the population for purposes of resource mobilization for investment, foreign investment can enable them to similarly overcome such a limitation. In other words, foreign investment can serve as a 'substitute' for local savings and investment that may be lacking.[5]

Some have held at one time or another that a significant factor that made for the success of the export-propelled strategy among the initial Northeast Asian Tigers was the greater equality resulting from land reform carried out under the auspices of Occupation regimes. That point about equality has considerable validity to it. Yet Malaysia, Indonesia, and Thailand were able to graduate to NIE status without the benefit of similar land reform through a combination of the export-propelled growth strategy and foreign investment. It may well

---

[5] On the notion of substitutions in development, see Alexander Gerschenkron, *Economic Backwardness in Historical Perspective* (Cambridge, MA: Belknap Press, 1966), 529.

be that there was greater equality to begin with in these ASEAN countries, but it would certainly be difficult to make a similar assertion about Mexico. It would seem that the fulfilling of one or another requisite for development is often read back into the situation after the demonstration of success. A similar comment would seem to apply to cultural requisites, with the very values that were at one time considered to be obstacles to development, such as those belonging to Confucianism, being subsequently regarded as having contributed to the advance made in East Asia and Southeast Asia.

What emerges from the record, then, is the receding nature, one by one, of what had at one time been regarded as requisites for development, underlining in the process the importance of the state pursuing appropriate policies. From the experience of the NIEs, such policies would seem to include an increased openness to the world economy in terms of trade and foreign investment, adopting a pragmatic approach to geopolitical opportunities, providing an adequate economic and social infrastructure, and ensuring macroeconomic stability. It would be simpleminded to assume that success in the implementation of these policies was all accomplished smoothly and without pain. But the reward has been the lifting of the NIEs out of their earlier low-income status, as compared to those countries that did not follow such policies.

The world economy is a dynamic arena, as noted earlier. It constantly undergoes change, and through such change it provides new opportunities as well as creates new threats. The past cannot simply be projected into the future. Expert opinion is no reliable indicator of future trends. If the export pessimists had been listened to, countries that benefited from opening up their economies would not have so benefited. In 1992, the eminent economist and management expert Lester Thurow had warned of the closing of the space for exports from LDCs:

> Market access is central in export-led growth. To become a little economic dragon, such as Singapore or Taiwan, two requirements must be met. A country must get itself organized to compete; but it must also have a place where market access is relatively easy—a 'market of first resort'. In the past half century the market of first resort has been the United States. But generating just 23 per cent of the world GNP America cannot continue to buy almost half of the Third World's manufactured exports. During the 1990s the United States will probably be forced to cure its balance of payment deficit. When it does, imports will have to go down and exports

will have to go up. As this happens, the American market, for a time, will effectively be closed to the developing world.[6]

A year later, on the other hand, the World Bank, in its report on *The East Asian Miracle*, provided a more comforting vision of the future, declaring: 'Export drives can succeed even when industrial-economy markets are not expanding rapidly…. The scope for export expansion remains substantial. Indeed, individual developing economies, particularly smaller economies currently contemplating an export-led expansion, could safely assume that demand for their products is infinitely elastic.'[7] The record indicates that the World Bank's assessment had greater validity, with exports having continued to expand. At least, that much is evident between 1993 and 2000 for the set of countries analysed in this study (see Table 13.1). The exports of these countries (plus Vietnam) expanded from $888.9 billion in 1993 to $1,525.6 billion in 2000 in constant US dollars; that represents a net addition of $636.7 billion and an increase of 71.6 per cent in seven years. Particularly noteworthy are the increases in respect of China, India, Korea, Malaysia, Thailand, and, especially, Vietnam. The rise in exports for the select group of countries would perhaps have been even higher were it not for the fiscal crisis in

Table 13.1: Exports of Goods and Services
(Constant 1995 US$) (Billion)

Country	1993	2000	Increase (Per Cent)
China	123.5	239.0	93.5
India	27.6	56.5	104.7
Indonesia	44.9	54.4	21.2
Japan	446.2	563.8*	26.4
Korea	102.2	320.6	213.7
Malaysia	57.6	135.7	135.6
Pakistan	9.8	9.9	1.0
Philippines	20.1	31.8	58.2
Thailand	53.2	97.1	82.5
Vietnam	3.8	16.8	342.1

* Figure for 1999.
Source: Based on World Bank Indicators.

[6] Thurow, *Head to Head*, 209.
[7] World Bank, *The East Asian Miracle*, 361.

Southeast Asia from 1997 to 1999, which affected Indonesia most severely.

The increase in exports of these select economies testifies to the dynamism of the world economy. At the same time, it suggests that the NIEs themselves, as they advance, are likely to become a source of opportunities for the exports from other countries. Expanding exports are not a zero-sum game or a one-way traffic. The developed countries need not be regarded as the only markets available for LDC exports.

For at least some countries, such as Mexico, that are able to get into regional economic blocs, the creation of such blocs provides opportunities for expanded exports even though it means trade diversion for others. More broadly, there now exist rule-based international institutions like the World Trade Organization (WTO) that can facilitate the expansion of LDC exports. To be sure, the organization is at the present time considerably rigged in favour of the developed countries, but it is better for LDCs to have such a rule-based organization than not to have one at all. It is precisely for that reason that China was eager to enter the WTO. Besides, there have been cases where the WTO settlement mechanism has worked in favour of the LDCs. In short, the situation is not as grim as export pessimists have painted it in terms of prospects for development, provided the LDCs can set their own internal house in order, so as to exploit the opportunities in the world economy for development.

National Autonomy and Development

One of the objections that critics often raise against participating in economic globalization is that it is likely to adversely affect the national autonomy of the LDCs, especially at the hands of the powerful MNCs. It would be difficult to deny that any state, to the extent that it allows the national economy to become integrated into the world economy, loses some control over its domestic economy as the latter is exposed to the workings of the world economy.

However, the assumed existence before economic globalization of greater national autonomy on the part of states, as reflected in the notion of sovereignty, has largely been a myth. Contrary to that notion, national autonomy is not something absolute. In actual fact, the autonomy of states has largely been a function of their capabilities rather than of legal concepts. To the extent that capabilities are in considerable part, other things being equal, a result of development, underdevelopment renders a country more vulnerable to interventions from outside than it would be if it were developed. If globalization helps to advance development, then it adds to the capabilities of a country rather than detracting from them. On the other hand, opting out of globalization is likely to retard development and therefore reduce, rather than enhance, autonomy.

There is necessarily some trade-off between autonomy and development through globalization. China, for example, has chosen to compromise on its founding ideology and to take part in the global economy aggressively in order to build up its capabilities, so that it can as a result become a more formidable actor in the global economy as well as in global politics. It may well be that China will become economically and politically constrained as a result of its integration in the international economy. But it chose to reject being totally self-reliant and autonomous, for it found that the cost of economic ghettoization was worse because of the economic marginalization that would follow.

The basic issue for a state is how to preserve its national autonomy to the maximum while pushing development forward. Economic insulation as such does not guarantee autonomy, rather, in the ultimate analysis, it threatens it. Through opting out of globalization, a state may retain its autonomy in form, but the resultant retarding of capabilities is likely to render it more vulnerable. If, on the other hand, globalization helps in building capabilities then, by compromising some on autonomy, a state may actually increase its capabilities, and thus, its autonomy. What any state interested in expanding its autonomy has to do is to build its economic and military capabilities through a combination of liberal and mercantilist policies.

If autonomy is a function of capabilities relative to other actors in the international system, then size matters for actors. Large states are perhaps at an advantage in that they can advance their capabilities relative to the major powers, and thus their national autonomy, through participation in globalization. The state may or may not be anachronistic, but autonomy may be more problematic for small states compared to their larger competitors. One way out of the predicament for small states may be to join a regional economic bloc en route to the pooling of sovereignty in a larger federal unit. Ironic as it may seem, a small state may have to lose its autonomy, even identity, in order to regain it as part of a larger state.

BIBLIOGRAPHY

Abramowitz, Morton and Stephen Bosworth, 'Adjusting to the New Asia', *Foreign Affairs*, 84, 4 (July–August 2003), 119–31.

Ahmad, Aijaz, 'Globalization and the Nation-State', *Seminar*, No. 437 (January 1996), 43–8.

Ahmed, Rashmee Z., 'Beware, the Raj is Retro-chic', *Times of India* Online, 7 March 2004.

Ahmed, Sultan, 'Growth without Relief', *Dawn* Online, 1 April 2004.

Ahsan, Syed Aziz-al, *Islamization of the State in a Dualistic Culture: The Case of Bangladesh*, Ph.D. dissertation, (Montreal: McGill University, 1990).

Aiyar, Swaminathan S. Anklesaria, 'The 1980s Revisited', *Economic Times* Online, 17 March 2004.

Akbar, M.J., 'Know Thine Friend', *Dawn* Online, 8 July 2003.

Akram, Lt General A.I., 'Security and Stability in South Asia', in *The Security of South Asia: American and Asian Perspectives,* Stephen Philip Cohen (ed.), (Urbana: University of Illinois Press, 1987).

Alperovitz, Gar, *Atomic Diplomacy: Hiroshima and Potsdam, the Use of the Atomic Bomb and the Confrontation with Soviet Power*, (New York: Simon and Schuster, 1965).

Amin, Samir, *Accumulation on a World Scale: A Critique of the Theory of Underdevelopment*, (New York: Monthly Review Press, 1974).

Amir, Ayaz, 'Platos from the Drill Square', *Dawn* Online, 9 April 2004.

Anandalingam, G., 'China Expands Its Influence', *Economic Times* Online, 25 April 2003.

Bagchi, Amiya Kumar, 'Globalization, Liberalization and Vulnerability', *Economic and Political Weekly*, 34, 35 (6 November 1999), 3219–30.

Baker, Dean *et al.* (eds), *Globalization and Progressive Economic Policy*, (Cambridge: Cambridge University Press, 1998).

Bank for International Settlements, *71st Annual Report: 1 April 2000—31 March 2001*, Basel, (Switzerland: BIS, 2001).

Barraclough, Geoffrey, 'Wealth and Power: The Politics of Food and Fuel', *New York Review of Books* (7 August 1975).

Barrett, Richard E. and Soomi Chin, 'Export-Oriented Industrialization States in the Capitalist World System: Similarities and Differences', in *The Political Economy of the New East Asian Industrialism*, Frederic C. Deyo (ed.), (Ithaca, NY: Cornell University Press, 1987).

Barry, Donald and Ronald C. Keith (eds), *Regionalism, Multilateralism, and the Politics of Global Trade*, (Vancouver: UBC Press, 1999).

Baru, Sanjaya, 'A Win-Win Race in South Asia', *Financial Express* Online, 13 June 2003.

Bergsten, C. Fred, *Managing International Economic Interdependence: Selected Papers of C. Fred Bergsten, 1975–76*, (Lexington, MA: Lexington Books, 1977).

Bhaduri, Amit and Deepak Nayyar, *The Intelligent Person's Guide to Liberalization*, (New Delhi: Penguin Books, 1996).

Bhagwati, Jagdish N. and Anne O. Krueger, *The Dangerous Drift to Preferential Trade Agreements*, (Washington, DC: AEI Press, 1995).

Bhagwati, Jagdish N. and Padma Desai, *India: Planning for Industrialization*, (London: Oxford University Press, 1970).

Bhagwati, Jagdish N., 'Bhagwati on Trade: Fast Track to Nowhere', *The Economist*, 18 October 1997, 21–3.

——— *Political Economy and International Economics*, (Cambridge, MA: MIT Press, 1991).

——— *The Wind of the Hundred Days: How Washington Mismanaged Globalization*, (Cambridge, MA: MIT Press, 2000).

Bhambhri, C.P., *The Indian State after Independence*, (Delhi: Shipra, 2000).

Blair, Tony, 'A Global Threat Needs a Global Response', *The Guardian* Online, 7 April 2004.

Borden, William S., *The Pacific Alliance: United States Foreign Economic Policy and Japanese Trade Recovery, 1947–1953*, (Madison, WI: University of Wisconsin Press, 1984).

Bowie, Alasdair and Danny Unger, *The Politics of Open Economies: Indonesia, Malaysia, the Philippines, and Thailand*, (Cambridge: Cambridge University Press, 1997).

Brawley, Mark R., *Turning Points: Decisions Shaping the Evolution of the International Political Economy*, (Peterborough, Ontario: Broadview Press, 1998).

Burki, Shahid Javed, 'Trading with America', *Dawn* Online, 29 July 2003.

——— *Pakistan: The Continuing Search for Nationhood*, (Boulder Co: Westview Press, 1991).

Cao, Yuanzheng, 'World Economic Restructuring and China's Economic Transformation', in *China, the United States, and the Global Economy*, Shuxun Chen and Charles Wolf, Jr (eds), (Santa Monica, CA: RAND, 2001).

Cardoso, Fernando Henrique and Enzo Faletto, *Dependency and Development in Latin America*, (Berkeley: University of California Press, 1978).

Carr, Edward Hallett, *The Twenty Years' Crisis, 1919–1939*, (New York: Harper & Row, 1964).

Chelliah, Raja J., *Towards Sustainable Growth: Essays in Fiscal and Financial Sector Reforms in India*, (New Delhi: Oxford University Press, 1996).

Chen, Shuxun and Charles Wolf, Jr (eds), *China, the United States, and the Global Economy*, (Santa Monica, CA: RAND, 2001).

Chopra, Ajai, *India: Economic Reform and Growth*, (Washington, DC: IMF, 1995).

Cline, William R., 'Can the East Asian Model of Development Be Generalized?', *World Development*, 10, 2 (1982), Reprinted in Charles K. Wilber (ed.), *The Political Economy of Development and Underdevelopment*, (New York: Random House, 1988).

Cockcroft, John D., Andre Gunder Frank and Dale L. Johnson, *Dependence and Underdevelopment: Latin America's Political Economy*, (Garden City, NY: Anchor Books, 1992).

Cohen, Jerome, *Economic Problems of a Free Japan*, (Princeton: Princeton University Center for International Studies, 1952).

Cohen, Stephen Philip, 'The Nation and the State of Pakistan', *The Washington Quarterly*, 25, 3 (2002), 109–22.

Communist Party of China, *Report on the Proposals for the Second Five Year Plan for Development of the National Economy*, (Peking: Foreign Language Press, 1956).

Cooper, Robert, 'Why We Still Need Empires', *The Observer*, Sunday, 7 April 2002.

Crouzet, Francois, *The Victorian Economy*, (New York: Columbia University Press, 1982).

Cumings, Bruce, 'The Origins and Development of the Northeast Asian Political Economy: Industrial Sectors, Product Cycles, and Political Consequences', in *The Political Economy of the New Asian Industrialism*, Frederic C. Deyo (ed.), (Ithaca, NY: Cornell University Press, 1987).

———— 'Webs with No Spiders, Spiders with No Webs: The Genealogy of the Developmental State', in *The Developmental State*, Meredith Woo-Cumings (ed.), (Ithaca, NY: Cornell University Press, 1999).

de Toledano, Ralph, *Nixon*, (New York: Henry Holt, 1956).

Deutsch, Karl W., 'Social Mobilization and Political Development', *American Political Science Review*, 55, 3 (September 1961).

Deyo, Frederic C. (ed.), *The Political Economy of the New Asian Industrialism*, (Ithaca, NY: Cornell University Press, 1987).

Diamond, Larry and Marc F. Plattner, *Economic Reform and Democracy*, (Baltimore, MD: Johns Hopkins University Press, 1995).

Dollar, David and Aart Kraay, 'Spreading the Wealth', *Foreign Affairs*, 81, 1 (January–February 2002), 120–33.

Draft Defence Planning Guidance Paper, *New York Times*, 8 March 1992, A14.

Dumbaugh, Kerry, 'Interest Groups: Growing Influence', in *Making China Policy: Lessons from the Bush and Clinton Administrations*, Ramon H. Myers, Michel C. Oksenberg, and David Shambaugh (eds), (Lanham, MD: Rowman & Littlefield, 2001).

Edwards, Sebastian, 'How Effective are Capital Controls?', *Journal of Economic Perspectives*, 13, 9 (1999), 65–84.

European Commission, *European Social Statistics: Demography*, (Luxembourg: 2001).

Evans, Peter, 'Class, State, and Dependence in East Asia: Lessons for Latin Americanists', in *The Political Economy of the New Asian Industrialism*, Frederic C. Deyo (ed.), (Ithaca, NY: Cornell University Press, 1987).

Falk, Richard, *Predatory Globalization: A Critique*, (Cambridge UK: Polity Press, 1999).

Ferguson, Niall, *Empire: The Rise and Demise of the British World Order and the Lessons for Global Power*, (New York: Basic Books, 2003).

Foot, Rosemary, 'Bush, China and Human Rights', *Survival*, 45, 2 (Summer 2003).

Frankel, Francine R., *India's Political Economy, 1947–1977: The Gradual Revolution*, (Princeton: Princeton University Press, 1978).

Frankel, Jeffrey A. (ed.), *Regionalization of the World Economy*, (Chicago: University of Chicago Press, 1998).

Frankel, Jeffrey and David Roemer, 'Does Trade Cause Growth?' *American Economic Review*, 89, 3 (1999), 379–99.

Freeman, David, *Energy: The New Era*, (New York: Vintage, 1974).

Frieden, Jeffry A. and Ronald Rogowski, 'The Impact of the International Economy on National Politics: An Analytical Overview', in *Internationalization and Domestic Politics*, Robert O. Keohane and Helen V. Milner (eds), (Cambridge: Cambridge University Press, 1996).

Friedman, Thomas L., *The Lexus and the Olive Tree*, (New York: Anchor Books, 2000).

———— 'Sleeping Americans, Working Indians', *Indian Express* Online, 5 March 2004.

Fukuyama, Francis, *The End of History and the Last Man*, (New York: Free Press, 1992).

Garnaut, Ross, 'Twenty Years of Economic Reform and Structural Change in the Chinese Economy', in *Growth Without Miracles: Readings on the Chinese Economy in the Era of Reform*, Ross Garnaut and Yiping Huang (eds), (Oxford: Oxford University Press, 2001).

Garrett, Geoffrey, 'The Causes of Globalization', *Comparative Political Studies*, 33, 6–7 (August–September 2000), 941–91.

Gerschenkron, Alexander, *Economic Backwardness in Historical Perspective*, (Cambridge, MA: Belknap Press, 1966).

Ghosh, D.N., 'Globalization and National Politics', *Economic and Political Weekly*, 37, 39 (25 September 1999), 2770–1.

Ghosh, Santanu, '*Dil Hai Hindustani* for Indians Abroad', *Indian Express* Online, 3 April 2003.

Gilpin, Robert, *The Challenge of Global Capitalism: The World Economy in the 21st Century*, (Princeton: Princeton University Press, 2000).

———— *The Political Economy of International Relations*, (Princeton: Princeton University Press, 1987).

———— *US Power and the Multinational Corporation: The Political Economy of Foreign Direct Investment*, (New York: Basic Books, 1975).

———— *War and Change in World Politics*, (Cambridge: Cambridge University Press, 1981).

Gowa, Joanne, *Cooperation Among Nations: Europe, America and Non-Tariff Barriers*, (Princeton: Princeton University Press, 1994).

Graubard, Stephen R., *Kissinger: Portrait of a Mind*, (New York: W.W. Norton, 1974).

Gray, Colin S., *The Geopolitics of the Nuclear Era: Heartland, Rimlands, and the Technological Revolution*, (New York: Crane, Russak, 1977).

Grieco, Joseph M., 'Realism and Regionalism: American Power and German and Japanese Institutional Strategies During and After the Cold War', in *Unipolar Politics: Realism and State Strategies After the Cold War*, Ethan B. Kapstein and Michael Mastanduno (eds), (New York: Columbia University Press, 1999).

Grieco, Joseph M. and G. John Ikenberry, *State Power and World Markets: The International Political Economy*, (New York: W.W. Norton & Company, 2003).

Haggard, Stephan, *Pathways from the Periphery: The Politics of Growth in the Newly Industrializing Countries*, (Ithaca, NY: Cornell University Press, 1990).

Haider, Mehtab, '$1 b Debt Write Off', *The Nation* Online, 6 April 2003.

Haqqani, Husain, 'Causes for Concern', *The Nation* Online, 30 July 2003.

Hardt, Michael and Antonio Negri, *Empire*, (Cambridge, MA: Harvard University Press, 2000).

Harrison, Selig S., 'America, India, and Pakistan: A Chance for a Fresh Start', *Harper's*, No. 233 (July 1966).

———— *The Widening Gulf: Asian Nationalism and American Policy*, (New York: The Free Press, 1978).

Hathway, Robert M., 'Everybody Wants to Go to Heaven, but No One Wants to Die: The US Congress and the South Asian Nuclear Tests', (1 November 1999 Draft).

Heginbotham, Eric and Richard J. Samuels, 'Mercantile Realism and Japanese Foreign Policy', in *Unipolar Politics: Realism and State Strategies After the Cold War*, Ethan B. Kapstein and Michael Mastanduno (eds), (New York: Columbia University Press, 1999).

Hennessy, Peter, *Never Again: Britain, 1945–1951*, (London: Jonathan Cape, 1992).

Herring, Ronald J., 'Embedded Particularism: India's Failed Developmental State', in *The Developmental State*, Meredith Woo-Cumings (ed.), (Ithaca, NY: Cornell University Press, 1999).

Hirst, Paul and Grahame Thompson, *Globalization in Question: The International Economy and the Possibilities of Governance*, (Cambridge, UK: Polity Press, 1996).

Hodgson, Geoffrey M., 'Economic Evolution: Intervention Contra Pangloss', *Journal of Economic Issues*, 25, 2 (June 1991), 519–33.

Hoeffding, Oleg, 'State Planning and Forced Industrialization', *Problems of Communism*, 8, 6 (November–December 1959).

Horowitz, Irving Louis, *Three Worlds of Development: The Theory and Practice of International Stratification*, (New York: Oxford University Press, 1966).

Huang, Yasheng, *Selling China: Foreign Direct Investment during the Reform Era*, (Cambridge: Cambridge University Press, 2003).

——— 'The Role of Foreign-Invested Enterprises in the Chinese Economy: An Institutional Foundation Approach', in *China, the United States, and the Global Economy*, Shuxun Chen and Charles Wolf, Jr (eds), (Santa Monica, CA: RAND, 2001).

Huntington, Samuel P., 'The Lonely Superpower', *Foreign Affairs*, 78 (March–April 1999), 35–49.

——— 'Why International Primacy Matters', *International Security*, 17, 4 (1993), 68–83.

Ikenberry, G. John (ed.), *America Unrivaled: The Future of the Balance of Power*, (Ithaca, NY: Cornell University Press, 2002).

——— *After Victory: Institutions, Strategic Restraint, and the Rebuilding of Order After Major Wars*, (Princeton: Princeton University Press, 2001).

——— 'Liberal Hegemony and the Future of American Post-War Order', in *International Order and the Future of World Politics*, T. V. Paul and John A. Hall (eds), (Cambridge: Cambridge University Press, 1999).

——— *Reasons of State: Oil Politics and the Capacities of American Government*, (Ithaca, NY: Cornell University Press, 1988).

IMF, *Direction of Trade Statistics Yearbook* (various years).

International Institute for Strategic Studies, *The Military Balance 2002–2003* (London: Oxford University Press, 2002).

Irwin, Douglas A. and Mario Tervio, 'Does Trade Raise Income? Evidence from the Twentieth Century', National Bureau of Economic Research Working Paper W7745, (Cambridge, MA: June 2000).

Ito, Takatoshi and Anne O. Krueger (eds), *Regionalism versus Multilateral Trade Arrangements*, (Chicago: University of Chicago Press, 1997).

Jahan, Rounaq, *Pakistan: Failure in National Integration*, (New York: Columbia University Press, 1972).

James, William E., Seiji Naya, and Gerald M. Meier, *Asian Development: Economic Success and Policy Lessons*, (Madison, WI: University of Wisconsin Press, 1989).

Jessop, Bob, 'Accumulation Strategies, State Forms, and Hegemonic Projects', *Kapitalistate*, 10–11 (1983), 89–111.

Johnson, Chalmers, *Blowback: The Costs and Consequences of American Empire*, (New York: Henry Holt, 2004).

——— *MITI and the Japanese Miracle: The Growth of Industrial Policy, 1925–1975*, (Stanford, CA: Stanford University Press, 1982).

———— 'Political Institutions and Economic Performance: The Government-Business Relationship in Japan, South Korea and Taiwan', in *The Political Economy of the New Asian Industrialism*, Frederic C. Deyo (ed.), (Ithaca, NY: Cornell University Press, 1987).

———— 'The Developmental State: Odyssey of a Concept', in *The Developmental State*, Meredith Woo-Cumings (ed.), (Ithaca, NY: Cornell University Press, 1999).

Jomo, K.S., 'Rethinking the Role of Government Policy in Southeast Asia', in *Rethinking the Asian Miracle*, Joseph E. Stiglintz and Shahid Yusuf (eds), (Oxford: Oxford University Press, 2001).

Joshi, Vijay and I.M.D. Little, *India: Macroeconomics and Political Economy 1964–1991*, (Washington, DC: World Bank, 1994).

———— *India's Economic Reforms 1991–2000*, (New Delhi: Oxford University Press, 1996).

Kagan, Robert, *Of Paradise and Power: America and Europe in the New World Order*, (New York: Knopf, 2003).

Kahn, Herman, *The Emerging Japanese Superstate: Challenge and Response*, (Englewood Cliffs, NJ: Prentice-Hall, 1970).

Kalb, Marvin and Bernard Kalb, *Kissinger*, (Boston: Little, Brown, 1974).

Kapstein, Ethan B., 'Does Unipolarity Have a Future?', in *Unipolar Politics: Realism and State Strategies After the Cold War*, Ethan B. Kapstein and Michael Mastanduno (eds), (New York: Columbia University Press, 1999).

Kataoka, Tetsuya, *Waiting for A 'Pearl Harbour': Japan Debates Defence*, (Stanford, CA: Hoover Institution Press, 1980).

Katzenstein, Peter J., Robert O. Keohane, and Stephen D. Krasner, 'International Organization and the Study of World Politics', *International Organization*, 52 (1998), 647–86.

Kautsky, John H. (ed.), *Political Change in Underdeveloped Countries: Nationalism and Communism*, (New York: John Wiley, 1962).

Kawai, Kazuo, *Japan's American Interlude*, (Chicago: University of Chicago Press, 1960).

Kennan, George F., *Memoirs, 1925–1950*, (Boston: Little, Brown and Company, 1967).

———— 'X' [George F. Kennan], 'The Sources of Soviet Conduct', *Foreign Affairs*, 25, 4 (July 1947).

Kennedy, Paul, *The Rise and Fall of Great Powers: Economic Change and Military Conflict from 1500 to 2000*, (London: Unwin Hyman, 1988).

Keohane, Robert, 'The Theory of Hegemonic Stability and Change in International Economic Regimes, 1967–1977', in *Changes in the International System*, Ole R. Holsti *et al.* (eds), (Boulder, CO: Westview Press, 1980).

Kirshner, Jonathan, 'The Political Economy of Realism', in *Unipolar Politics: Realism and State Strategies After the Cold War*, Ethan B. Kapstein and Michael Mastanduno (eds), (New York: Columbia University Press, 1999).

Kitching, Gavin, *Seeking Justice Through Globalization: Escaping a Nationalist Perspective*, (University Park, PA: Pennsylvania State University Press, 2001).

Kohli, Atul, 'Where Do High-Growth Political Economies Come From? The Japanese Lineage of Korea's "Developmental State"', in *The Developmental State*, Meredith Woo-Cumings (ed.), (Ithaca, NY: Cornell University Press, 1999).

Koo, Hagen, 'The Interplay of State, Social Class, and World System in East Asian Development: The Cases of South Korea and Taiwan', in *The Political Economy of the New Asian Industrialism*, Frederic C. Deyo (ed.), (Ithaca, NY: Cornell University Press, 1987).

Krasner, Stephen D. (ed.), *International Regimes*, (Ithaca, NY: Cornell University Press, 1981).

——— *Sovereignty*, (Princeton: Princeton University Press, 1999).

——— *Structural Conflict: The Third World Against Global Liberalism*, (Berkeley: University of California Press, 1985).

Kupchan, Charles, 'Hollow Hegemony or Stable Multipolarity?', in *America Unrivaled: The Future of the Balance of Power*, G. John Ikenberry (ed.), (Ithaca, NY: Cornell University Press, 2002).

Kurlantzick, Joshua, 'China: Economic Power, Political Enigma', *Washington Quarterly*, 25, 3 (Summer 2002), 50–67.

Kux, Dennis, *The United States and Pakistan, 1947–2000: Disenchanted Allies*, (Washington, DC: Woodrow Wilson Centre Press, 2001).

Lardy, Nicholas R., 'The Role of Foreign Trade and Investment in China's Economic Transformation', in *Growth Without Miracles: Readings on the Chinese Economy in the Era of Reform*, Ross Garnaut and Yiping Huang (eds), (Oxford: Oxford University Press, 2001).

Layne, Christopher, 'The Unipolar Illusion: Why New Great Powers Will Rise', *International Security*, 17, 4 (1993), 5–51.

Lieven, Anatol, 'The Pressures on Pakistan', *Foreign Affairs*, 81, 1, January–February 2002.

Lin, Justin Yifu, Fang Cai, and Zhou Li, 'Pre-Reform Economic Development in China', in *Growth Without Miracles: Readings on the Chinese Economy in the Era of Reform*, Ross Garnaut and Yiping Huang (eds), (Oxford: Oxford University Press, 2001).

Lipset, Seymour Martin, *Political Man: The Social Bases of Politics*, (Garden City, NY: Doubleday, 1960).

——— 'Social Requisites of Democracy: Economic Development and Political Legitimacy', *American Political Science Review*, 53, 1 (May 1959), 69–105.

Liska, George, 'The Third World: Regional Systems and Global Order', in *Retreat From Empire*, Robert E. Osgood *et al.* (eds), (Baltimore, MD: The Johns Hopkins University Press, 1973).

List, Friedrich, *The National System of Political Economy*, (New York: August M. Kelley, 1966).

Livi-Baci, Massimo (ed.), 'South-North Migration: A Comparative Approach to North American and European Experiences', in *The Changing Course of International Migration*, OECD, (Paris: OECD, 1993).

Lord, Winston, 'America's Purposes in an Ambiguous Age', *Department of State Bulletin*, No. 1845 (4 November 1974), 617–22.

Loriaux, Michael, 'Realism and Reconciliation: France, Germany, and the European Union', in *Unipolar Politics: Realism and State Strategies After the Cold War*, Ethan B. Kapstein and Michael Mastanduno (eds), (New York: Columbia University Press, 1999).

MacArthur, Douglas, *Reminiscences*, (New York: McGraw-Hill, 1964).

Mackinder, H.J., 'The Geopolitical Pivot of History', *Geographical Journal*, 23 (1904), 421–44, Reprinted in Harm J. de Blij, *Systematic Political Geography*, second edn, (New York: John Wiley & Sons, 1973).

Mahalanobis, P.C. (ed.), 'Draft Recommendations for the Formulation of the Second Five Year Plan 1956–61', in *Papers Relating to the Formulation of the Second Five Year Plan, 1955*, Government of India, Planning Commission, (Delhi: Manager of Publications, 1962).

——— 'Some Observations on the Process of Growth of National Income', *Sankhya*, 12, 4 (1953).

Malik, Brigadier S.K., *The Quranic Concept of War*, (Lahore: Wajidalis, 1979).

Mann, James, *About Face: A History of America's Curious Relationship with China, from Nixon to Clinton*, (New York: Alfred A. Knopf, 1999).

Mann, Michael, 'Has Globalization Ended the Rise and Rise of the Nation-State?', in *International Order and the Future of World Politics*, T.V. Paul and John A. Hall (eds), (Cambridge: Cambridge University Press, 1999).

Marchand, Marianne H., 'The Political Economy of North–South Relations', in *Political Economy and the Changing Global Order*, Richard Stubbs and Geoffrey D. Underhill (eds), (Toronto: McClelland & Stewart, 1994).

Marx, Karl and Frederick Engels, 'The Communist Manifesto', in *Karl Marx: Selected Writings*, David McLellan (ed.), (Oxford: Oxford University Press, 1977).

Mastanduno, Michael, *Economic Containment: CoCom and the Politics of East-West Trade*, (Ithaca, NY: Cornell University Press, 1992).

Mathias, Peter, *The First Industrial Nation: An Economic History of Britain, 1700–1914*, (London: Methuen, 1969).

Mayers, David, *George Kennan and the Dilemmas of US Foreign Policy*, (New York: Oxford University Press, 1988).

McMillan, John and Barry Naughton, 'How to Reform a Planned Economy: Lessons from China', in *Growth Without Miracles: Readings on the Chinese Economy in the Era of Reform*, Ross Garnaut and Yiping Huang (eds), (Oxford: Oxford University Press, 2001).

Mearsheimer, John J., *The Tragedy of Great Power Politics*, (New York: W.W. Norton, 2001).

Middleton, Drew, *Retreat from Victory: A Critical Appraisal of American Foreign and Military Policy from 1920 to the 1970s*, (New York: Hawthorn Books, 1973).

Miscamble, Wilson D., *George F. Kennan and the Making of American Foreign Policy, 1947–1950*, (Princeton: Princeton University Press, 1992).

Morgenthau, Hans J., *Politics Among Nations*, fourth edition, (New York: Alfred A. Knopf, 1967).

Mukherji, Joydeep, 'Commentary: India Seeks an Economic "Tryst with Destiny"', *Standard & Poor's*, December 1999, 1–6.

Mustafa, Zubeida, 'A Curriculum of Hatred', *Dawn Online*, 31 March 2004.

Myers, Ramon H. and David Shambaugh, 'Introduction: The Legacy of US–China Policy, 1989–2000', in *Making China Policy: Lessons from the Bush and Clinton Administrations*, Ramon H. Myers, Michel C. Oksenberg, and David Shambaugh (eds), (Lanham, MD: Rowman & Littlefield, 2001).

Myint, Hla, 'Inward and Outward-Looking Countries Revisited: The Case of Indonesia', *Bulletin of Indonesian Economic Studies*, 20, 2 (August 1984), 41–42.

Naravane, Vaiju, 'The Surrender', *The Hindu Online*, 28 May 2003.

Nayak, Gayatri, 'NRIs Send Home Maximum Funds', *Economic Times Online*, 5 April 2004.

Nayar, Baldev Raj and T.V. Paul, *India in the World Order: Searching for Major-Power Status*, (Cambridge: Cambridge University Press, 2003).

Nayar, Baldev Raj, *The Modernization Imperative and Indian Planning*, (New Delhi: Vikas, 1972).

——— 'Opening Up and Openness of Indian Economy', *Economic and Political Weekly*, 36, 37 (15–21 September 2001), 3529–37.

——— 'Globalization and India's National Autonomy', *Journal of Commonwealth and Comparative Politics*, 41, 2 (July 2003), 1–34.

——— *Globalization and Nationalism: The Changing Balance in India's Economic Policy, 1950–2000*, (New Delhi: Sage Publications, 2001).

——— 'The Political Mainsprings of Economic Planning in the New Nations: The Modernization Imperative versus Social Mobilization', *Comparative Politics*, 6, 3 (April 1974), 341–66.

Nayar, Kuldip, *India After Nehru*, (Delhi: Vikas, 1975).

Nayyar, Deepak, 'Globalization: The Game, the Players and the Rules', in *The Political Economy of Globalization*, Satya Dev Gupta (ed.), (Boston: Kluwer Academic Publishers, 1997).

Nehru, Jawaharlal, *Jawaharlal Nehru's Speeches: Volume Three: March 1953–August 1957*, (Delhi: Ministry of Information and Broadcasting, 1958).

Newell, Peter, 'Global Challenges to the Future State', *Seminar*, No. 503 (July 2001).

Nixon, Richard, *Beyond Peace*, (New York: Random House, 1994).

Noman, Omar, *Economic and Social Progress in Asia: Why Pakistan Did Not Become a Tiger*, (Karachi: Oxford University Press, 1997).

North, Douglass C., *Institutions, Institutional Change and Economic Performance*, (Cambridge: Cambridge University Press, 1990).

Nye, Joseph S. Jr, 'East Asian Security: The Case for Deep Engagement', *Foreign Affairs*, 74, 4 (July–August 1995), 90–102.

——— *Bound to Lead: The Changing Nature of American Power*, (New York: Basic Books, 1990).

O'Connor, James, *The Fiscal Crisis of the State*, (New York: St. Martin's Press, 1973).

Odell, John, *US International Monetary Policy: Markets, Power and Ideas as Sources of Change*, (Princeton: Princeton University Press, 1982).

OECD, *Trends in International Migration*, (Paris: OECD, 2001).

Ohmae, Kenichi, *The Borderless World: Power and Strategy in the Interlinked Economy*, (New York: Harper Business, 1990).

Palma, Gabriel, 'Dependency: A Formal Theory of Underdevelopment or A Methodology in the Analysis of Concrete Situations of Underdevelopment', *World Development*, 6 (1978), 881–922.

Panagariya, Arvind, *Regionalism in Trade Policy: Essays on Preferential Trading*, (Singapore: World Scientific Publishing, 1999).

Papanek, Gustav F., *Pakistan's Development: Social Goals and Private Incentives*, (Cambridge, MA: Harvard University Press, 1967).

Parker, W.H., *Mackinder: Geography as an Aid to Statecraft*, (Oxford, UK: Clarendon Press, 1982).

Patrick, Hugh and Henry Rosovsky, *Asia's New Giant: How the Japanese Economy Works*, (Washington, DC: Brookings Institution, 1976).

Paul, T.V., *Asymmetric Conflicts: War Initiation by Weaker States*, (Cambridge: Cambridge University Press, 1994).

Pempel, T.J., 'The Developmental Regime in a Changing World Economy', in *The Developmental State*, Meredith Woo-Cumings (ed.), (Ithaca, NY: Cornell University Press, 1999).

People's Republic of China, *First Five Year Plan for Development of the National Economy of the People's Republic of China in 1953–57*, (Peking: Foreign Language Press, 1956).

Perkins, Dwight, 'Completing China's Move to the Market', in *Growth Without Miracles: Readings on the Chinese Economy in the Era of Reform*, Ross Garnaut and Yiping Huang (eds), (Oxford: Oxford University Press,' 2001).

Pfaff, William, 'Bush's New Global Order Will Generate Resistance', *International Herald Tribune* Online, 17 April 2003.

——— 'Europe Can Gently Check America', Ibid., 2 May 2003.

——— 'Europe Will Follow France: A Contest of Identities', Ibid., 22 May 2003.

——— 'Seeing Mortal Danger in a Superpower Europe', Ibid., 3 July 2003.

Pirzada, Moeed, 'Camp David and Beyond', *Dawn* Online, 11 July 2003.

Plumptre, A.F.W., *Three Decades of Decision: Canada and the World Monetary System*, (Toronto: McClelland & Stewart, 1977).

Polanyi, Karl, *The Great Transformation*, (New York: Rinehart, 1957).

Posen, Barry R. and Andrew L. Ross, 'Competing Visions for US Grand Strategy', *International Security*, 21 (Winter 1996–97), 5–53.

Powell, Robert, 'Absolute and Relative Gains in International Relations Theory', *American Political Science Review*, 85, 4 (December 1991), 1303–20.

Putzel, James, 'Developmental States and Crony Capitalists', in *Rethinking Development in East Asia: From Illusory Miracle to Economic Crisis*, Pietro P. Masina (ed.), (Richmond, Surrey, UK: Curzon Press, 2002).

Qureshi, Saleem, 'Military in the Polity of Islam: Religion as a Basis for Civil–Military Interactions', *International Political Science Review*, 2, 3 (1981), 271–82.

Raby, Geoff, 'The "Neither This Nor That" Economy', in *Growth Without Miracles: Readings on the Chinese Economy in the Era of Reform*, Ross Garnaut and Yiping Huang (eds), (Oxford: Oxford University Press, 2001).

Raghavan, Chakravarthi, *Recolonization: GATT, the Uruguay Round & the Third World*, (London: Zed Books, 1990).

Randall, Willard Sterne, *Alexander Hamilton: A Life*, (New York: HarperCollins, 2003).

Rhodes, Carolyn (ed.), *The European Union in the World Community*, (Boulder, CO: Lynne Reinner, 1998).

Rodrik, Dani, *Has Globalization Gone Too Far?*, (Washington, DC: Institute for International Economics, 1997).

———*The New Global Economy and Developing Countries: Making Openness Work*, (Washington, DC: Overseas Development Council, 1999).

Rodrik, Dani and Arvind Subramanian, 'From "Hindu Growth" to Productivity Surge: The Mystery of the Indian Growth Transition', Available online; (Cambridge, MA and Washington, DC: March 2004).

Rosecrance, Richard, *The Rise of the Trading State*, (New York: Basic Books, 1986).

Ross, Robert S., 'Engagement in US–China Policy', in *Engaging China: The Management of an Emergent Power*, Alastair Iain Johnston and Robert S. Ross (eds), (London: Routledge, 1999).

———'The Bush Administration: The Origins of Engagement', in *Making China Policy: Lessons from the Bush and Clinton Administrations*, Ramon H. Myers, Michel C. Oksenberg, and David Shambaugh (eds), (Lanham, MD: Rowman & Littlefield, 2001).

Rostow, Walt W., *Politics and the Stages of Growth*, (Cambridge: Cambridge University Press, 1971).

Rowen, Henry S., 'China and the World Economy: The Short March from Isolation to Major Player', in *China, the United States, and the Global Economy*, Shuxun Chen and Charles Wolf. Jr. (eds), (Santa Monica, CA: RAND, 2001).

Ruggie, John Gerard, 'International Regimes, Transactions, and Change: Embedded Liberalism in the Post-War Economic Order', in *International Regimes*, Stephen D. Krasner (ed.), (Ithaca: Cornell University Press, 1983).

Sachs, Jeffrey D. and Andrew Warner, 'Economic Reform and the Process of Global Integration', *Brookings Papers on Economic Activity 1995*, No. 1 (1995), 1–118.

Samuels, Richard J., *Rich Nation, Strong Army: National Security and the Technological Transformation of Japan*, (Ithaca, NY: Cornell University Press, 1994).

Sayeed, Khalid B., *Politics in Pakistan: The Nature and Direction of Change*, (New York: Praeger, 1980).

———— *The Political System of Pakistan*, (Boston, MA: Houghton Mifflin, 1967).

Scalapino, Robert A., 'Democracy in Taiwan and Asia—Advances and Challenges', in *Taiwan's Modernization in Global Perspective*, Peter C.Y. Chow (ed.), (Westport, CT: Praeger, 2002).

Schaller, Michael, *Altered States: The United States and Japan Since the Occupation*, (New York: Oxford University Press, 1997).

———— *The American Occupation of Japan: The Origins of the Cold War in Asia*, (New York: Oxford University Press, 1985).

Shaw, Martin, *Theory of the Global State: Globality as Unfinished Revolution*, (Cambridge: Cambridge University Press, 2000).

Shonfield, Andrew, *Modern Capitalism: The Changing Balance of Public and Private Power*, (London: Oxford University Press, 1965).

Shourie, Arun, 'Getting Our Act Together', *Indian Express* Online, 21 March 2003.

Shroff, Manu, 'Globalization: A Stock-Taking', *Economic and Political Weekly*, 34, 40 (2 October 1999), 2845–49.

Siddiqui, Kalim, 'Pakistan's External Environment', *Asian Review*, 2, 2 (January 1969).

Skidelsky, Robert, *John Maynard Keynes: Volume Three: Fighting for Freedom 1937–1946*, (New York: Viking Press, 2002).

Sklair, Leslie, *Globalization: Capitalism and Its Alternatives*, (Oxford: Oxford University Press, 2002).

Spykman, Nicholas John, *The Geography of the Peace*, (New York: Harcourt, Brace and Company, 1944).

Strange, Susan, *States and Markets*, (New York: Basil Blackwell, 1988).

———— 'Cave! Hic Dragones: A Critique of Regime Analysis', in *International Regimes*, Stephen D. Krasner (ed.), (Ithaca, NY: Cornell University Press, 1981).

———— 'The Future of the American Empire', *Journal of International Affairs*, 42 (Fall 1988).

Sullivan, Michael P., *Power in Contemporary International Politics*, (Columbia, SC: University of South Carolina Press, 1990).

Suroor, Hasan, 'Blair Advocates Pre-emptive Strikes', *The Hindu* Online, 7 March 2004.

Sutter, Robert G., 'Domestic Politics and the US–China–Taiwan Triangle: The 1995–96 Taiwan Strait Conflict and Its Aftermath', in *After the Cold War:*

Domestic Factors and US–China Relations, Robert S. Ross (ed.), (New York: M.E. Sharpe, 1998).

Syed, Anwar, 'The Right Policy Recipe', *Dawn* Online, 25 May 2003.

Tammen, Ronald L. *et al.*, *Power Transitions: Strategies for the 21st Century,* (New York: Chatham House, 2000).

Teles, Steven M., 'Public Opinion and Interest Groups in the Making of US–China Policy', in *After the Cold War: Domestic Factors and US–China Relations,* Robert S. Ross (ed.), (New York: M.E. Sharpe, 1998).

Thompson, William J., *Khrushchev: A Political Life,* (New York: St. Martin's Press, 1995).

Thucydides, *Pelopennesian War,* (trans. by Richard Crawley), (London: J.M. Dent, 1903).

Thucydides, *History of the Pelopennesian War,* (trans. by Rex Warner), (London: Penguin, 1972).

Thurow, Lester, *Head to Head: The Coming Economic Battle Among Japan, Europe and America,* (New York: William Morrow, 1992).

Tucker, Nancy Bernkopf, 'The Clinton Years: The Problem of Coherence', in *Making China Policy: Lessons from the Bush and Clinton Administrations,* Ramon H. Myers, Michel C. Oksenberg, and David Shambaugh (eds), (Lanham, MD: Rowman & Littlefield, 2001).

Tussie, Diana, *The Less Developed Countries and the World Trading System: A Challenge to the GATT,* (New York: St. Martin's Press, 1987).

UNCTAD, *World Investment Report* (various years).

——— *World Investment Report 1991:The Triad in Foreign Direct Investment.*

Vedrine, Hubert, *Les Cartes de la France a l'heure de la Mondialization,* (Paris: Fayard, 2000).

Vernon, Raymond, *Sovereignty at Bay: The Multinational Spread of US Enterprises,* (New York: Basic Books, 1971).

Vinocur, John, 'After the Iraq War: A New Balancing Act in US–European Relations', *International Herald Tribune* Online, 13 May 2003.

Virmani, Arvind, 'India's Economic Growth: From Socialist Rate of Growth to Bharatiya Rate of Growth', Working Paper No. 122, (New Delhi: Indian Council for Research on International Economic Relations, February 2004).

Wade, Robert, *Governing the Market: Economic Theory and the Role of Government in East Asian Industrialization,* (Princeton: Princeton University Press, 1990).

Waleed, Hamid, 'Exports Touch $11 Billion', *The Nation* Online, 11 July 2003.

Walters, Robert E., *The Nuclear Trap: An Escape Route,* (Harmondsworth, UK: Penguin Books, 1974).

Waltz, Kenneth N., 'Structural Realism after the Cold War', in *America Unrivaled: The Future of the Balance of Power,* G. John Ikenberry (ed.), (Ithaca, NY: Cornell University Press, 2002).

——— 'The Emerging Structure of International Politics', *International Security,* 18, 2 (1993), 44–79.

———— *Theory of International Politics*, (New York: Random House, 1979).

Wang, Hui, 'US–China: Bonds and Tensions', in *China, the United States, and the Global Economy*, Shuxun Chen and Charles Wolf, Jr (eds), (Santa Monica, CA: RAND, 2001).

Wang, Jisi, 'A View From China', *Foreign Policy*, July–August 2003, 31.

Warren, Bill, *Imperialism, Pioneer of Capitalism*, (London: Verso, 1980).

Weiner, Myron, *The Indian Paradox: Essays in Indian Politics*, (New Delhi: Sage Publications, 1989).

Wilcox, Wayne A., 'India and Pakistan', in *Conflict in World Politics*, Steven L. Spiegel and Kenneth N. Waltz (eds), (Cambridge, MA: Winthrop Publishers, 1971).

Wohlforth, William C., 'The Stability of a Unipolar World', *International Security*, 24, 1 (Summer 1999), 5–39.

Woo-Cumings, Meredith, 'Introduction: Chalmers Johnson and the Politics of Nationalism and Development', in *The Developmental State*, Meredith Woo-Cumings (ed.), (Ithaca, NY: Cornell University Press, 1999).

Woods, Randall Bennett, *A Changing of the Guard: Anglo-American Relations, 1941–1946*, (Chapel Hill: University of North Carolina Press, 1990).

World Bank, *India: Five Years of Stabilization and Reform and the Challenges Ahead*, (Washington DC: 1996).

———— *Rethinking the East Asian Miracle*, Joseph E. Stiglitz and Shahid Yusuf (eds), (New York: Oxford University Press, 2001).

———— *The East Asian Miracle: Economic Growth and Public Policy*, (New York: Oxford University Press, 1993).

———— *World Development Indicators*.

———— *World Development Report* (various years).

Wriston, Walter B., *The Twilight of Sovereignty: How the Information Revolution is Transforming Our World*, (New York: Scribners, 1992).

Xu, Xianquan, 'Sino-US Economic and Trade Relations', in *China, the United States, and the Global Economy*, Shuxun Chen and Charles Wolf, Jr (eds), (Santa Monica, CA: RAND, 2001).

INDEX

9/11 116–17, 212, 256, 261, 265

Abramowitz, Morton 214
accommodation, policy of 90
Afghanistan 111, 199, 252–3, 256, 265
agnostics [on globalization] 1–2, 259
agriculture, subsidization of 66, 260
Ahmad, Aijaz 4
Ahmadiyyas 242
Ahmed, Sultan 257
Ahsan, Syed Aziz-al 244
Aiyar, Swaminathan S. Anklesaria 234
Akbar, M.J. 256–7
Albright, Madeleine 115
Alperowitz, Gar 77
al-Qaeda 117
Ambition 225
Amery, Leo 65
Amin, Samir 103
Amir, Ayaz 240
Anandalingam, G. 194
ASEAN (Association of Southeast Nations). See Southeast Asia
ASEAN Four. See Southeast Asia

Asian Tigers 142, 168, 171, 176, 179, 235, 238, 264, 268
autonomy, national 19, 225, 227–8, 271–2
Axis Powers 63, 73, 79
Ayub Khan 247, 249, 251

Bagchi, Amiya Kumar 47
Baker, Dean et al. 20–1, 25, 31
balancing. See counterbalancing
Ball, George 106
bandwagoning 127–9, 135, 209–16
Bangladesh 218, 229
Bangladesh War 229
Barrett, Richard E. 162, 165
Baru, Sanjaya 257
Bergsten, C. Fred 101
Berkeley mafia 173
Bhaduri, Amit 4
Bhagwati, Jagdish 21, 52, 54, 126, 147, 227, 229, 266
Bhambhri, C.P. 4
Bhutto, Benazir 254
Bhutto, Zulfikar Ali 252
bipolarity 89, 94, 113
Blair, Tony 120–1
blowback 167, 254
Borden, William S. 75, 146, 149–51, 153–5